BENGAL DISTRICT GAZETTEERS

CHAMPARAN

BENGAL DISTRICT GAZETTEERS

Burdwan/ **J.C.K. Paterson**
Darjeeling/ **L.S.S. O'Malley**
Howrah/ **L.S.S. O'Malley**
Hooghly/ **L.S.S. O'Malley**
Santal Parganas/ **L.S.S. O'Malley**
Sambalpur/ **L.S.S. O'Malley**
Puri/ **L.S.S. O'Malley**
Gaya/ **L.S.S. O'Malley**
24 - Parganas/ **L.S.S. O'Malley**
Purnea/ **L.S.S. O'Malley**
Bhagalpur/ **J. BYRNE**
Feudatory States of Orissa/ **L.E.B. Cobden-Ramsay**
Singhbhum, Saraikela and Kharsawan/ **L.S.S. O'Malley**
Cuttack/ **L.S.S. O'Malley**
Darbhanga/ **L.S.S. O'Malley**
Champaran/ **L.S.S. O'Malley**

BIHAR AND ORISSA DISTRICT GAZETTEERS

Patna/ **L.S.S. O'Malley**
Shahabad/ **L.S.S. O'Malley**
Monghyr/ **L.S.S. O'Malley**
Saran/ **L.S.S. O'Malley**

EASTERN BENGAL DISTRICT GAZETTEERS

Dacca/ **B.C. Allen**

BENGAL DISTRICT GAZETTEERS

CHAMPARAN

L. S. S. O' MALLEY

LOGOS PRESS
New Delhi-110 002

ISBN-13: 978-81-7268-228-6

First Published 1907
Reprinted 2013

Printed and Published by
LOGOS PRESS

Building No. 4788-90, Street No. 23, Ansari Road, Darya Ganj,
New Delhi-110 002 (India)
Phone : 23272187
Email : mail@logospressindia.com
Website : www.logospressindia.com

PREFACE

I desire to acknowledge the great assistance I have derived in compiling this volume from the Champāran Survey and Settlement Report (1990) by Mr. C.J. Stevenson Moore, I.C.S. I also beg to express my thanks to Mr. W. R. Gourlay, I.C.S., formerly Collector of Champāran, for the ready assistance he has given in supplying materials and revising the proofs.

L. S. S. O' MALLEY

PLAN OF CONTENTS

TABLE OF CONTENTS

CHAPTER I

PHYSICAL ASPECTS

CHAPTER II

HISTORY

CHAPTER III

THE PEOPLE

CHAPTER XIII

LOCAL SELF-GOVERNMENT

CHAPTER XIV

EDUCATION

CHAPTER XV

GAZETTEER

GAZETTEER

OF THE

CHAMPARAN DISTRICT.

CHAPTER I.

PHYSICAL ASPECTS.

GENERAL DESCRIPTION.

THE district of Champāran, which forms the extreme north-western portion of the Patna Division and of the Province of Bengal, is situated between 26° 16′ and 27° 31′ north latitude, and between 83° 50′ and 85° 18′ east longitude. It extends over an area of 3,531 square miles, and contains a population, according to the census of 1901, of 1,790,463 persons. The principal civil station is Motīhāri, but Bettiah, the headquarters of the subdivision of that name, is the most populous town in the district and also the chief centre of commerce. The name Champāran is a corruption of Champā-aranya, *i.e.*, the forest of *champā* trees (Michelia Champaca), a designation which is popularly believed to date back to the time when the district was a vast forest, uninhabited except by solitary ascetics.

Boundaries.

The district is bounded on the north and north-east by Nepāl; on the south-east and south by the district of Muzaffarpur; on the south-west by Sāran; and on the north-west by the Gorakhpur district of the United Provinces. To the north and north-east the boundary marches with the Nepalese *Zilās* of Parsā and Bārā; and here the frontier, where not naturally formed by rivers, is marked by ditches and masonry pillars, and for a considerable distance runs along the crest of the Sumeswar range. On the north-east the Uriā, and on the south-east the Lāl Bakyā and Bāghmati constitute natural boundaries; and on the west the district is separated from Gorakhpur and Sāran by the present channel and an old bed of the Gandak.

B

Configuration. In shape, Champāran roughly resembles an irregular parallelogram, extending along the eastern bank of the Gandak for 100 miles, and having a breadth of 20 miles at the northern and of 40 miles at the southern extremity. The general aspect of the greater part of the district is very similar to that of the rest of North Bihār, a flat cultivated expanse diversified by numerous large groves of mango trees and intersected by a number of rivers and streams debouching from Nepāl. In the south and east the country is almost perfectly level with a very slight declination to the south; and the general character of the scenery is tame and monotonous. Towards the north and north-west the country begins to undulate, and the alluvial plain gives place to a broken hilly region known as the Dūn or Rāmnagar Dūn. This consists of a range of low hills, about 20 miles long, north of which the Sumeswar range extends for about 46 miles along the northern frontier. Below these hills extend southwards and eastwards large grassy prairies watered by numerous hill-streams, while in the back-ground tower the Himālayas of Nepāl in an imposing arc of eternal snow.

Natural divisions. The district includes four distinct tracts. To the extreme north are the outliers of the Himālayas known as the Sumeswar and Dūn ranges, which with their foot hills encroach for some 15 miles into the alluvial plain. These hills still contain large stretches of jungle and forest, though the finest timber has long since been cleared away. Skirting these hills is the unhealthy submontane tract, known as the Tarai, consisting mostly of prairie land and forest, in which the scattered clearances of the aboriginal Thārus afford the only evidence of human occupation. The rich and fertile plain which occupies the rest of the district is divided by the Little Gandak into two well defined tracts with markedly different characteristics. The northern portion is composed of old alluvium, and contains much low land admirably suited for rice, but unfit for the cultivation of indigo and *rabi* crops; it is a great rice-producing area traversed by a number of streams flowing southwards. The southern tract, which is composed of recent alluvium deposited during the oscillations of the Gandak while it shifted westwards to its present channel, is characterized by stretches of upland varied in places by large marshy depressions known as *chaurs*; here the soil is generally lighter, and grows indigo, millets, pulses, cereals and oilseeds.

HILL SYSTEM. To the extreme north the Dūn and Sumeswar Hills extend over an area of about 364 square miles. The Sumeswar Hills form part of a long range, which, under different names, runs in practical continuity along the whole length of Nepāl, the only breaks in the chain being caused by rivers seeking an outlet. It is the lowest and outermost of all the Himālayan ranges, immediately overlooking the plains of Hindustān; and at its base lies the swampy feverish Tarai. The hills of this range are mainly composed of imperfectly compacted sandstone, in which are imbedded rocks and pebbles of the same formation. Owing to this ill-formed sandstone, the hills have been worn by the action of rainfall into a series of steep ravines and almost inaccessible summits; and bare steep crags rise from the midst of the luxuriant vegetation with which many of its slopes are clothed.

The average height of the range in this district is 1,500 feet, but the hills vary in altitude from a few hundred feet to 2,884 feet above sea level at Fort Sumeswar, which commands a superb view of the Himālayas. This peak overlooks the Mauri valley in Nepāl and in the back-ground stretches the main range of the Himālayas, hill succeeding hill and peak rising above peak until they culminate in the vast snowy range to the north. The great peaks of Dhaulāgiri (26,826), Gosainthān (26,305) and Gaurīsankar are clearly visible; and the view is said to be, for extent, one of the finest obtainable from any place on the frontier line in British India. The ascent lies along the Sumeswar pass up the bed of the Jūri Pānī stream amid romantic scenery; this pass was commanded by a hill fort during the Nepāl War of 1814-15. About 200 feet below the summit a bungalow has been erected, as it was once hoped that the place might develop into a sanitarium for North Bihār. For this it is in many ways well adapted, as the temperature does not exceed 80° in the hot weather and there is a supply of pure water; but the place has the reputation of being unhealthy except from December to May. At the eastern extremity of the range, where the Kūdi river pierces it, is situated the Bhikhnā Thorī pass through which a British force successfully marched into Nepāl in 1815; and the other principal passes are the Kāpan and Harhā, also leading to Deoghāt in that State.

The only other hills in the district are the Dūn hills, a range of low hills which extends for about 20 miles in a south-easterly direction from the north-west corner of the district, and has an average breadth of 4 to 5 miles. Between this and the Sumeswar range lies what is known as the Dūn valley, an elevated table-land inhabited by aboriginal Thārus.

RIVER SYSTEM.

The general line of drainage is first from north to south, and then from north-west to south-east, the latter being the predominant course of the rivers. To the west the Gandak flows along the whole length of the district, except for a small strip of land, forming the Dhanahā outpost, which lies to the west of it adjoining Gorakhpur. To the north-east the Uriā forms part of the boundary, while to the south-east the district is bounded throughout its length by the Lāl Bakyā and Bāghmati rivers. Besides these boundary rivers, there are a considerable number of rivers and streams, of which the most important is the Little Gandak or Sikrāna. The whole of the country north of this river is watered by a number of tributaries flowing almost due south from Nepāl or the Sumeswar range; to the south there are only two considerable streams, both sluggish and with tortuous channels, in which the water remains almost stagnant except during the rains. The following is a description of the principal rivers; an account of their liability to flood will be found in Chapter VII.

Great Gandak.

The Gandak, or Great Gandak, rises in the central mountain basin of Nepāl, which has been called, from time immemorial, the Sapt Gandaki or the country of the seven Gandaks, from the seven main streams which unite to form this river. After passing through the Deoghāt Hills, 30 miles north of British territory, the united stream flows southwards in a succession of rapids and pools until it reaches the Sumeswar range near Tomāspur. Here the descent is very rapid, and its course lies through a narrow gorge between high cliffs crowned with trees. The Gandak finally leaves the hills through a pass in the sandstone range to the west of the Sumeswar Hills, at Tribenī, where it is joined by the Pānchnad and Sonāha, the name Tribenī being suggested by the confluence of the three streams.

It then flows in a south-easterly direction separating the district from Gorakhpur for a distance of 28 miles, as far as Sattar Ghāt. From this point down to Rājghāt in the Bettiah subdivision the present channel of the Gandak ceases to be the natural boundary, and some 35 villages, in the jurisdiction of the Dhanahā outpost, are situated between it and the old channel of the river; the latter follows a tortuous course of 44 miles along the boundary of the Gorakhpur district until it joins the present channel near Pīpra Ghāt. The united stream then forms a natural boundary between Champāran and Sāran till it leaves the district in the extreme south near Tājpur. A number of streams fall into it during its course through Champāran, such as the Rohuā, Manaur and Bhabsā, which drain the low hills to the south of Tribenī; and several minor streams, which rise in the south of the tract known as the Rāmnagar Dūn, pour their combined waters into it at Rajwatiā near Bagahā.

At first a snow-fed torrent, the Gandak becomes much wider and its stream more equable in velocity after debouching into the plains at Tribenī; and boats come up thus far and take away cargoes of timber. Navigation, however, is difficult owing to the narrow and tortuous course of the river during the hot and cold seasons, and the impetuosity of its current during the rains; large boats rarely go beyond the shoals and rapids near Bagahā, but smaller craft ply as far as Lehra Ghāt in Nepāl. South of Bagahā it becomes a wide-spreading river, with sandy banks, frequently changing its course and exhibiting the operations of alluvion and diluvion on a large scale, wide sandy tracts being formed one year to be swept away the next. It is on record that the main stream was once diverted for over a mile in consequence of the obstruction caused by a boat laden with rice being sunk in its channel. In the rains the stream attains a breadth of 2 to 3 miles, and even in the hot and cold weather it is a quarter of a mile broad. After its entry into British territory, the Gandak first flows over a rocky bed between high banks bordered with forests, but it soon acquires the character of a deltaic river, its bed being raised considerably above the level of the surrounding country. The south of the district is consequently liable to inundation from the river overflowing its banks, but is now protected from its once disastrous floods by an embankment extending from near Bagahā to the southern extremity of Champāran.

The Gandak has been identified with the Kondochates of the Greek geographers and, according to Lassen, is the Sadanīra or everflowing river of the epics. It is also known as the Nārāyani and the Sālgrāmi, the latter name being derived from the *sālgrām* stones found in the bed of the river.

Little Gandak.

Next to the Great Gandak, the largest river in Champāran is the Little Gandak, which rises in the western extremity of the Sumeswar hills and flows through the centre of the district from north-west to south-east till it enters Muzaffarpur. During the first portion of its course, until it turns southwards at Lakhaurā, north of Motihāri, it is joined by a number of hill-streams, which make it an impetuous torrent in the rains. In the dry weather it is generally fordable, and it is navigable for a portion of its course towards the south by boats of small burden. This river rises with great rapidity in the rains, when it sometimes overflows its banks, causing serious inundations. It has frequently changed its course, its oscillations from side to side being facilitated by its banks being composed of sandy friable soil. In the northern portion of its course it is known as the Harhā and in the southern portion as the Burh Gandak, but it is most commonly called the Sikrāna by the local inhabitants.

Lālbegī and Dhanauti. Between the Sikrāna and the Great Gandak, the only important rivers are the Lālbegī and the Dhanauti. The former flows into the Gandak to the north of Gobindganj. The latter was formerly a branch of the Lālbegī, but its upper reaches have silted up, and it is now a sluggish stream falling into the Sikrāna to the east of Pīpra factory. The area on its banks is reported to be very unhealthy, and a large tract of country to the north-west of Motihāri is uninhabited on this account. A proposal was made during the famine of 1897 to reopen the connection which once existed between the Gandak and Dhanauti, so as to ensure a flow of water along the bed of the latter, and thus render the neighbouring country more healthy; but the project was not carried out.

Bāghmati. The Bāghmati forms part of the eastern boundary from Adauri on the north to Norwā on the south, a distance of about 35 miles. Its current is very rapid, sometimes reaching 7 miles an hour in its upper reaches during heavy freshets. It runs low during the cold season, and also when no rain has fallen; but after a few days' rain it often inundates the country far inland. It has changed its course several times, for the soil along its banks, being very light and friable, is easily washed away. In this portion of its course the river is navigable by boats of 15 to 18 tons burthen as far as Maniāri Ghāt. Its principal tributary is the Lāl Bakyā, which joins it near Adauri.

Minor rivers. The other rivers are of minor importance, most of them being hill streams flowing into the Little Gandak in the northern portion of its course. Some of the streams, such as the Uriā, Dhoram and Pandai, are used for irrigation, but the supply in many cases is dependent on the Nepalese, who are able to control it by building embankments across the streams in their own territory. Some, such as Bhabsā, Manaur, Rohuā, and Pānchnad, present some very picturesque scenes in the upper portion of their course, where the current strikes against high sandstone cliffs 20 to 90 feet high. The following is an account of the more important of these streams.

Uriā. The Uriā, which flows due south from Nepāl, separates Champāran from Nepāl for 12 miles, and then flows southwards through the district for 14 miles. It joins the Dhoram near Mainpur, and the united stream joins the Little Gandak about 3 miles west of Ahirauliā.

Dhoram. The Dhoram rises in the Churiā Ghāti hills, a low range of hills in Nepāl, known locally as the Chiriaghatti hills, and enters Champāran, about 5 miles south of the Nepāl outpost station of Thorī. At first it flows in a westerly direction for about 5 miles, but soon turns to the south and is joined by the Pandai, the united stream falling into the Uriā near Mainpur, about 10 miles from the frontier.

Pandai. The Pandai rises on the north of the Sumeswar range, and enters the district through a pass between that range and the Churiā Ghāti range; at Bhikhnā Thorī. After it debouches from the hills, it flows for a few miles towards the west over a rocky bed and then curves to the south-east, in which direction it flows until it joins the Dhoram, about 2 miles east of Shikārpur.

Masān. The Masān rises in the Sumeswar range, close to Fort Sumeswar, and flows in a southern direction until it turns to the east near Barbīro. It drains a large tract of country, receiving nearly all the flood water of the Dūn, and is liable to heavy floods. Its catchment area is 150 square miles, three-fourths of which is hilly ground. It has a broad sandy bed throughout its course, and soon runs dry after the rains stop.

Other rivers. The four rivers last mentioned all traverse the north of the district; and the same tract is watered by a number of smaller streams such as the Harborā, Balaurā and Rāmrekhā. To the south-east one of the largest rivers debouching from Nepal is the Tilāri, locally known as the Telāwe, immediately to the north of Sugauli; this river is said never to run dry, and in October there is a depth of 4 to 5 feet in the stream, which is from 150 to 180 feet broad. The Gadh, an adjoining stream, has a smaller supply, and the next stream of importance is the Pūsa. The only other river in this portion of the district calling for separate mention is the Tiar, which feeds the canal of the same name.

Lakes and marshes. A remarkable physical feature of Champāran is a chain of lakes, 43 in number, running through the centre of the district. These lakes, of which the largest are at Lālsaraiyā, Sugāon, Turkauliā, Motihāri, Pīpra, Sirahā, Nawāda and Tetāria, extend over an area of 139 square miles, and evidently mark an old bed of the Great Gandak. Their depth varies from 3 to 20 feet, and the water, which is considered very unhealthy, never entirely dries up. They contain a number of fish; and indigo factories are built on the banks of the greater number of them.

There are also a number of swamps and marshes scattered over the district, of which one of the most remarkable is the one known as Bahās, along the borders of *tappās* Bahās and Balthar. This is a genuine bog during the greater part of the year, and even in the hot weather the prudent wayfarer cautiously feels his way with a stick or bamboo across the treacherous ground. This unpromising marsh, however, produces fine crops of rice, the seed being sown broadcast from canoes.

FORESTS. The only forests left in the district are situated in the Bagahā and Shikārpur thānas to the north, where a belt of forest and jungle stretches over an area of 427 square miles. Those on the Sumeswar range, which belong to the Rāmnagar Rāj, have been leased for many years past to European capitalists and have been systematically worked, with the result that the best timber has been removed. The most valuable trees found in these forests are *sāl* (Shorea robusta), *sisū* (Dalbergia Sissoo) and *tūn* (Cedrela Toona). The minor products consist of *sabai* grass, *narkat* reeds, honey, bees' wax, lac and various medicinal plants. There is also a large tract of forest, belonging to the Bettiah Rāj, in Rājpur Sihoriā in the extreme north-west corner of the district. This forest-bearing tract extends over 77 square miles, and is divisible into two portions separated from each other by the Tribenī Canal, that to the east being a fairly compact area consisting mainly of low hills and plateaux, and that to the west being a low-lying area adjoining the Gandak river. The eastern tract extends over an area of 50 square miles, and is a hilly region intersected by small nullahs, which cut up the hills into narrow sharp-edged ridges. The western tract extends over an area of 27 square miles and consists of a straggling narrow belt of forest, scarcely over 3 miles wide, along the bank of the Gandak.

In the eastern area, which is the only one containing *sāl*, it is estimated that workable *sāl* of 4 feet in girth or more extends over 36½ square miles. Large areas in this tract, however, situated in recent alluvial lands in the valleys, are either unproductive or grow *khair* (Acacia Catechu) and *sisū*; and on somewhat older or higher land there is a mixed forest of Terminalia, Adina cordifolia, *simul* or red cotton tree (Bombax malabaricum), Odina, etc. The outer flanks of this tract are generally occupied by mixed forests, in which *sāl* appears as soon as the ground rises. The best *sāl* attains a height of 80 or 90 feet, the usual girth being 2 to 5 feet. The bulk of the *sāl* area, however, is only moderately stocked, the trees being of indifferent height and girth, while crooked and unsound trees are numerous.

In the western area *sisū* is found in a few localities in or close to the Gandak, where it attains a girth of 6 feet, but the timber has been heavily felled, so that trees over 4 feet in girth are now scarce. *Khair* covers a larger area, but is usually very small and under 3 feet in girth. Large areas are covered with red cotton trees and grass only, heavy grazing and annual fires precluding the development of other species; while owing to the injuries so caused the trees are often badly shaped, diseased or dead.

The Dūn and Sumeswar hills in the extreme north, which are a continuation of the Siwālik range, are formed of ill-compacted sandstone, scored by the bare stony beds of the water-courses which rush down in the rains. There is little doubt that the rocks of these hills are of the same horizon as the Churiā Ghāti range south of Kātmāndu, *i.e.*, Siwālik or Upper Tertiary.* The beds of the Churiā Ghāti range dip at 30° N. N. W., and we may regard the structure of these Himālayan foot-hills as having been originally anticlinal, the southern half of the anticline having disappeared. No older rocks are exposed *in situ* in this area, but traces of them as boulders may be found in the gravel beds at the foot of the hills. These gravel beds form the slope known as *bhābar*, and are covered with forest, in which *sāl* (Shorea robusta) predominates; this slope is traversed by a number of streams issuing from the northern hills, which lose a part of their water by percolation through the gravel. In the Tarai, at the base of the slope, much of the water which has percolated the gravel reissues in the form of springs; here the ground is marshy, and high grass replaces the forest. The remainder of the district is an alluvial plain, a large portion of which has been formed by the Great Gandak, a river which now forms the south-western boundary, but formerly flowed through the centre of the district along the course indicated on the maps as the Little or Burh Gandak. The whole of the tract between the latter river and the present channel of the Great Gandak has been subject to fluvial action within comparatively recent times, and the soil is the *bāngar* or older alluvium which is a characteristic feature of the Gangetic valley. Gold is washed in minute quantities from the Gandak river and from the Pānchnad, Harhā, Bhabsā and Sonāha hill-streams in the north of the district. Beds of *kankar* or nodular limestone are found in workable quantities near Lauriyā Ararāj, and along the banks of the Harhā river in Bagahā thāna; it is used for road metal and for burning into lime. Saliferous earth is found in all parts of the district, and a special caste, the Nuniās, earn a scanty livelihood by extracting saltpetre.† GEOLOGY.

Botanically, Champāran may be divided into several distinct areas. To the north are the Sumeswar and Dūn ranges covered with forest and scrub wood, and next comes a narrow, more or less BOTANY.

---

* *See* Mr. Medlicott's Account of a Journey to Kātmāndu, Records, Geological Survey of India, Vol. viii, p. 93.

† I am indebted to Mr. G. de P. Cotter, Assistant Superintendent, Geological Survey of India, for revising this account of the geology of Champāran.

sloping, gravelly, submontane tract covered, except along river-beds, with forest, the constituent species of which are those that occur on the lower slopes of the mountains themselves. In existing river beds only a few tough flexible bushes occur; along abandoned shingly river courses the jungle is open and park-like, and the species are those characteristic of a drier climate than obtains in the forest alongside. The submontane forest is succeeded by a belt of swampy land of varying width, covered with long reedy grasses. Further out into the plain the ground, if so high as to be free from inundation, is in waste tracts usually covered with open jungle of a bushy character.

Nearly the whole of the rest of the district is under cultivation, and is bare or diversified with bamboos, palms, and orchards of mangoes, or less often groves of other trees. The tracts liable to inundation are mainly confined to the banks of the larger rivers, and are there often covered with a jungle of reeds and bushes, largely tamarisk, with a few trees. To the south, however, the river courses widen considerably in proportion to their streams, and their beds contain little or no vegetation. The powerful current in the rains sweeps everything away; the shingly or sandy banks are at other seasons too dry to admit of much growth. But old river beds, marshes, lakes and such streams as are stagnant or nearly so except after heavy rains, have a mass of vegetation, while even small rivers with a gentle stream abound with water plants.*

The belt of forest along the northern border of the district contains *sāl* (Shorea robusta), *sisū* (Dalbergia Sissoo) and *tūn* (Cedrela Toona); the red cotton tree (Bombax malabaricum) and *khair* (Acacia catechu) are also common. Bamboos thrive in the moist Tarai tract, *sabai* grass (Ischœmum angustifolium) and the *narkat* reed (Amphadonax falcata) are also valuable products, and extensive thickets of tamarisk line the Gandak river. In the south cultivation is closer, and the crops leave room for little besides weeds, grasses and sedges, chiefly species of Panicum and Cyperus, though on patches of waste land thickets of *sisū* very rapidly appear. The sluggish streams and lakes are filled with water weeds, the sides being often fringed by reedy grasses, bulrushes and tamarisk. Near villages, small shrubberies may be found containing mango, *sisū*, Eugenia jambolana, various species of Ficus and occasional tamarind, and a few other semi-spontaneous and more or less useful species. Both the palmyra (Borassus flabellifer) and date-palm (Phœnix sylvestris) occur planted and at times self-sown, but neither in great abundance.

* D. Prain, *Bengal Plants*, Calcutta, 1903.

The carnivora of Champāran comprise tiger, leopard, bear and other smaller species. The ungulata are represented by *sāmbar*, spotted deer, hog deer, barking deer, *nīlgai*, antelope and wild pig. Tigers are only found in the jungles in the extreme north of the district bordering on the Nepāl hills. Even here they are not very numerous, though one or two are shot every year; and as the population is sparse and game fairly plentiful, they do comparatively little damage. Occasionally, however, one takes to man-eating, as happened in 1903 and 1904, when one of these brutes, carried off several wood-cutters in the Rāmnagar forests, until he was finally destroyed by poison on one of his kills. Among his victims was a priest of the Roman Catholic Mission at Bettiah, who was killed close to the Sumeswar bungalow while making the ascent of the hills. Leopards (Felis pardus) are found in the same tract; they seem never to be found in the central and southern parts of the district, though suitable cover exists in many places. Bears are occasionally met with in the lower ranges of hills in the north of the district, but they do little or no damage and are by no means common. Wolves and hyænas were, it is said, formerly fairly common, but seem now to be nearly, if not quite, extinct. FAUNA.

Wild pig (Sus cristatus) are numerous on the *diāras* of the Gandak, and are fairly common throughout the district in any place where suitable cover is found. Pigsticking is a favourite form of sport among the European residents, 10 to 15 boars being sometimes got in a day. *Sāmbar* (Cervus unicolor) are only found in the hills and heavy jungle in the north; as a rule, they have poor heads, as compared with those of Central India. Spotted deer (Cervus axis) are found in the same tract and in one or two other places where they have been preserved. Barking deer (Cervulus muntjac) are also met with in the north, but are not common. Hog deer (Cervus porcinus) are found on some of the *diāras* of the Gandak; and black buck (Antilope cervicapra) are fairly numerous in a few localities in the north of the district, but, in common with all the species enumerated above, are on the decrease, being shot at all seasons and without regard to age or sex. *Nīlgai* (Boselaphus tragocamelus) are fairly common all over the district and do a good deal of damage; they appear to be on the increase, as the population, being largely composed of Hindus, regard them as a species of cow. Possibly, however, if they become too much of a nuisance, these scruples may be got over by inventing a new name for them, as is said to have been done in Sāran, where, it is reported, Hindus kill them and salve their consciences by calling them *ban bakri* or jungle goat.

Game birds. The game birds of Champāran consist of peafowl, jungle fowl, *kālij* pheasant, black, grey and marsh (or kyah) partridge (Ortygornis gularis) and florican, both the Bengal (Sypheotides bengalensis) and the lesser florican (Sypheotides auritus), although neither can be said to be common. Woodcock and wood-snipe are said to be occasionally obtained in the north; and pintailed snipe and common snipe are found in suitable localities throughout the district, but never in very large numbers, 15 to 20 couple being an unusually good bag. Among duck the red-headed and white-eyed pochard, the pintail, and the gadwall are most common, but several other species are met with. Grey quail and button quail are common, the former affording excellent sport in the early hot weather.

Fish. The rivers contain *buāli*, *rohu*, *tengrā*, *bachwā* and other species; and the numerous so-called lakes found all over the district, as well as the artificial tanks, are well stocked with *rohu*, *naini*, *katlā* and *buāli*. Mahseer are found in the upper reaches of the Great Gandak. Both the *gariāl* or fish-eating alligator and the mugger or snub-nosed species are common in the Gandak. Some of the latter occasionally carry off women and children, but they are neither so large nor so destructive as those found in the Sundarbans.

CLIMATE. Champāran has the reputation of having the worst climate in Bihār, but this is only true of the Tarai in the neighbourhood of Rāmnagar and of the sub-montane tract included in thānas Bagahā and Shikārpur. The evil reputation which attaches to this part of the district is well illustrated by an old legend which says that once a stalwart wrestler (*pahlwān*) came to the court of the Rājā of Rāmnagar or Bettiah, and boasted of his prowess, saying he would defeat all the wrestlers in the Rājā's service. On this, the Rājā asked him to wait for six months, after which period a match would be arranged, at which he might vindicate his boast. To this the stranger agreed; so he was told off to live in a Tarai village, where he soon contracted fever. At the end of six months, he reappeared before the Rājā, pale, weak and emaciated, and saying that he had been defeated by the greatest *pahlwān* in the Rājā's service—fever—and implored permission to return to his home.

Except in these notoriously unhealthy tracts the climate is comparatively pleasant and cool throughout the year. From November to March it is cold and bracing, especially at night, but cloudy skies and cold-weather showers are more frequent than in districts further removed from the hills; light fogs occur occasionally in the day time. The hot weather begins in the middle of March and is at its height in May, a hot, dry month, when westerly winds prevail; but compared with other districts, the temperature is not excessive. In the rainy season the climate is damper and cooler than in the adjoining districts, but the nights are hot and disagreeable, except when there is an east wind to temper the atmosphere. In October the steamy heat begins to be less oppressive, and in November the cold weather is ushered in by a chilly north wind blowing from the hills. It is said that owing to the progress made in clearing the forests and the extension of cultivation in the north of the district, the rainfall is decreasing, while the extremes of temperature are becoming more marked and the mean temperature is rising.

On the whole, the temperature is comparatively low, the mean for the year being 76°. The mean maximum temperature rises to 97° in April and May and falls to 73° in January, more than half the change taking place in November and December. The mean minimum temperature varies from 47° in January to 78° in July and August. The mean humidity for the year is 83 per cent. of saturation; it varies from 68 per cent. to 72 per cent. from March to May, and between 82 per cent. and 93 per cent. in other months, the greatest humidity being in January. **Temperature and humidity.**

The rainfall is heavier than in any other district in West Bihār, and is especially heavy in the sub-montane tract, partly owing to the heavy showers which fall when cyclonic storms break up on reaching the hills, and partly because the monsoon current is stronger towards the west over the districts just under the hills. The average annual rainfall for the whole district is 54·09 inches, of which 2·61 inches fall in May, 9·34 inches in June, 13·71 inches in July, 12·81 inches in August, 9·89 inches in September and 3·27 inches in October. Rainfall in the latter two months is very capricious, and on the other hand there are sometimes very heavy falls in August; thus in August 1906 there were no less than 32·47 inches at Motīhāri or 20 inches above the normal. The following table shows the rainfall recorded at the various registering stations during the cold, hot and rainy seasons, the figures shown being the averages recorded in each case— **Rainfall.**

STATION.	Years recorded.	November to February.	March to May.	June to October.	Annual average.
MOTIHARI ...	40-43	1·19	3·81	46·47	51·47
BETTIAH ...	29-30	1·36	3·78	48·61	53·75
BAGAHA ...	15-16	1·79	4·07	56·74	62·60
BARHARWA ...	15-16	1·29	2·91	44·33	48·53
AVERAGE ...		1·41	3·64	49·04	54·09

CHAPTER II.

HISTORY.

LEGENDARY HISTORY.

LEGENDARY history, local tradition,[1] the names of places and archæological remains, all point to a prehistoric past. Local tradition asserts that in the early ages Champāran was a dense primeval forest, in whose solitude Brāhman hermits studied the *aranyakas*, which, as their name implies, were to be read in silvan retreats; and the name Champāran itself is said to be derived from the fact that the district was formerly one vast forest (*aranya*) of *champā* trees. It is, at least, certain that in the Vishnu and other Purānas mention is often made of a Champak-aranya stretching along the Sālgrāmi or Nārāyani river, which is another name for the Gandak; and according to the descriptions contained in ancient writings, it was a place of retreat for Hindu ascetics, where, removed from worldly ambitions, they could contemplate the Eternal Presence in the silence of a vast untrodden forest. Various parts of the district are also connected by immemorial tradition with many of the great Hindu *rishis*. Thus, *tappā* Duho Suho is said to be so-called after the two wives of Rājā Uttānpāda, Du Rānī and Su Rānī, and to have been the *tapoban* or silvan retreat of his son Dhruba. Legend relates that in consequence of the jealousy of his favourite wife, Su Rānī, the Rājā sent Du Rānī into exile. Shortly afterwards, while hunting in the forest, he lost his way, took shelter in the humble cottage belonging to the banished queen, and spent the night there. Dhruba was subsequently born in the forest, and there gave himself up from early infancy to the contemplation of heavenly things.

Other *tappās* have also names associated with different Hindu sages, such as Chānkī, Deorāj, Māndo, Sugāon and Jamhaulī; and the whole district is dotted over with places held in religious esteem as the traditional abodes of Hindu *rishis*, such as Vālmīki, in whose hermitage Sītā, the banished spouse of Rāma, is said to have taken shelter. This great sage is reputed to have resided near Sangrāmpur, and the village is believed to be indebted for its name (which means the city of the battle) to the famous fight between Rāma and his two sons, Lava and Kusha. The popular belief also is that within this district lay the kingdom of Virāt mentioned in the Mahābhārata as the tract within which the Pāndavas spent the last year of their weary 12 years' exile; and that its capital, where the five brothers resided a year, was situated at or near a village called Vairāti, 6 or 7 miles west of Rāmnagar.

Apart, however, from these traditions, it seems probable that Champāran was occupied at an early period by races of Aryan descent and formed part of the country in which the Videhas settled after their migration from the Punjab. According to the legend preserved in Vedic literature, Agni, the god of fire, accompanied the Videhas in their march eastwards from the banks of the Saraswatī, and when they came to the broad stream of the Gandak, informed them that their home lay to the east of that river. Thenceforward the Videhas lived to the east of the Gandak, where they cleared the forests, cultivated the virgin soil, and founded a great and powerful kingdom. This kingdom was in course of time ruled over by king Janaka, who is said by local legend to have lived at Chānkīgarh, known locally as Jānkīgarh, 11 miles north of Lauriyā Nandangarh. Under his rule, according to Hindu mythology, the kingdom of Mithilā was the most civilized kingdom in India. His court was a centre of learning and attracted all the most learned men of the time; Vedic literature was enriched by the studies of the scholars who flocked there; his chief priest, Yājnavalkya, inaugurated the stupendous task of revising the Yajur Vedas; and the speculations of the monarch himself, enshrined in the sacred works called the Upanishads, are still cherished with veneration by the Hindu community.

EARLY HISTORIC PERIOD.

The earliest event which can claim historic reality is the rise of the Vrijjian oligarchical republic, which apparently replaced the old monarchical rule of Videha, while the centre of power shifted from Mithilā to Vaisāli, the modern Basārh in the adjoining district of Muzaffarpur. The Vrijjians, it has been suggested, were in all probability Scythian invaders whose power reached as far as the Ganges to the south and the Himālayas on the north.* They founded a confederacy consisting of several clans, among whom the most powerful were the Lichchhavis, who held the tract now known as Tirhut. At the close of the 6th century B. C. the growing power of the latter brought them into collision with the rising kingdom of Magadha, the limits of which roughly corresponded with the present districts of Patna and Gayā. For some time Ajātasatru, the king of this tract, had been engaged in extending his rule over neighbouring states, and his ambition now

* S. Beal, *Buddhist Records of the Western World* (1884), p. xvi.

induced him to undertake the conquest of the Lichchhavis. The invasion was successful; the Lichchhavi capital, Vaisāli, was occupied; and Ajātasatru became master of Tirhut. It is probable that the invader carried his victorious arms to their natural limit, the foot of the mountains, and that from this time the whole country between the Ganges and the Himālayas became subject, more or less directly, to the suzerainty of Magadha.*

But few remains of the early period are left, though it has been suggested that in this district Motīhāri, Kesariyā, Simrāon and Lauriyā Nandangarh were once capitals of the Vrijjian tribes.† At Nandangarh great mounds of earth are still extant which have been attributed to this race; and it has been conjectured that they were erected to serve as sepulchral barrows for their rulers. In one of them a small punch-marked silver coin has been found, which is anterior to the time of Alexander the Great and may be as old as 1000 B.C.; and it seems at least certain that they were erected before the rise and spread of Buddhism. A few places in Champāran may be associated with the life of the great founder of that religion. According to Buddhist tradition, Buddha rode forth by night from his father's house on his favourite white steed, Kanthaka, accompanied by his charioteer, Chandaka, and after crossing the river Anoma bade him return with the horse, stripped himself of his princely dress and ornaments, cut his hair, and assumed the outward aspect and character of an ascetic. The village of Bihār in this district, east of the Gandak, is said to mark the traditional site of Chandaka's return, and the name at least indicates that it once contained a Buddhist monastery (*vihāra*).‡ Buddha subsequently returned in answer to an appeal from the Vrijjians, who implored him to deliver them from a pestilence which devastated their country. Here he made many converts; and at the end of his long ministry he passed through Champāran on his last march from Vaisāli to Kusinārā, the scene of his death: Lauriyā Nandangarh or its neighbourhood is believed by some to be the site of the "Ashes stūpa" erected over the ashes or charcoal taken from his funeral pyre.‡

Asoka's reign. Although the Lichchhavis had been defeated, the powerful Vrijjian confederacy does not appear to have been broken up; and this district and Muzaffarpur continued to form part of their territory, under the suzerainty of the king of Magadha. In the

* V. A. Smith, *Early History of India* (1904), p. 30.

† A. Cunningham, *Ancient Geography of India* (1871), p. 445.

‡ V. A. Smith, *Kusinārā or Kusinagara,* Journal of the Royal Asiatic Society, 1902.

fourth century B.C. it passed under the sway of the Mauryan Emperor; and records and memorials of that dynasty exist to this day in the great pillars erected by Asoka, in the 21st year of his reign, when he made a tour to the sacred sites of Buddhism. The Emperor's line of march probably followed the route taken by Buddha on the way to his death, and is marked in this district by a stūpa at Kesariyā and by the pillars of Lauriyā Ararāj, Lauriyā Nandangarh and Rāmpurwā. Nepāl was at this time an integral part of the empire and was probably administered directly from the capital as one of the home provinces. The royal road to it from Pātaliputra led first to Vaisāli and then passed Kesariyā, Lauriyā, Ararāj, Bettiah, Lauriyā Nandangarh, Chānkīgarh and Rāmpurwā in this district, entering the hills by the Bhikhnā Thorī pass.

Chinese pilgrims.

This appears also to have been a pilgrim road, and was followed at least in part by the Chinese pilgrim Fa Hian, who about 400 A.D. visited the site of Chandaka's return, then proceeded to the Ashes stūpa and after going on to Kusinagara returned to Vaisāli. The next mention of this part of the country appears to occur in the account of his travels left by Sung-yun, who visited the north-west of India in 518, and found it in possession of a race of Huns, who had conquered or received tribute from more than 40 countries, among which he mentions Tieh-lo in the south. The symbols Tieh-lo possibly represent Tīrabhukti, the present Tirhut and the old land of the Vrijjians. This conquest was achieved two generations before Sung-yun's time, and from other sources we know that towards the close of the fifth century the White Huns of the Oxus valley penetrated into the heart of the Gangetic provinces and overcame the Gupta Emperor, who at this time ruled Champāran.*

Neither Fa Hian nor Sung-yun left any account from which an insight can be gained into the conditions prevailing in this part of the country, but a detailed description is given by Hiuen Tsiang, the prince of Chinese pilgrims, who travelled through Champāran in the first half of the seventh century, on his way from the Lumbini Garden to Kusinagara. The first place which he visited in this district was the site of Chandaka's return, which he mentions as being situated in the kingdom of Rāma, a kingdom which had been waste and desolate for many years, the towns being decayed and the inhabitants few. The site of Chandaka's return

---

* A sculptured column at Kahāon in the east of the Gorakhpur district records the fact that the rule of Skandagupta included the Eastern Provinces in the year 460, and characterizes his rule as tranquil. V. A. Smith, *Early History of India* (1904), p. 629.

was commemorated by a great stūpa built by Asoka in the midst of dense forest. Leaving this place, he proceeded south-east through the middle of a desert to the stūpa built over the ashes of Buddha, by which were an old Buddhist monastery and another large stūpa built by Asoka, mostly in ruins but still 100 feet high. From this place he went north-east to Kusinagara "through a great forest along a dangerous and difficult road, where wild oxen and herds of elephants, and robbers and hunters cause incessant troubles to travellers." This account sufficiently shows that the northern part of Champāran was still almost an uninhabited waste.

Tibetan invasion. At the time of Hiuen's Tsiang's visit Tirhut formed part of the territory acknowledging the sway of Harshavardhana or Silāditya, who possessed full sovereign power over Western and Central Bengal, and exercised a certain amount of control as far east as Assam. On his death in 648, one of his ministers, Arjuna, usurped the throne, and attacked a mission which was on its way from the Emperor of China. "The members of the escort were massacred, and the property of the mission plundered; but the envoys, Wang-hiuen-tse and his colleague, were fortunate enough to escape into Nepāl by night. The reigning king of Tibet, the famous Strongtsan Gampo, who was married to a Chinese princess, succoured the fugitives, and supplied them with a force of 1,000 horsemen, which co-operated with a Nepalese contingent of 7,000 men. With this small army Wang-hiuen-tse descended into the plains, and, after a three days' siege, succeeded in storming the chief city of Tirhut. Three thousand of the garrison were beheaded, and 10,000 persons were drowned in the neighbouring river. Arjuna fled, and having collected a fresh force, offered battle. He was again disastrously defeated and taken prisoner. The victor promptly beheaded a thousand prisoners; and in a latter action captured the entire royal family, took 12,000 prisoners, and obtained 30,000 head of cattle."* Five hundred and eighty walled towns made their submission, and Arjuna was carried off in chains to China. Wang-hiuen-tse once more visited the scene of his adventures, being sent by Imperial order in 657 A.D. to offer robes at the Buddhist holy places. He entered India through Nepāl, probably by the old pilgrim route through the Bhikhnā Thorī pass, and thence marched through to Vaisāli, Bodh Gayā and other sacred spots.*

MEDIÆVAL PERIOD. From this time there is no clear record of the history of Tirhut until the ascendency of the Pāla dynasty (800—1200). We know that Nepāl, which had been a tributary state, recovered

* V. A. Smith, *Early History of India* (1904), pp. 298-99.

its independence 10 years after the death of Harsha; and it appears probable that in Champāran also the local chiefs asserted their autonomy and that the country was divided among a number of petty potentates. Early in the ninth century Gopāla, the founder of the Pāla dynasty, became ruler of Bengal, and towards the close of his life (cir. 850 A.D.) he extended his power westward over Bihār. In the 10th century we find the Mithilās mentioned among the races against whom Yasovarman, the Chandella king of Jejabhukti (cir. 925), claimed to have warred successfully;* and early in the 11th century Tirhut seems to have passed under the rule of the Kalachuri kings of Chedi, a tract corresponding to the present Central Provinces, for in 1019 A.D. it acknowledged the sovereignty of Gangeyadeva,† one of the most ambitious of the Chedi kings, who aimed at attaining paramount power in Northern India. The end of that century witnessed the rise of the power of the Sena kings, who not only wrested the eastern provinces from the Pālas, but also appear to have carried their arms northwards to North Bihār. Mithilā formed the north-western province of the kingdom of the Senas, and their rule in this part of Bihār is still commemorated by the use of the Lakshmana Sena era, the first current year (1119-20 A.D.) of which was apparently the date of either the accession or the coronation of Lakshmana Sena, the last great king of the Sena dynasty.

MUHAMMADAN PERIOD.

In the beginning of the 13th century the tide of Muhammadan conquest swept over Bihār, but it does not appear to have reached far north of the Ganges; for it is not till the time of Ghiās-ud-dīn Iwaz, the Muhammadan Governor of Bengal between 1211 and 1226, that we learn that the banner of Islām was triumphantly carried into the territories of the Rājā of Tirhut, which had never before been subdued, and the Rājā compelled to pay tribute. This appears, however, to have been rather a successful invasion than an effectual conquest of the country; for a local dynasty of Hindu kings was established about this time‡ at Simrāon in the north-east corner of the district; and these kings succeeded in maintaining their rule over Tirhut for

* C. M. Duff, *Chronology of India* (1899), p. 87.

† Prof. C. Bendall, *History of Nepal and Surrounding Kingdoms*, J. A. S. B., Part I, 1903.

‡ The traditional date of the foundation of Simrāon is the Samvat year 1154 or 1097 A.D. But as Hara Singh Deva, the fifth in descent from its founder Nānyupa, fled to Nepāl in 1323 A.D., the date should probably be referred to the Saka era, which would place the foundation of the capital in 1232 A.D. See Reports Arch. Surv. Ind., Vol. XVI, pp. 1—5.

over a century, until the invasion of Tughlak Shāh in 1323 put an end to their independence.

Simrāon dynasty.

Of the earlier kings of this dynasty we have only traditional accounts. Its founder was one Nāna or Nānyupa Deva, who is said to have established himself at Simrāon, to have subdued the whole of Mithilā, and to have overcome the king of Nepāl. Tradition relates that one of his sons reigned in Nepāl, and the other, Gangā Deva, in Mithilā. The latter is credited with having introduced the system of fiscal divisions or *parganas* for the purposes of revenue administration ; while a *chaudhri* or headman was appointed in each *pargana* to collect the revenue, and a *panchāyat* was chosen to settle all disputes. Gangā Deva was succeeded by his son Narsingh Deva, who is said to have had a quarrel with his kinsman, the king of Nepāl, the upshot of which was that Mithilā and Nepāl were separated never to be united again. Rām Singh Deva, who succeeded his father on the throne, was a pious devotee and a firm patron of sacred literature. Under his auspices, several well-known commentaries on the Vedas were compiled ; rules were framed for the guidance of Hindus in their religious and social observances ; and an officer was appointed in each village to adjudicate upon all questions arising from the working of these new canons of conduct. Various reforms in the system of internal administration are also attributed to this king. In every village a police officer was appointed whose duty it was to make a daily report of all occurrences worthy of note to the *chaudhri* or head revenue-collector of the *pargana;* the latter being assigned, in return for his services, a certain quantity of land, the produce of which was appropriated by him and his heirs in office. To the same period too is assigned the rise of the system of *pātwarīs* or village accountants, who were, it is said, paid at the rate of Rs. 10 a month from the village funds. On the death of Rām Singh Deva, his son Sakti Singh ascended the throne, but his despotism appears to have offended the nobles, and one of his ministers established a council of seven elders as a check upon the autocratic power of the king.

Hara Singh Deva, the son of Sakti Singh, was the last but, in popular esteem, the greatest of the line. It was this king, it is believed, who grouped the Maithil Brāhmans into the three main divisions of Srotiya, Jog and Jaiwār, made a classification of the sub-castes according to *mels* and *dihs*, introduced the other matrimonial arrangements prevailing to this day, and established the order of Panjiāras or genealogists, who keep intact the purity of the Brāhman blood ; the latter measure is said to have been taken by him in consequence of one of his ministers having married, in ignorance, a lady within the prohibited degrees of relationship. With this king at least we enter upon historical ground. In 1323 the Emperor Tughlak Shāh led his victorious forces into Tirhut on his march back from the defeat of Bahādur Shāh, the rebellious Governor of Bengal, and proceeded to reduce this outlying portion of the empire. Hara Singh fell back on the capital, Simrāon, but this was soon taken and reduced to ruins. Ferishta gives the following account of its capture:—"As the king was passing near the hills of Tirhut, the Rājā appeared in arms, but was pursued into the woods. Finding his army could not penetrate them, the king alighted from his horse, called for a hatchet, and cut down one of the trees with his own hand. The troops, on seeing this, applied themselves to work with such spirit that the forest seemed to vanish before them. They arrived at length at a fort surrounded by seven ditches, full of water, and a high wall. The king invested the place, filled up the ditches, and destroyed the wall in three weeks. The Rājā and his family were taken and great booty obtained." The account generally received is that Hara Singh escaped to Nepāl and conquered it, and that his descendants continued to rule that country till they were displaced by Prithwī Nārāyan on the Gurkha conquest of Nepāl in 1769.* Recent researches, however, seem to show that neither Hara Singh nor his ancestors succeeded in maintaining any effectual authority over Nepāl, and Professor Bendall sums up the position of this dynasty as follows:—"Until more evidence is forthcoming, it seems safer to regard Hara Singh and his ancestors, who reigned in Tirhut, Simrāon, and also possibly other parts of the Nepāl Tarai, as at most titular kings of Nepāl, even if they really claimed sovereignty over the valley of Nepāl at all."†

Sugāon or Thākur dynasty.

With the flight of Hara Singh, Tirhut became a dependency of the empire of Delhi, and Tughlak Shāh placed it under Kāmeswara Thākur, the founder of the Sugāon or Thākur dynasty, which continued to rule over Tirhut till early in the 16th century. Here, as elsewhere, the Muhammadan conquest passed over the land without sweeping away all the ancient landmarks. So long as they acknowledged their submission to the Muhammadans by the payment of an annual tribute, the Hindu rulers of Tirhut were practically independent; but their tenure of power

* See Oldfield's Sketches from Nepal, Vol. I, 1880.

† Prof. C. Bendall, *History of Nepal and Surrounding Kingdoms*, J. A. S. B., Vol. LXXII, Part I, 1903.

always depended solely on the pleasure of their Muhammadan over-lords. The first of the line, Kāmeswara, was deposed by Firoz Shāh (1353), who gave the empty throne to Bhogiswara, the younger son of Kāmeswara and his own personal friend. Kīrtti Singh, the second in descent from Bhogiswara, was also a younger son, who similarly obtained a principality as a personal favour from the Emperor, as a result of a visit to Delhi.

The most famous of the whole line, Siva Singh, rebelled in 1402 A.D., and succeeded in establishing his independence, but his triumph was short-lived, as three years afterwards he was conquered by the Musalmāns and carried off to Delhi; while his wife, Lakshimā Thākurānī, accompanied by the poet Vidyāpati, took refuge in Nepāl, and there committed *satī* when no news of her husband had been received for 12 years. The memory of Siva Singh is still preserved among the people as the greatest of their kings, but his chief claim to fame is that he was a royal patron of learning. Not only was his wife, Lakshimā, one of the few learned women of India, but his court was frequented by poets and scholars, of whom Vidyāpati was at once the most famous and the most faithful. In this respect, Siva Singh was true to the traditions of his house. Like the Senas, who are said to have devoted their efforts to collecting troops of poems rather than to marshalling armies of soldiers, these Brāhman princes were noted for their encouragement of learning and the fine arts. Their courts were said to be the asylum of Sanskrit *belles lettres* and philosophy; and they lived immersed in the study of sacred books and poems.*

The Sugāon dynasty continued to hold the north of Tirhut as tributary princes for about a century after the capture of Hara Singh. Towards the close of the 15th century it appears to have been included within the territory of Husain Shāh, king of Bengal (1493—1518), who built a line of forts from Kāmrūp in Assam as far as Bettiah to protect the country against the hill tribes; but by a treaty, concluded at Bārh in 1499, between him and the Emperor Sikandar Lodī it was agreed that the latter should retain Bihār, Tirhut and *Sarkār* Sāran on condition that he did not invade Bengal; and Sikandar Lodī then swept down upon Tirhut. Unable to face the imperial forces, the Rājā of Tirhut advanced to meet him, made his submission and was allowed to make terms on the payment of a fine amounting to

* *Vidyāpati and His Contemporaries*, and *Some Mediæval Kings of Mithilā*, by Dr. Grierson, Indian Antiquary, Vol. XIV, 1885, and Xol. XXVIII, 1899.

several lakhs of rupees;* this Rājā was probably Rāmbhadra or Rūp Nārāyan, the tenth of the line, who is known to have ruled over Tirhut in 1495 when the Gangākrityaviveka was composed.† The treaty between the Emperor and the Bengal king was not long observed, for in the early part of the 16th century Nasrat Shāh (1518—32) conquered Tirhut and extended his kingdom across the Gogra into the modern district of Ballia. The Rājā of Tirhut (probably Lakshmināth or Kansa Nārāyan) was put to death, and with him the Thākur dynasty was extinguished. Nasrat Shāh appointed his son-in-law Viceroy of Tirhut, and thenceforward the country was administered by Muhammadan Governors.

Invasion of Champāran.

Of Champāran itself we find no separate mention except in the Wākiat-i-Mushtāki by Sheikh Rizkullā Mushtāki, in which a spirited description is given of its invasion in the reign of Sikandar Lodī (1489–1517). According to the account left by this historian, Miān Husain Farmulī was *jāgīrdār* of Sāran and Champāran, which were called *jalkhet* or the field of water, and he had taken no less than 20,000 villages from the infidels, besides those comprising his *jāgīr*. When he marched to attack the Rājā of Champāran, he found his advance checked by a flood of the Gandak and was obliged to encamp on its banks, while the Rājā remained secure in his fort on the other side of the river. One of his nobles, Mughūlā Kirāni, however, was not daunted by this obstacle, though he was told that the breadth of the river was 7 *kos* (14 miles). Having taken a vow to hold all food and drink as unlawful as a carcase, until he had attacked the Rājā, he mounted his horse and plunged into the river. Stimulated by this example, Miān Husain and the whole army began to cross the Gandak, and at sunset dashed upon the Rājā, who had been lulled into security by the thought that he was protected from attack by the flooded state of the Gandak. "Suddenly," it is said, "an uproar rose in the city, for it was reported from the watch-tower that the Afghāns had arrived; but the infidel did not credit it and was engaged in his pastimes, when the Afghāns were upon him and forced him to fly for his life. By the will of God that day Mughūlā became a martyr. Miān Husain greatly lamented his loss, and said—'Would to God that to-day there had been no victory, for that and the plunder combined are no compensation for the loss sustained in the death of Mughūlā.' Thus, after a duration of 200 years, destruction fell upon the kingdom of

* Sir H. Elliot, *History of India*, Vol. V (1873), p. 96.

† C. M. Duff, *Chronology of India* (1899), p. 266.

the Rājā ; and all the riches and treasures which were amassed during that period were dispersed in plunder. The shoes of the infidels who lost their lives in this action were collected; and when melted down no less than 20,000 mohurs of gold were obtained from them." *

Last days of Muhammadan rule.

Campaigns of Alī Vardi Khān.

After this, Champāran does not come into prominence until the last days of Muhammadan rule, when it appears that the Hindu chiefs were still practically independent.† In 1729 Alī Vardi Khān, who had been appointed Governor of Bihār under Shujā-ud-dīn, was sent to Patna at the head of a force of 5,000 men. On his arrival there he found the province in a state of disorder. It was infested by a band of robbers, called Banjārās, who, in the guise of peaceful traders and travellers, laid the country under contribution and plundered right and left. The zamīndārs of Bettiah and other places were also in a state of insurrection and had for some time set at defiance the authority of the Governor. In order to reduce these marauders and rebels, Alī Vardi Khān took into his service a body of Afghāns under Abdul Karīm Khān, who is described as being the chief of the Afghāns of Darbhangā, and first sent them against the Banjārās. The expedition was successful, the Banjārās were routed, made to disgorge their plunder, and driven out of the country. Then, according to the Riyazu-s-Salātin, "Alī Vardi Khān, being aided by the Afghāns, advanced with his forces against the tracts of the Rājās of Bettiah and Bhawārah, who were refractory and turbulent. Their regions had never previously been trod by the feet of the armies of former Nāzims, nor had their proud heads ever bent before to any of the former Sūbahdārs. Indeed, they had never before paid the imperial revenues and taxes. After fighting with them incessantly, Alī Vardi Khān became victorious and triumphant. Raiding and pillaging their tracts, Alī Vardi Khān carried off a large booty, amounting to several lakhs in specie and other effects; and settling with the Rājās the amounts of tribute, presents and the imperial revenue, he raised an immense sum. The soldiery also were enriched by the booty, and the strength of Alī Vardi's administration increased." ‡

---

* Sir H. Elliot, *History of India*, pp. 546-47, Vol. IV, 1873.

† The Cheros of Palāmau have a tradition that thay invaded Champāran under one of their great chiefs, Sahābal, drove out the Rājā, and laid waste the country to the foot of the Tarai. The Rājā fled, it is said, to the court of Jahāngīr, who ordered Islām Khān, the Viceroy of Bengal, to march to Champāran and reinstate him.

‡ Maulavī Abdus Salām, *Translation of the Riyazu-s-Salātin*, Calcutta, 1904.

Subsequently, in 1748, Alī Vardi Khān, who had in the meantime been raised to the Nawābship of Bengal, was forced to return to Champāran in consequence of the rebellion of his former allies, the Afghāns of Darbhangā. The latter had risen under Shamsher Khān, murdered Ali Vardi's son-in-law Zain-ud-dīn or Hiābat Jang, the Governor of Bihār, and sacked Patna. Alī Vardi Khān hurried up by forced marches from Bengal, completely defeated the Afghāns and their allies, the Marāthas, and marched in triumph to Patna. There he received a message from the Rājā of Bettiah, saying that he had given shelter to the families of Shamsher Khān and Sardār Khān, another Afghān leader, and was ready to pay the Nawāb 3 lakhs of rupees if he would agree not to demand their surrender. The Nawāb refused to treat with him, insisted on the unconditional surrender of the families of the Afghān chiefs, and advanced towards Bettiah to enforce his demands. The Rājā, thereupon, quietly gave up the wife and daughters of Shamsher Khān, who were treated with the utmost courtesy by Alī Vardi Khān.*

In 1760 Champāran again witnessed the march of contending armies. At this time the Emperor, Shāh Alam, was engaged in the invasion of Bihār, and Khadīm Husain Khān, the Governor of Purnea, marched to join him with an army composed of 6,000 horse, 10,000 foot, and 40 pieces of cannon. Before, however, he could effect a junction with the Emperor, Captain Knox had marched to the relief of Patna and driven off the besieging force. He followed up this blow by defeating the Governor of Purnea at Hājīpur, and Khadīm Husain fled precipitately northwards towards Bettiah. Shortly after this, a force commanded by Major Caillaud and Miran, the son of Mīr Jafar Khān, hurried up and set out in pursuit. In an action fought on the 25th June the enemy were routed, leaving behind their guns, a large quantity of ammunition and stores, and all their heavy baggage. The rains had now set in, the Gandak was in flood, and Khadīm Husain Khān was unable to procure boats and cross it. He, therefore, fell back towards the hills, closely pressed by Caillaud and Miran; and here his army lost their way and were dispersed in the dense forest. "At day-break," it is said, "his people could not discover the morning star, and concluded that it must be hidden by the chain of mountains close to which they supposed themselves to

Caillaud's campaign.

* Sair-ul-Mutākharin, Raymond's Translation (reprinted, Calcutta, 1902), Vol. II, p. 58.

be."* Their position was, in fact, desperate, with a river in front, an enemy in their rear, and the soldiers dispirited and scattered; but fortunately for them, the plans of the invading force were completely altered by Miran being struck by lightning while sleeping in his tent near Bettiah. Thereupon, Caillaud, on whom the command of the allied forces now devolved, abandoned the campaign. He moved the army before the fort of Bettiah, received the submission of the Rājā, and then marched off to Patna.†

Capture of Bettiah.

This submission appears to have been merely a shift to gain time, for we find that in 1762 Mīr Kāsim Alī was forced to send an expedition against the Rājā. "The command of it," says the author of the Sair-ul-Mutākharin, "was given to Bahādur Ali Khān, who had been for a long time Grandmaster of Artillery to Alī Vardi Khān and now enjoyed a small part of that office under Mīr Kāsim Khān. He had with him several commanders with their corps, together with some pieces of cannon in the English fashion, and some regiments of Talingas, disciplined by Gurgan Khān. His orders were to take the fortress of that name, and to chastise the zamīndār of that country, who had proved unruly." This expedition appears to have been completely successful, for we learn later from the same work that, as the fortress of Bettiah had been taken but freshly and the country had been but lately brought under control, the Nawāb availed himself of the pretence of establishing order in that region to set out on an expedition against Nepāl.

Invasion of Nepal.

This expedition, it is said, was undertaken at the instigation of the Nawāb's Armenian General, Gurgan Khān. "As the country of Nepāl was known to produce gold, as well as to be full of riches, Gurgan Khān, who had as much ambition as covetousness in his composition, wished to undertake an expedition thither. But he had another object in view; he wanted also to make a trial of the troops which he had disciplined, and of the

* The translator of the Sair-ul-Mutākharin gives a vivid picture of these forests:—"No man that has not seen the forests of India can have an idea of the darkness and horror by which a visitor is at once surrounded. Lofty trees eternally green, growing close together, intercept not only the light of the sun, but the very sight of the sky. Not a leaf is seen moving, not a bird is seen hopping about, save some crows; and chirping is as unknown there as would be an organ touched by a Handel. Such are the *sāl* forests that bound Bengal on the north. Myriads of red ants, still more formidable by their enormous bigness than by their voracity, seem, as well as stupendous serpents, to be the only inhabitants of those lonely woods, that is, the western ones."

† Sair-ul-Mutākharin, and Broome's History of the Rise and Progress of the Bengal Army

artillery which he had trained. With this view, he had long before commenced connections with those crowds of Cashmirians and Sanyasis and Fakirs who yearly frequented those parts ; he had likewise procured much information from some French priests that live at Latsa (Lhāsa), insomuch that he became a proficient in the knowledge of the passes over the mountains and of the entrances into the country. He even attached to his service some of those men, whom he found to be endowed with understanding and capable of serving as guides in his expedition; for they had of themselves tendered their services on that head, and had first inspired him with the thoughts of conquering so wealthy a country." *

In spite of these allies, the invasion was a disastrous failure. An advance force entered Champāran under Gurgan Khān and was followed by the main body under Mīr Kāsim Alī, who pitched his camp at Bettiah. Gurgan Khān then advanced to the north, and commenced the ascent of a pass through the hills. Here he was met by the Nepalese, and a short fight took place in which the Bengal army was successful. They pushed on to the summit and halted for the night, but no sooner was it dark than the Nepalese attacked and drove them back in disorder to the bottom of the pass. The whole force then fled in rout back to the main camp at Bettiah; and the Nawāb, without making any further attempt to pierce the Nepalese defence, broke up his camp, and marched off to Patna (1763).

EARLY ENGLISH ADMINISTRATION.

Campaign of 1766.

In 1764 Champāran passed with the rest of Bengal under British rule after the decisive battle of Buxar. A short campaign, however, was necessary before the authority of the British was acknowledged. Of this campaign there is the following account in Broome's History of the Rise and Progress of the Bengal Army (1850):—"In the beginning of 1766, Sir Robert Barker moved from Bankipore with a considerable detachment of his Brigade into the Bettiah country, to reduce a number of the refractory zamīndārs of that district, who, taking advantage of the troubles that had existed for the last two years, had shut themselves up in their strongholds and refused to pay any revenue, of which considerable arrears were now due. The judicious arrangements of Sir Robert Barker, and the efficient force at his disposal, led to a speedy and satisfactory adjustment of affairs in this quarter. Some little resistance appears to have been offered

* This appears to be a reference to the Capuchin Mission which had established itself at Lhāsa, but had by this time retired to Nepāl and set up a branch station at Bettiah. A brief account of the fortunes of this Mission will be found in the articles on Bettiah and Chuhāri in Chapter XV.

at first, but the inutility of such attempts being rendered very apparent, served to prevent any subsequent efforts of the same nature, and in a few months the whole country was brought into a state of complete subjection.

"Sir Robert Barker, in a letter to the Select Committee, dated from Camp at Rāmpur, 6th March 1766, gave a very favourable account of the resources of this district, with which even at the present time we are but scantily acquainted. He observes:—'Bettiah will, I think, be of considerable consequence to the Company. Its firs will afford masts for all the ships in India, which must produce a new and considerable trade with the other nations in India, as well as advantage to our own shipping. Gold and cinnamon are also here (the latter we gather in the jungles); timbers as large as any I have seen; musk and elephants' teeth; besides many other commodities I have not yet got the knowledge of.' The Select Committee reported this circumstance to the Court of Directors, stating that they looked upon it 'rather as an article of curious intelligence than mere prospects of advantage to the Company.' At the same time, they expressed their determination of pushing the discovery to the utmost advantage, if the advices received met with confirmation."

In spite of this campaign, the early days of British administration were troubled ones. The Rājā of Bettiah, Jugal Keshwar Singh, fell into arrears of revenue, and in the words of the Judges of the Dīwāni Adālat, "rebelled and fought with the forces of the British Government, was defeated and fled to Bundelkhund for safety, and his *Rājgi* was seized upon and brought under the direct management of the Company." This change only made matters worse, and in 1771 Mr. Golding, the Supervisor of *Sarkār* Champāran, reported that the country was in a state of desolation and ruin, hardly to be credited by any one who had not been a witness to it. As a remedy for the mischief he urged the restoration of the Rājā to his estate. The Patna Council, accordingly, made conciliatory overtures to Jugal Keshwar Singh and persuaded him to return.*

Relations with Nepāl. In the meantime, the British Government had come into collision with Nepāl, where the Gurkhas under Prithwī Nārāyan were engaged in the conquest of the whole country. In order to explain the position of Government in their relations to the Nepalese, the following sketch of the previous history of the frontier is quoted, with some abbreviations, from Prinsep's

* See also Chapter XI, in which a brief account has been given of the system of administration introduced.

Political and Military Transactions in India (1812—23), published in 1825. "From time immemorial the country within the hills and on the borders has been divided amongst petty Hindu Rājās, and the forest and Tarai had naturally been a perpetual bone of contention to them; a chieftain possessing fastnesses in the hills could always enforce contributions, by issuing thence and carrying off booty from those who hesitated to comply. Hence every hill Rājā had a sweep of the forest and low country attached to his estate, and this he was continually endeavouring to extend either by intrigue or by violence. The superior wealth and greater number of followers at the command of some of the Rājās of the plains enabled them occasionally to penetrate and reduce to subjection a hill neighbour; but, ordinarily, such enterprizes were beyond their skill or resources; and the border war was handed down from father to son, in their respective families."

"Neither Akbar nor any of his descendants on the throne of Delhi made any attempt to add the tract of hills to the Mughal empire; its revenue was not an object of cupidity, nor was its population sufficiently formidable to make the subjugation of the country necessary as an act of political precaution. The Rājās of the plains, on the other hand, though compelled to submit to the Musalmān yoke, retained their territories, and became tributaries of the empire, which did not prevent their prosecuting their hereditary feuds with their neighbours.

"Such continued to be the state of this frontier, until the low countries fell under the British dominion, and the hills were gradually overrun by the Nepalese, and consolidated by them into one sovereignty. The British Government, assimilating its conduct to that of its predecessors, did not interfere with the possession of the Rājās in the plains; but contented itself with the regular payments of revenue. The Gurkhas, on the other hand, as each Rājā in the hills successively fell before them, exterminated the family; and, becoming heir to all its possessions, took up likewise the old Rājā's claims and contests with his neighbours. This brought them into contact with our zamīndārs, who were unable to maintain themselves against such an enemy, and generally therefore had to resign the object in dispute; for unless the encroachment was gross and easy of proof, it was vain to hope to interest the British Government in their favour."

Frontier disputes.

Shortly after the British occupation such an encroachment was brought to notice. The Rājā of Bettiah had for a long time past been at war with the hill Rājā of Makwānpur for the possession of different portions of the Tarai; and among other sources of dispute, each claimed part of the Simraon *pargana*. In 1743 the

Makwānpur family granted Rautahat and Pachrautī, two *tappās* or subdivisions of this *pargana*, in *jāgīr* to one Abdullah Beg, who had influence enough with the Nawāb of Bengal to have the tenure confirmed by him. The Bettiah Rājā, who, there is reason to believe, was then in possession, at first resisted; but in the end, also gave Abdullah a *sanad* for the same lands. Abdullah's tenure was thus secure, whichever claimant established his claims; but as the Makwānpur grant was the oldest in date and had been acknowledged at Murshidābād, this Rājā's title to resume eventually acquired a kind of preference. In 1763, Prithwī Nārāyan, having subdued the Makwānpur Rājā, claimed to succeed to his rights as Abdullah's feudal superior, with authority to resume the *jāgīr;* and after a year or two seized not only Abdullah's lands, but also 22 more villages, which he claimed as part of Rautahat. Abdullah fled to the English authorities, who took up his cause and subsequently made it a pretext for declaring war on Nepāl.

The ulterior motive, however, appears to have been a desire to re-establish our trade with Nepāl, which had been interrupted for some years in consequence of the subjugation of Makwānpur. In 1767 the Newār Rājā of Kātmāndu, being hard-pressed by the Gurkhas, appealed to the British for assistance, and Mr. Golding, the Commercial Agent at Bettiah, who feared that the success of the Gurkhas would ruin the trade with Nepāl, recommended that the opportunity should be taken to send an expedition to his succour. The British, accordingly, responded to the appeal of the Rājā and sent a force under Major Kinloch to march to his relief.

Expedition into Nepāl.

Major Kinloch advanced into the hills in October 1767, but had not strength enough to establish a chain of depôts to secure his communications with the plains. Having penetrated as far as Hariharpur, he was detained there by an unfordable torrent, which carried away a bridge and raft he constructed. The delay thus caused exhausted his supplies, the deadly climate brought on sickness among the soldiers, and he was obliged to return early in December, the time when, properly, he should have set out. Having failed to penetrate into the hills, he was directed in January 1768 to occupy the whole Tarai as a means of recouping the expenses of the expedition. Abdullah then claimed his *jāgīr*, and Rautahat and Pachrautī were, accordingly, given up to him; but when peace was restored, the Nepalese sent an Agent to claim this territory as part of Makwānpur. This claim was opposed by the Bettiah Rājā, and a long investigation ensued; but eventually in 1781 Warren Hastings decided, on the strength of the first deed of grant to Abdullah, that Rautahat and Pachrautī belonged to Makwānpur, and were not part of Bettiah or Champāran. The 22 villages seized by Prithwī Nārāyan, and subsequently occupied by Major Kinloch in 1768, had, however, never been given up. Their restoration was not demanded, and the revenue due from them was collected as part of the *tappā* of Nonaur, which with Rautahat belonged to the *pargana* of Simrāon but fell in the portion annexed to Champāran. At the Permanent Settlement Nonaur formed part of the land for which the Rājā of Bettiah engaged; and till 1810 the 22 villages continued in his possession.

The Gurkhas, meanwhile, continued to present yearly to the British Government a large elephant as tribute for the cultivated lowlands occupied by them until 1801, when this tribute was relinquished by a treaty concluded at Dinapore, by which the Nepalese also agreed to the establishment of a residency at Kātmāndu. The alliance with the Darbār was dissolved in 1804 in consequence of their deliberate breach of faith and the indignities offered to the Resident; and for the next six years our transactions with Nepāl consisted entirely of unavailing remonstrances against stealthy but systematic encroachments on our territory. In 1811, one Lakshmangīr, the Gurkha Governor of Rautahat, crossed the frontier with a party of armed men, seized and stockaded Kewayā, one of the 22 villages occupied in Prithwī Nārāyan's time and began plundering and making collections in eight other villages alleging that they belonged to Rautahat. The Rājā of Bettiah's people resisted this aggression, and an affray followed, in which Lakshmangīr was killed. Nepalese aggressions.

The British Government directed the Assistant to the Magistrate of Sāran to proceed to the frontier and make an enquiry; but, before he arrived there, a reinforcement had been sent down from Kātmāndu, which immediately seized the 22 disputed villages. Commissioners were now appointed by both Governments to enquire into and adjust all the frontier disputes, Major Bradshaw being appointed Commissioner on the part of the British Government and instructed to insist on the restitution of the 22 villages occupied by the Nepalese as a preliminary to any investigation of the claims set up by the Gurkhas. After much evasion, this condition was agreed to; but when he proposed to open the enquiry, the Nepalese Commissioners, pretending to have taken some personal offence against the Major, refused to enter into any discussion with him, and suddenly returned to Kātmāndu, leaving him alone on the frontier (1814). Lord Hastings, thereupon, threatened the forcible occupation of the lands, if they were not evacuated by a fixed date; and the

Gurkhas having failed to restore them, the disputed tracts were occupied by the British in April 1814. War was now inevitable, and it was formally declared on the 1st November 1814.*

The Nepāl war.

An arduous campaign ensued, but little fighting took place near this district. The plan of campaign provided for the main attack being delivered through the passes between the Great Gandak and Bāghmati by a force of nearly 8,000 men with a strong force of artillery under General Marley, while another brigade was to follow the army and secure its depôts and rear as it advanced into the hills. Before these forces took the field, Major Bradshaw, the British Commissioner, who was in military charge of the frontier and the disputed lands of Simrāon, advanced against the Nepalese post of Barharwā prior to occupying the whole of the Tarai. The attack was successful, and the Tarai was evacuated by the Gurkhas and occupied by the British troops, the headquarters of the Champāran Light Infantry being posted at Baragarhi and two other stations established at Samanpur and Parsā. General Marley arrived at the frontier early in December, but he did little more than hold his position. He was staggered by the activity and enterprise of the Gurkhas, and was apprehensive for his train of heavy artillery which was coming up from Bettiah; and eventually he was superseded for incompetence.

In the meantime, the force under General Ochterlony had been most successful, and on the 28th November 1815 a treaty was concluded with the Nepalese at Sugauli. The ratification of the treaty, however, was withheld by the Darbār, who formally announced their intention of trying the result of a second campaign; and in 1816 General Ochterlony took command of the main army, which numbered nearly 20,000 men. This force was collected at Sugauli, where the General established his headquarters on the 22nd January 1816, and was divided into 4 brigades, one being directed to march through Rāmnagar, while the main force under Ochterlony marched due north to Makwānpur. The invasion, as is well known, was successful, and on the 2nd December 1816, the Nepalese at last delivered the treaty of Sugauli duly signed and executed, by which the British were granted the Tarai between the Rāpti and Gandak, excepting Butwal Khās, and retained the portion between the Gandak and Coosah (Kosi) which they already occupied.

Raid of 1840.

After the conclusion of this treaty, there was peace on the frontier until 1840, when the Nepalese took advantage of our reverses in Afghānistān to seize part of the north of the district.

* This sketch of the early relations with Nepāl is based on the account given in Prinsep's Political and Military Transactions in India (1813—23), Vol, I, 1825,

A party of about 40 or 50 Gurkha sepoys, under the command of an officer, entered the Rāmnagar territory, on the occasion of a large fair, at which most of the inhabitants were present, and issued a proclamation notifying that the tract of land in question (7 or 8 miles wide, and 25 to 26 miles in length), which had formerly belonged to Nepāl, but had been given to the Rāmnagar Rājā on the occasion of his marrying a Nepalese princess, had now, on the death of that princess, been resumed by Nepāl; all local authorities were therefore directed on pain of severe punishment, not only to acknowledge the authority of the Darbār, but to pay their taxes and revenue into the treasury of Nepāl. Friendly remonstrances were made, but were unattended to; and at last, in October 1840, Government ordered the advance of a brigade under Colonel Oliver to enforce, if necessary, the immediate evacuation of our territory by the Gurkha troops, to watch the movements of the Nepalese, and to protect our subjects against any further aggressions. Seeing that we were in earnest in our demands, the Darbār reluctantly, but completely, yielded. The Gurkha troops were recalled, and 91 villages, which they had occupied, were restored to their rightful and original owners. A corps of soldiers was, however, retained on the frontier till 1842.*

Since that time the peace of the district has only been broken by the Mutiny of 1857. Major Holmes was at this time in Command of the 12th Irregular Cavalry at Sugauli. As soon as danger began to threaten Bihār, he wrote to Canning, expressing, with great freedom and plainness, the view that stern and instant repression was the only policy for the times. Canning told him in reply that he was entirely wrong, and that his "bloody, off-hand measures" were not the cure for the disease. "I am determined," he rejoined, "to keep order in these districts, and I will do it with a strong hand." His method was simple, but very effective. On his own responsibility, he placed the whole country between Patna and Gorakhpur under martial law. His only instrument for enforcing it was his single native regiment; but he thoroughly trusted his men, and, if they were not loyal to him in their hearts, they were so carried along by his daring spirit that they could not choose but do his bidding. Sending out parties to seize evil doers and protect the civil stations, and declaring that he would visit with instant death any one who showed the slightest sign of disaffection, he soon established such a terror of his name that none dared to stir a finger in the cause of rebellion. **THE MUTINY.**

These measures were set aside by the Local Government as soon as it learnt of them; but up to the 25th July there appeared

* H. A. Oldfield, *Sketches from Nepal*, 1880.

to be no signs of disaffection in the regiment, and the men were doing splendid service. Holmes had reported most favourably of them, and had himself been quoted as an example of the truth of Lord Canning's axiom, that no regiment which was properly commanded would mutiny. But on the evening of the 26th, as he was driving out with his wife, a daughter of Sale, the heroic defender of Jalālābād, 4 sowārs rode up to him with their swords drawn; and almost before he knew what they wanted, they had beheaded both himself and Mrs. Holmes. The regiment then rose, cut down the Deputy Post-Master, murdered the doctor (Dr. Gardiner), his wife and children (except one who escaped their notice), and fired their bungalow. After plundering the treasury, they marched to Siwān, where they attacked the house of Messrs. Lynch and McDonnell, the Deputy Magistrate and Sub-Deputy Opium Agent, and then marched towards Azimgarh. The bodies of Major and Mrs. Holmes and of Mr. Bennett were brought into Motihāri by the police, those of Dr. Gardiner and his family being burnt in his bungalow. In view of the defenceless state of the station and the probability that the mutineers would attack it, Mr. Raikes, the Magistrate, left it, with the other civil officers and their families, and took refuge in a factory some miles away; but he returned almost immediately and refused again to abandon it, even on receipt of the Commissioner's order.

On the 30th July martial law was proclaimed by Government, and shortly afterwards Honorary Magistrates were appointed from among the indigo-planters, and authorized to raise small bodies of police for the protection of their immediate neighbourhood. The arrival in August of two Gurkha regiments from Nepāl soon restored confidence, and though there was some fear of an advance of rebels from Gorakhpur, the presence of the Gurkhas prevented any attack from that direction. An attempt was, indeed, made by a party of rebels, but they were quickly dispersed by a detachment of Gurkhas stationed at Bagahā Ghāt. Towards the end of December Jang Bahādur with his Nepalese army arrived at Bettiah, and on the 26th a fight took place at Sāhibganj, 5 miles from Pīpra, between two regiments sent by Jang Bahādur and a party of rebels, who were completely defeated. On the same day a successful action was fought by Colonel Rowcroft at Sohanpur on the Gorakhpur frontier, and these successes had the effect of clearing the districts north of the Ganges.*

* This account of the Mutiny has been compiled from The Parliamentary Papers, The Mutiny of the Bengal Army (1857-58), and Holmes' History of the Indian Mutiny (1891).

FORMATION OF THE DISTRICT.

The only other event calling for record in the history of Champāran is its formation into a district. It originally formed part of the district of Sāran with headquarters at Chaprā, but in 1837 a Magistrate was stationed in Motīhāri; in 1852 the Bettiah subdivision was established; and in 1866 Champāran was converted into an independent district.

ARCHÆOLOGY.

"Champāran," it has been said, "presents an immense field o archæological research." * Many sites still await scientific exploration, but the remains already discovered are extremely interesting. Three of the pillars erected by Asoka are found in this district, viz., one at Lauriyā Ararāj near Gobindganj, another at Lauriyā Nandangarh, 15 miles north of Bettiah, and a third, commonly known as the Rāmpurwā pillar, near Pīpariyā in the Shikārpur thāna; these pillars which are perhaps the most important remains in the district, rank among the most valuable ancient monuments of India. Two miles south-west of Kesariyā is an ancient Buddhist stūpa, and on the road from that place to Pīpra is a mound, called Sāgardih, which evidently marks the ruins of another Buddhist stūpa. At Lauriyā Nandangarh are a great number of earthen barrows, possibly sepulchral mounds erected by the Lichchhavis, besides a great mound which may represent the Ashes stūpa of Buddhist historians; and at Chānkīgarh, 3 miles west of Shikārpur, is another remarkable mound. All these places, as already mentioned, were probably situated on the imperial road from Pātaliputra (Patna), the capital of Asoka, to Kusinagara, the scene of Buddha's death, which is believed to have passed Basārh (Vaisāli), Kesariyā, Lauriyā Ararāj, Bettiah, Chānkīgarh, Rāmpurwā and the Bhikhnā Thorī pass. Remains of the ancient capital of Mithilā are still extant at Simrāon, 5 miles from the Purnahiā factory; and other monuments and buildings of archæological interest are found at Nonāchar, 5 miles east of Motīhāri, at Sītākund and Bediban close to the Pīpra railway station, and at Bāwangarhi near Sohariā in the extreme north-west of the district. A detailed description of these remains will be found in Chapter XV.

---

* V. A. Smith, *Introduction to Report on a Tour of Exploration of the Antiquities in the Tarai, Nepal*, by P. C. Mukerji, Calcutta 1901.

CHAPTER III.

THE PEOPLE.

GROWTH OF THE POPULATION.

THE first census of the district was taken in 1872, and the result was to disclose a total population of 1,440,815 persons, but there is little reason to doubt that the efficiency of this census was marred in some degree by popular suspicion. The lower classes believed that the census was preliminary to a poll-tax; that some of them would be sent to Mauritius to work in Government gardens; that the English were at war with the Russians who were coming to invade India, and in order to repel them many men were to be sent down to Calcutta to be trained as soldiers. At the census of 1881 the population was returned at 1,721,608, representing an increase of 19·5 per cent., due partly to improved enumeration and partly to immigration from the adjoining districts to the sparsely inhabited thānas in the north. The next decade showed a further advance of 8 per cent., the population having risen to 1,859,465, mainly owing to a continuance of the stream of immigration, the total number of persons born elsewhere but residing in Champāran at the time of the census having reached the unprecedented total of 248,511.

Census of 1901.

At the census of 1901 it was found that the population had fallen to 1,790,463, representing a decrease of 69,002 persons or 3·7 per cent. This loss of population was due to the fact that during the preceding decade the district had been severely tried both by famine and disease. The first 7 years of the decade were lean years, and they culminated in the famine of 1897. Practically the whole district was affected; but the Dhāka thāna suffered most, and next to that the whole of the Bettiah subdivision except a narrow strip on the banks of the Gandak. No deaths occurred from starvation, but the vitality of the people was lowered, and the sequel of the famine was a reduced birth-rate. There were also several severe outbreaks of cholera during the decade, and fever was very prevalent. The net result of these combined influences was that the number of deaths reported exceeded that of births by 1,059. At the same time, immigration received a severe check, and not only did new settlers cease to arrive but many of the old immigrants returned to their homes.

These three factors—the unhealthiness of the decade, the diminished fecundity of the people consequent on a series of bad years, and the stoppage of immigration—led to a loss of population in every thāna in the district except Adāpur; but this thāna enjoys the advantage of irrigation and an exceptionally fertile soil, and in part of it a full rice crop was secured even in 1896, when there was a disastrous failure elsewhere. The decrease was greatest in Gobindganj and Motihāri thānas, but the reason for this is not apparent, for they suffered from the famine far less than Dhāka, in which the proportional decrease was only half as great as in the thānas to the north-west, where there was only a slight loss of population.

The principal statistics of the census of 1901 are reproduced below:—

SUBDIVISION.	Area in square miles.	Number of		Population.	Population per square mile.	Percentage of variation in population between 1891 and 1901.
		Towns.	Villages.			
Motihāri ...	1,518	1	1,304	1,040,599	686	—5·4
Bettiah ...	2,013	1	1,319	749,864	373	—1·3
DISTRICT TOTAL	*3,531*	*2*	*2,623*	*1,790,463*	*507*	*—3·7*

The population is sparse in comparison with the neighbouring districts, the density being only 507 persons to the square mile as compared with 901 in Sāran and 908 in Muzaffarpur. Generally speaking, the most populous part is the tract east of the Little Gandak; then comes the tract between that river and the Great Gandak; and lastly the north-western corner, where the surface rises towards the Sumeswar hills on the Nepāl frontier. Here a large portion of the country is still covered with forest, the climate is very unhealthy, and in many parts only the aboriginal Thārus and immigrants from the Nepāl Tarai—both races inured to malarial conditions—venture to settle. The most thickly populated thānas are Madhuban, with 810 persons to the square mile, Dhāka (771) and Adāpur (749) in the east of the district, where conditions are similar to those in Muzaffarpur; while in the north-western thānas of Shikārpur and Bagahā, where cultivation is still undeveloped and malaria is prevalent, there are only 270 and 301 persons respectively to the square mile.

GENERAL CHARACTERISTICS. Density of population.

The reason for the sparse population appears to be that the district generally is less healthy than other districts in the Patna Division; the soil is also less fertile, the land has more recently been reclaimed from forest, and large tracts still await the advent of the plough. More irrigation and better means of communication are also required, and when the railway and the canals now under construction have been completed, it seems probable that the less settled parts will be rapidly filled up. It is noticeable, however, that though Champāran is, next to Shāhābād, the most sparsely inhabited district in the Patna Division, the density of population has increased by no less than 24 per cent. since 1872, when the average number of persons per square mile was only 408.

Migration. Perhaps the most prominent feature in the history of Champāran during the last 20 years has been the extent to which immigration has gone on. In 1881 no less than 193,659 persons were residing in the district who were born elsewhere, and this great army of immigrants had increased to 248,511 in 1891, including 83,241 immigrants from Sāran, 56,076 from Muzaffarpur, 52,186 from the United Provinces and 34,626 from Nepāl. The census of 1901 shows that the tide of immigration has begun to ebb. The number of immigrants was found to be only 106,781, and it would appear therefore that the ranks of those enumerated in 1891 have not been swelled by the arrival of new-comers, and that many of those who were then in the district must since have returned to their former homes. Even so, however, no less than 59·6 per thousand of the present population are immigrants, and this is the highest proportion in the whole of Bihār.

The volume of emigration is far smaller, the number of natives of Champāran enumerated elsewhere in 1901 being only 36,077. Champāran is, indeed, the only Bihār district, except Purnea, where the immigrants outnumber those who have left the district. The people have ample land at home, and there is little emigration except to the contiguous districts. The bulk of the immigrants also come from the adjoining districts, especially from Gorakhpur in the United Provinces, from Sāran, and also, though to a less extent, from Muzaffarpur. The volume of migration between Champāran and distant places is comparatively small, but those who thus leave the district outnumber those who come into it in the ratio of more than 4 to 1.

Immigration from Nepāl to the half-reclaimed country in the north of Champāran formerly took place on a large scale, but it is believed that the influx is now counterbalanced by an ebb of population in the opposite direction; in 1901 the number of immigrants from Nepāl was 19,540, as compared with 34,626 in 1891. Rents, it is said, are lower in Nepāl, good land is plentiful, and settlers are particularly attracted by a strip of jungle in the Nepalese Tarai which is now being cleared for cultivation. There are, however, no statistics of population of Nepāl, and it is impossible to verify this inference. As a rule, it is reported, the emigrants only go a few miles inside Nepāl, and have their permanent homes in British territory.

The population is almost entirely rural, the only towns being Motīhāri and Bettiah. The population of these two towns has nearly doubled itself within the last 30 years, but even so, they contain only 2 per cent. of the total population of the district. The remainder of the population live in 2,623 villages, of which 20 per cent. contain a population of under 500, while 52 per cent. have a population of 500 to 2,000. The average area of the villages is a little over a square mile, and the largest village is Semralabedahā in Bagahā thāna, which has an area of over 40 square miles. **Towns and villages.**

The vernacular current in the district is a dialect of Bihāri Hindī called Bhojpurī, of which two main varieties are found, viz., a border subdialect called Madhesī and a broken form called Thāru, which is current along the Nepāl frontier. Muhammadans of the upper classes again mostly talk Awadhī, a dialect of Eastern Hindī. There are thus 3 dialects prevalent in the district, of which the following sketch is condensed from Dr. Grierson's Linguistic Survey of India. **LANGUAGE.**

The Champāran district is to the north of and separated by the Gandak river from Sāran, with which it has historical and political connections. On the other hand, it forms part of the ancient country of Mithilā. The language spoken in it illustrates this state of affairs. Although it is based in the main on the same stock as that of the Bhojpurī spoken in Sāran and East Gorakhpur, it has some peculiarities borrowed from the Maithilī spoken in the neighhouring district of Muzaffarpur. The Maithilī influence is strongest in the east of the district on the Muzaffarpur border, where Maithilī, and not Bhojpurī, is spoken in a strip of land, about 2 miles wide, and 18 miles long, in Dhāka thāna. As we go west, the influence decreases, till, on the banks of the Gandak, the language is the same as that spoken in North-east Sāran, and in Eastern Gorakhpur. This dialect is locally known as Madhesī, a word formed from the Sanskrit Madhya-desa, meaning midland, an appropriate name enough for the language of the country situated between the Maithilī-speaking country of Tirhut, and the Bhojpurī-speaking country of Gorakhpur. Some of the people actually name the form which the dialect takes in the western part of the district "Gorakhpuri," but such minute distinctions are not necessary, and, excepting the small strip in **Madhesī.**

which Maithilī is spoken, it is sufficiently accurate to say that the language spoken over the whole of Champāran is Madhesī. As its name implies, the dialect is a border form of speech, possessing some of the characteristics of both Bhojpurī and Maithilī, but its structure is in the main that of Bhojpurī. It shares with Maithilī a dislike to the cerebral *r*, frequently substituting the dental *r* for it. The Maithilī form *okni*, current in Muzaffarpur, is used for "to them," and the third person singular of the past tense of transitive verbs regularly ends in *ak*, as in Maithilī, *e.g.*, *kahlak*, he said, *delak*, he gave, etc. It is estimated that no less than 1,714,036 persons in this district speak Madhesī, while 28,800 persons speak Maithilī.

Thāru. Thāru is the dialect of the aboriginal tribe of Thārus, who inhabit the Tarai along the Nepāl frontier. They have no speech of their own, but have adopted more or less completely the language of their Aryan neighbours and speak a corrupt form of the local Bhojpurī mixed with aboriginal words. It is estimated that in Champāran 27,620 persons speak Thāru.

Awadhī. Awadhī, literally the language of Oudh, is a dialect of Eastern Hindī spoken by middle class Muhammadans and by people of the Tikulihār or spangle-maker caste, the total number of persons speaking it being estimated at 58,000. The Awadhī spoken by the Tikulihārs is locally known as Tikulihāri, and that spoken by the middle class Musalmāns is called Sheikhoi.

Domrā. Domrā is a gipsy dialect or kind of "Thieves' Latin" spoken by criminal tribes. It is merely a perversion of the local dialect deliberately intended to prevent outsiders from understanding what is meant, *e.g.*, *jamadār* becomes *majadār* and a rupee is called *bajaiyā*, *i.e.*, a thing which rings. It is estimated that in Champāran 4,000 persons speak Domrā, but it is probable that most of these are quite as much at home in the ordinary Bhojpurī of the district as in their own peculiar jargon.

RELIGIONS. The great majority of the inhabitants are Hindus, who, with a total of 1,523,949 persons, account for 85 per cent. of the population, while Muhāmmadans number 264,086 or nearly 15 per cent. The latter are considerably more numerous in Champāran than in any other district in Bihār except Purnea. Christians number 2,417, including 2,180 native converts; nearly all the remainder are Europeans, of whom there were 206 in the district at the time of the census, most of them being engaged in the indigo industry.

Hindus. Popular Hinduism in Champāran resembles in its general features the Hinduism of other districts of Bihār. The majority of Hindus are uneducated men of low caste, who know but little of the higher side of their religion. Reverence for Brāhmans and the worship of the orthodox Hindu gods are universal, but as a matter of every-day practice, the low-caste villager endeavours to propitiate the evil spirits and godlings which his ancestors have worshipped from time immemorial. Most of these are regarded as malignant spirits, who produce illness in the family and sickness among the cattle, if not appeased. They affect the ordinary life of the peasant more directly and vitally than the regular Hindu gods; and consequently, the great mass of the illiterate Hindus, as well as some of the most ignorant Muhammadans, are careful to make periodical offerings to them. They form no part of the orthodox Hindu pantheon, but are given a kind of brevet rank; and for practical purposes they are the gods most feared and therefore most worshipped by the lowest castes. One such spirit with a great local reputation is Bischha Barham, the spirit of a Brāhman who died a violent death. Bischha Barham is one of the most dreaded of all the malevolent spirits and has a famous temple in Motīhāri, where even Muhammadans make offerings through the Brāhman priest who presides there.

Religious movements.

It must not be supposed that practices of the type described above monopolize the religious life even of the most ignorant Hindus. The same village will contain a temple of the Siva or Vishnu with its regular Brāhman priest, as well as the little mound of earth, the tree, the block or the stone, which marks the haunt of the evil spirit. The worship of both go on side by side, and the same man will make his little offerings to the Grām Devatā or village god whom the Brāhman does not recognize, and to the orthodox gods of Brāhmanical worship. The latter has a very strong hold over the people generally, and striking proof of its strength was afforded in 1893-95, when there was an outburst of religious excitement, which here, as in other parts of Bihār, found expression in the anti-kine-killing agitation, the ploughmen's begging movement and the tree-daubing mystery.

Anti-kine-killing agitation.

The first movement appears to have been due to the activity of the Gorakshinī Sabhās or associations for the protection of cattle. These societies, the legitimate object of which is the care of diseased, aged, and otherwise useless cattle, started a crusade against the killing of kine, sent out emissaries to preach their doctrines and collected subscriptions to further their objects. The result was a series of outbreaks, large crowds of Hindus suddenly rising against their Muhammadan neighbours in order to prevent their sacrificing or slaughtering kine for food, and that though here was no sign of any attempt to wound the religious feelings of the Hindus. In this district there was great unrest along the border adjoining Muzaffarpur, where there are a number of villages containing a strong Muhammadan element. The measures taken to preserve the peace in these villages were successful, but the fanatical feeling spread beyond them, and large crowds of Hindus suddenly appeared in places where no disturbances were anticipated, bent upon attacking the Muhammadans wherever they could be found. In one large Muhammadan village, called Bijai, a Hindu mob carried all before them; the village was gutted, nearly all the houses being burnt; everything that could be carried away of any value was looted, while the men were mercilessly beaten and the women stripped of their ornaments. Additional police were quartered on 38 offending villages, and the excitement gradually died down.

Ploughmen's begging movement.

The ploughmen's begging movement, or, as it should more properly be called, the Mahādeo *pūjā*, was a curious exhibition of religious feeling which occurred soon afterwards. All ploughmen, the story goes, were obliged to give their cattle three days' rest and go round the neighbouring villages carrying the plough and begging. With the proceeds three wheaten cakes were prepared—one for the ploughman himself, one for his cattle, while the third had to be buried under their stalls. This penance was performed by the people in consequence of a rumour that it has been imposed by the god Mahādeo to expiate the sin committed by the agricultural community in overworking their cattle. One evening, it is said, as a poor ryot was ploughing his field, a man appeared before him and asked why he was working his cattle so late. He replied that his poverty compelled him to do so, and thereupon Mahādeo—for it was he—waved his hand and the cattle vanished. The peasant then begged that he would bring them back, and Mahādeo promised that the cattle would return, if he performed the penance above described for 3 days, otherwise the penance would be imposed for 8 months. For some time the people continued to carry out, with scrupulous care, the orders which they supposed had been given them by their god. The elaborate nature of the penance gives reason, however, to suppose that it had been carefully thought out; and its inception and spread among the villagers have been attributed to the efforts of those interested in the Gorakshinī agitation to keep the movement afloat.

Tree-daubing mystery.

Tree-daubing was another widespread movement, the meaning of which afforded many grounds for speculation. By the most reliable reports it commenced about the latter end of February 1894 in the north-east corner of Bihār in the neighbourhood of the Janakpur shrine, which lies across the border in Nepāl. The movement consisted in marking trees with daubs of mud, in which were stuck hairs of different animals. It slowly spread through the Gangetic districts eastwards into Bhāgalpur and Purnea, and westwards through many of the districts of the United Provinces. As an explanation of the movement, it was suggested at the time that the sign was intended as an advertisement of the shrine of Janakpur; and this view was accepted officially. Others, however, held that the marks originated merely with cattle rubbing themselves against trees. Others again pointed out that it was suspicious that it should follow the Gorakshinī agitation, which was hostile to the administration, and that it was intended to promote some movement antagonistic to British rule.

Muhammadans. The lower and uneducated classes of Muhammadans in the district are infected with Hindu superstitions, especially those regarding sickness and disease. As a rule, their knowledge of the faith they profess seldom extends beyond the three cardinal doctrines of the unity of God, the mission of Muhammad, and the truth of the Korān. Apart too from Hindu superstitions, there are certain practices not based on the Korān, the most common of which is the adoration of departed Pīrs or saints. These Pīrs are believed to have miraculous powers, and their *dargāhs* or tombs are places of pilgrimage to which Muhummadans resort for the cure of disease or the exorcism of evil spirits, or to obtain the fulfilment of some cherished wish.

Veneration of Pīrs. In Champāran one of the most famous of the local Pīrs is Khwāja Mīrza Halīm, who has a shrine at Mehsī. Many miraculous feats are attributed to this saint, such as drawing enough milk from a cow, which had never been in calf, to satisfy the thirst of his many followers. There is a date palm near the *dargāh*, and it is said that, when a Kalwār once attempted to tap it, in order to obtain the juice for the manufacture of intoxicating drink (which is forbidden to Muhammadans), blood flowed from the tree. There is also a tradition that there was formerly an inscribed stone at the gate of the tomb, with the magic aid of which thieves could be unerringly detected and stolen property recovered. Jang Bahādur, says the legend, removed this stone to Nepāl, and when the saint remonstrated, he promised to erect a cenotaph in his memory. The original *dargāh* is a favourite place of pilgrimage, and an annual fair is held there at which some thousands attend. It is visited by all kinds of persons and for all sorts of purposes, but mainly by those who desire to be blessed with children or who are suffering from some lingering disease.

One of the most modern saints is Patuki Sain, who lived near the Court House at Motīhārī and died only 30 or 40 years ago. He was illiterate, and in his lifetime had no great reputation. It was only after his death that he achieved the reputation of holiness; a striking illustration of the proverb—*Barhā to Mīr*, *Ghātā to Fakīr*, *Marā to Pīr*, *i.e.*, "If he grew rich, he became a chief; if poor, a beggar; and if he died, a saint." The tomb of this Pīr was erected by a Hindu money-lender of the Kalwār caste, and his reputation is already so great that about half the residents of the town believe in his miraculous powers and pray for his assistance. His aid is especially invoked by litigants in the Courts, and their offerings form a considerable addition to the income of the custodian, who was formerly a peon of the District Magistrate's establishment. The Mārwāris make annual offerings to this saint, and his aid is also sought by the women of the town, who visit his tomb in a body with a band playing various musical instruments.*

Wahābis. Such corrupt doctrines find no favour among the Wahābis, who have shown considerable activity in propagating their doctrines in Champāran, the movement in this and other districts in North Bihār being inaugurated by Maulvī Nāzir Husain, a native of Monghyr, and others. The members of the sect prefer, however, to call themselves Ahl-i-Hadīs or the people of the tradition, *i.e.*, they interpret for themselves the traditional sayings of Muhammad not embodied in the Korān, without following any particular Imām. Another name adopted by them is Ghair Mukallid, *i.e.*, those who do not wear the collar of any Imām. The main features of their creed are that Friday prayers are enjoined, the hands are raised in prayer, and the 'Amen' is pronounced in a loud voice. The use of music, the celebration of the Muharram festival, the offering of the *shīrnī* to the manes of ancestors, and the veneration of Pīrs are strictly forbidden. The movement is spreading, but it has been estimated that the total number of adherents is less than 1,000. It is noticeable that it is the Ajlaf or lower class of Muhammadans who are most attracted by the preaching of the reformers, and that the better classes generally hold aloof. The propagation of these new doctrines frequently leads to much ill-feeling between the members of the different sects, and the disputes between the Mukallids and Ghair Mukalldis would more than once have ended in bloodshed but for fear of the law.

It is reported that fresh accessions to the ranks of Muhammadans are still being received from without; and a Maulavi,

* E. A. Gait, *Bengal Census Report*, 1901.

who is one of the religious preceptors in this district, states that within his knowledge a little over a thousand persons have become Muhammadans within 15 or 16 years. The most important cause of conversion is poverty, especially in time of famine or scarcity, when poor people become Muhammadans or Christians by hundreds; for any Hindu who takes food cooked by a Muhammadan is outcasted, and his place of shelter is only among the Muhammadans or Christians. Some persons also embrace the Muhammadan faith in order to raise their social rank. Conversion for the sake of women is comparatively rare, and the number of persons who become Muhammadans from conviction is still less. There is no organised propaganda, but fresh accessions to the faith are slowly going on.*

Nearly all the Christians in Champāran are Roman Catholics, and are found in the Bettiah subdivision. Bettiah is the headquarters of the Prefecture Apostolic of Bettiah and Nepāl, which was constituted in 1892 and made over to the Capuchin Fathers of the Tyrolese Province. The Catholic Mission in this district dates back, however, to the 18th century, being the direct descendant of the great Capuchin Mission, which established itself in Lhāsa and Nepāl during the first half of that century. In 1745, compelled to leave Lhāsa by the persecution of the Tibetan authorities, the heroic Father Horace of Penna retired with his two companions to the Mission hospice at Pātan near Kātmāndu, where he died six weeks afterwards. One of these companions was Father Joseph Mary (Giuseppe Maria dei Bernini), who possessed some knowledge of medicine, and had previously attended Dhurup Singh, the Rājā of Bettiah, and cured the Rānī of a serious illness. The grateful Rājā had already invited him to establish a mission at Bettiah, and had even written to the Pope to obtain his sanction; and the opportunity was now taken to send Father Joseph Mary to Bettiah, where the Rājā assigned him a residence. Subsequently, in 1769, the Capuchins, being expelled from Nepāl by the victorious Gurkhas, took refuge at Chuharī with some of their Nepalese converts; many of the native Christians at the latter place are, in fact, descendants of the original fugitives from Nepāl. A fuller account of the history of the Mission will be found in the articles on Bettiah and Chuharī in Chapter XV. There are also outstations at Chakhnī, Chainpatiā, Rāmnagar and Rāmpur. Dispensaries for the poor are maintained at Bettiah, Chuharī and Chainpatiā and orphanages at the former two places, besides a Middle English school at Bettiah. A Protestant Mission styled

Christians.

* Bengal Census Report (1901), Appendix II.

the Regions Beyond Mission was opened at Motihāri in 1900, and has a branch at Chainpatiā in the Bettiah subdivision.

PRINCIPAL CASTES.

Among the Muhammadans the Jolāhās (73,999) and Sheikhs (71,617) are the most important communities. Among Hindus the most numerous castes are Ahirs or Goālās (189,090) and Chamārs (125,382), and there are 9 other castes numbering over 50,000, viz., Kurmīs (99,482), Brāhmans (84,949), Koiris (83,727), Dosādhs (79,182), Rājputs (75,949), Kāndus (65,322), Mallāhs (60,511), Telis (56,633), Nuniās (54,541) and Bābhans (52,453). The Goālās live almost entirely by cultivation and cattle breeding, and have a bad reputation for thefts and cattle stealing. The Chamārs are the village leather dressers and tanners, and their women serve as midwives. The Kurmīs are among the best cultivators, and are found in greatest strength in thānas Dhāka, Adāpur and Bettiah; the members of the Jaiswār sub-caste perform menial services, but other subdivisions are regarded as more respectable than most of the lower classes and include a number of land-owners. The Brāhmans also are largely supported by agriculture, and a number of them are petty *britdārs*, cultivators, and proprietors of small resumed estates; the principal divisions found are the Kanaujiā and Maithil Brāhmans. The connection which exists between the Mahārājās of Bettiah and Benāres has induced many Brāhmans from Benāres to settle in and about Bettiah, where costly temples have been built and endowed under their influence, and many villages have been let out to them at low rents. The Koiris are practically all pure cultivators or market gardeners; they are the best and most industrious of all the peasantry, and the cultivation of opium in this district is due to their exertions. The Dosādhs are cultivators and labourers, and have an evil reputation for criminal propensities. The Rājputs, like Brāhmans, are mostly dependent on agriculture, and include a large proportion of cultivating ryots and tenure-holders. The Kāndus are grain parchers and petty traders. The Mallāhs are a boating and fishing caste, and their women work in the villages and sell fish. The hereditary occupation of Telis is the manufacture and sale of oil, but a large number of them have engaged in trade and have become wealthy *mahājans*. The Nuniās' traditional occupation is the manufacture of saltpetre, and they make the best labourers in the district. The Bābhans are nearly all connected with agriculture in some form or another. They stand first in the category of landlords, both in respect of the number and extent of their estates; and with the Rājputs and Koiris, contain the largest number of cultivating ryots and tenure-holders. They number among them some of the most influential zamīndārs of the district, of whom the principal belong to the Bettiah Rāj family.

Among other high castes may be mentioned the Kāyasths or writer caste, in whom, it is said, that local intellect, such as it is, is concentrated. It is noticeable, however, that the term Majhawā, *i.e.*, resident of *pargana* Majhawā, which is a synonym for a fool, is applied to the Kāyasth of Champāran by his fellow Kāyasths of other districts. Among the low castes the Turāhās are specially numerous, this district containing 26,335 members of the caste out of the total of 74,712 found in the whole Province. They are a caste of musicians, but the men also gain a livelihood by carrying *pālkis* and catching fish, while the women sell the latter as well as vegetables.

It remains to notice a few castes peculiar to this district, viz., the Sarbhangs, Thārus, Thākurais and Magahiyā Doms.

Sarbhangs. The Sarbhangs form a small community, which is said to have sprung from promiscuous intercourse between Sannyāsi ascetics and loose women. No caste restrictions are observed; they admit outsiders of all castes and religions, and will take food from any one. They worship Rāmchandra and hold that the whole world is full of Rām, so everything is pure. The dead are buried. Their usual occupation is begging, but some have settled down to cultivation. The caste, if such it can be called, is said to rank with Aghoris and to be regarded with scorn by respectable Hindus.

Thākurais. The Thākurais are a Muhammadan community found only in Champāran. They are mostly cultivators of Hindu origin, and claim to have been Rājputs prior to their conversion to Muhammadanism. They observe the Hindu custom of *gaunā* or second marriage, and use brass vessels, like Hindus, instead of copper ones like Muhammadans. Most of them eschew beef and are still subject to many Hindu superstitions. They are the most respectable of the Ajlāf class.

Magahiyā Doms. The Magahiyā Doms are a sub-caste of Doms, who derive their name from the fact that their home is in Magah or Magadha, the old name of Bihār. In physical appearance, they are described as small and dark, with long tresses of unkempt hair and the peculiar beady eye of the non-Aryan; and there can be no doubt that they are of aboriginal descent. They are practically gipsies of predatory habits, whose manner of life has been described by Mr. Beames as follows:—" The Magahiyā Doms of Champāran are a race of professional thieves. They extend their operations into the contiguous districts of Nepāl. They are rather dainty in their operations, and object to commit burglary by digging through the walls of houses: they always enter a house by the door; and if it is dark, they carry a light. Of course, all this is merely done by way of bravado. Magahiyās never live long in one place. They move about constantly, pitching their ragged little reed tents or *sirkis* outside a village or on a grassy patch by the roadside, like our gipsies, till they have done all the plundering that offers itself in the neighbourhood, when they move off again." Such a wandering life is now precluded, as they are concentrated in two settlements, but when, as occasionally happens, they undertake thieving expeditions, they revert to the nomadic life of their ancestors. A fuller account of the Magahiyā Doms as a criminal caste will be given in Chapter XI, and it will suffice here to mention the way in which their criminal propensities have reacted on their religious ceremonies.

"Systematic robbery," writes Sir H. H. Risley in "The Tribes and Castes of Bengal," "is so far a recognized mode of life among the Magahiyā Doms that it has impressed itself on their religion, and a distinct ritual is ordained for observance by those who go forth to commit a burglary. The object of veneration on these occasions is Sansāri Māi, whom some hold to be a form of Kālī, but who seems rather to be the earth-mother known to most primitive religions. No image, not even the usual lump of clay, is set up to represent the goddess: a circle one span and four fingers in diameter is drawn on the ground and smeared smooth with cowdung. Squatting in front of this, the worshipper gashes his left arm with the curved Dom knife, and daubs five streaks of blood with his finger in the centre of the circle, praying in a low voice that a dark night may aid his designs; that his booty may be ample; and that he and his gang may escape detection."*

Thārus. The Thārus are an aboriginal tribe who inhabit the sub-Himālayan Tarai from Jalpāigurī on the east to Kumāon on the west. In Bengal and Eastern Bengal they number 27,884 souls, and of these no less than 26,687 are found in Champāran, mostly in the frontier thānas of Shikārpur and Bagahā, where they live in scattered clearings in the midst of jungle, forest and prairie land. The origin of the Thārus has formed the subject of much controversy, but the most probable explanation seems to be that they are a Dravidian race, whose ancestors ruled at one time in the valley of the Ganges and were gradually driven up into the sub-Himālayan forests. There they have been brought into contact with the Nepalese and other hill tribes, and their physiognomy has acquired in some instances a slightly

* See also *The Outcasts*, by G. R. Clarke, Calcutta, 1903.

Mongolian cast, which shows itself chiefly, but not to a striking degree, in slanting eyes, high cheek-bones, and scanty beards and moustaches. In other respects, their physical characteristics are of the strictly Indian type. They have long, wavy hair, a dark, almost a black, complexion, and in stature, build and gait they resemble other natives of India. It seems possible that they are the people mentioned by Alberuni (*cir.* 1030) as living in Tilwat, a country immediately to the south of and bordering on Nepāl, the inhabitants of which were called "Taru, a people of a very black colour and flat nosed like the Turks."

Originally of nomadic habits, many have now taken to settled cultivation and make honest and industrious husbandmen, damming up the hill streams to irrigate their scanty patches of rice land. They are among the most prosperous of the ryots and possess large herds of cattle and well-filled granaries. Traces of their nomadic ancestry, however, are still found. Thus, their houses are made of grass and reeds; the headmen farm the villages, each Thāru paying rent according to the number of ploughs he owns, and ploughing as much as he can; and they move off and go elsewhere at the slightest sign of oppression. These features of a nomadic life have gradually become less pronounced, especially in the last 10 years, their lands having been settled in 1897. They have an intense repugnance to service; nothing will induce them to hire themselves out as labourers to Hindu landlords; and it is said that the only kind of service they will undertake is that of elephant drivers, in which they display no mean skill. They are simple in their habits, contented and averse to litigation; they eat flesh, drink spirits, and are expert sportsmen; and those who have dealings with them find them more upright and honest than the ordinary ryot of Champāran.

The Thārus are the pioneers of cultivation in the undeveloped tract to the north. When a village is founded, the site is marked off by cross stakes of wood driven into the ground, which are solemnly worshipped on the day of the completion of the settlement, and then lapse into neglect unless some indication of the displeasure of the deity again directs attention to them. These crosses may be found in groups of ten or more on the edge of the cultivated lands.* "Every little village," says Mr. Nesfield, "is a self-governing community. Disputes are decided by a council of elders; and this is sometimes presided over by a headman, who in the Thāru language was formerly

* W. Crooke, *Popular Religion and Folklore of Northern India*, Allahabad, 1894.

called *barwaik*, but who is now dubbed even by themselves with the ordinary Hindī title of *chaudhri*. The office of headman is not hereditary. The man selected is one whose age, experience, and knowledge of the magical and medicinal arts entitle him to more respect than the rest; and he acquires the status of headman by tacit consent, and not by formal election. The decisions of the council or the headman are obeyed unreservedly, and there is no such thing known as a Thāru taking a fellow tribesman before a tribunal outside his own community. Litigation between Thārus and Hindus is equally unknown. Among themselves the Thārus are for the most part a peaceful and good-natured race, following without question, as if by a law of nature, the customs and maxims of their ancestors."* It may, however, be added that they occasionally call in the Collector, Subdivisional Officer, and Manager of the Bettiah Rāj to settle a point of law for them.

Their religion is a veneer of Hinduism over Animism. A prominent place in their pantheon is taken by the tribal hero Rikheswar, who, according to their legends, was the son of Rājā Ben. Rikheswar or Raksha was banished, it is said, from his father's court, and ordered with his band of male followers to seek a new home in the north, from which they were never to return. Setting out on their wanderings, they took as wives any women whom they could steal or capture on the road, and in this way the Thāru tribe was founded. It was not till they had reached the sub-Himālayan forest in which they still dwell that they decided to rest and settle. The soul of Raksha is still believed to hover among the people of his tribe. Just as in ancient days he led them safely through the wide wilderness into a new and distant settlement, so at the present day he is said to be the guardian and guide of men travelling on a distant journey. No Thāru sets out from his village for such a purpose without propitiating him with gifts and promising him a sumptuous feast of flesh, milk, and wine on his return. His presence is represented by a mound of mud, with a stone fixed in the middle; and he delights in seeing the head of a live capon dashed against this stone, and to feel its blood trickling down the side. One peculiarity of this god is that he is deaf, an emblem of his antiquity; and hence vows and prayers are addressed to him in a stentorian voice. Another popular deity is Dharchandī, whose shrine is a mound of clay studded with short wooden crosses, on which rice, pulse and other

* J. C. Nesfield, *The Thārus and Bogshas of Upper India*, Calcutta Review, Vol. LXXX, 1885.

produce of the fields are offered, and always on plates of leaf. Her shrine is so placed that all the cattle of the village, together with the swine, sheep, and goats, pass it on going out to graze, and repass it on their return. When cattle sicken or die, larger and more valuable offerings are made. Kuā is another village deity peculiar to the Thārus in Champāran, who is worshipped by casting sweetmeats down a well (*kuā*) and smearing vermilion on its rim.

These and other primitive deities are now rapidly losing ground in the estimation of the people, and giving way to the more popular worship of Siva and his consort Kālī. Although, however, modern Hinduism is fast displacing the earlier gods of the Thāru religion, it seems probable that the principles of their primitive belief will long survive in the strong fear of evil spirits which continually haunts the tribe. It is to the action of these spirits that fever, ague, cough, dysentery, fainting, headache, madness, bad dreams, and pain of all kinds are ascribed. In fact, the Thārus have no conception of natural disease, and no belief in natural death, except what is faintly conceived to be the result of natural decay. Their state, therefore, would be one of utter helplessness were it not for the reputed skill of medicine-men or sorcerers, who profess to have the power to control the spirits of the air or to interpret their grievances and wants. The power of the medicine-man is tremendous. He has a host of spirits at his command. Not only can he expel a fiend from the body of the sufferer, but he can produce suffering or death by driving a malignant spirit into the body of his foe. This belief in evil spirits also finds expression in the funeral ceremonies; for the corpse is painted with turmeric or vermilion, yellow and red being colours particularly dreaded by evil spirits, and the night after death it is placed on the village fetish mound. Thārus themselves are supposed to possess special powers as sorcerers, and Thāruhat or the land of the Thārus is a synonym for "witches' country."*

SOCIAL LIFE.

Houses.

No people in this Province, it is said, are so badly housed as the people of Champāran; and it cannot be denied that, taking the district as a whole, the houses are at least the worst in Bihār. The majority are squalid huts with walls made of mats, straw, or the branches and leaves of the *tāri* palm; the framework consists of a few bamboos lightly strung together, while the roof, which is supported on the trunk of a palm tree, is thatched with grass or reeds.

---

* W. Crooke, *Popular Religion and Folklore of Northern India*, Allahabad, 1894. The above account of the Thārus has been compiled mainly from Risley's Tribes and Castes of Bengal.

In the north of the Bagahā thāna and in the country round Tribenī hardly a mud hut is to be seen, but towards the south mud huts become more numerous. The well-to-do alone can afford tiled roofs and masonry or brick houses. The latter generally consist of four buildings facing one another with a court-yard in the centre. In one of these some members of the family sleep; a second is used as a store-room for rice, etc.; a third serves as a cook-house; and the fourth is given up to the cows and live-stock. The furniture is generally meagre. A few rough beds made of coarse string with a bamboo or wooden frame-work, some brass utensils for eating and washing purposes, some earthen cooking vessels and receptacles for water, a chest or two, and a circular receptacle for grain (*kothī*), with a mud cover and mud sides, are all that is usually found.

Food. Rice, which is the staple food of the people in Bengal, is not the staple food of the poor in Champāran, but rather that of the fairly well-to-do. The mass of the people live on bannocks made of flour prepared from one of the many kinds of coarse grains and pulses. These cakes are accompanied by vegetables, salt and a few simple condiments; and the meal is varied by a porridge of the same. Maize is eaten whenever it can be procured, and also *arhar* (Cajanus indicus) either in the form of flour or as a thick pottage; and besides these, many kinds of millets and pulses form part of the cultivator's dietary. Among the poorer classes the morning meal usually consists of parched or boiled grains of various sorts, and the evening meal of boiled rice (*bhāt*) with *dāl* or pulse and occasionally vegetable curries.

Dress. The poorest classes wear nothing more than a *langota*, *i. e.*, a narrow strip of cloth fastened to a cord round the waist, but the cultivator wears a *dhotī* and a piece of cloth (*gamchā*) worn over the shoulder or on the head with one end hanging down; a corner of this cloth is often knotted and used like a purse for keeping spare cash, receipts, etc. The man who habitually wears a *pagrī* belongs to a higher grade, and the average tenant wears a head-dress on special occasions only. As we get higher up the scale, we find a *mirzāi* or coat added to the *dhotī* and *pagrī*. A Muhammadan, however, wears a *chapkan*, *i. e.*, a long coat coming down to the knees, a small cap or *pagrī*, and trousers (*pāijāmā*), which are sometimes long loose drawers and sometimes tight-fitting pantaloons. Women of the cultivating class generally wear a *sārī*, a long piece of cloth thrown over the head and wound round the body, and women of the poorer classes a coarse cotton sheet called *putli*; the women-folk of the more prosperous tenants also wear a *jhulā* or bodice.

The following account of the agricultural, marriage and funeral ceremonies observed in Champāran is quoted, with some slight abbreviation, from Mr. Stevenson-Moore's Settlement Report:—

Agricultural ceremonies.

Before sowing, a Pandit is consulted for an auspicious hour. On being served with *purota* (a dole of rice, some *haldī* (turmeric), and one to four annas in pice), the Pandit unfolds his *patra* and proceeds to study the stars. After fixing the time, he selects a male member of the family whose horoscope is favourable, and at the appointed hour the man chosen proceeds to the field with a *kodālī* on his shoulder and a *lotā* of water in the right hand. Digging for five steps each way in the middle of the field, he scatters seed and pours out the hallowed water from his *lotā* there. This preliminary ceremony is technically called *muth lagāna*.

The crops, when ready, are cut on a day again named by the Pandit, for which he gets another *purota*. They are harvested and brought to the threshing floor, where a mango or *dhip* post is set up in the centre, after a few nuts (*kasaili*) and some pice have been placed in the hole made for the purpose. To this post the bullocks that tread out the grain are fastened. During the subsequent process of husking, any grain that falls outside the basket is jealously guarded and reserved for the consumption solely of members of the family; this is called *agwar*. After the *agwar* has been gathered up, the grain has to be weighed, but before the actual weighment begins, a religious ceremony takes place. A fire is ignited on the spot; some *ghī*, linseed, *dhip* wood and rice are mixed, and poured over it. A *mantra* is meanwhile recited by the priest, who again comes in for a gratuity, generally of a *paseri* of rice and 4 annas with some *haldī*. The heap is then smoothed, and a ball of cowdung is placed in the centre of the heap, as an emblem of good luck. Three *sūps* of grain are next taken out, one set apart for Brāhmans, another distributed to beggars, and the third reserved for the *gorait*. A *sūp* usually contains a *paseri* of grain. Finally, the grain is brought home and stored without any further ceremony.

Marriage ceremonies.

When a match is proposed, the *kundali* (an abstract of the *janam patra* or horoscope) of the boy is brought by a Pandit and a barber to the girl's father. The Pandit is paid handsomely according to the means of the parties, receiving also various articles of clothing. The boy's *kundali* is compared with that of the girl, and if there is no astrological obstacle, the match is accepted. A rupee and *dhotī* are then sent to the boy as a token of confirmation; if a Brāhman or Khattrī by caste, a sacred thread is also added. This present is locally called by that familiar word *parcha*. Then follows the settlement between the two parties of the *tilak* or dowry. The amount of *tilak* knows no bounds. From one rupee and a *dhotī* it may rise to thousands, according to the means of the bride's guardian; but for an ordinary ryot it would seldom exceed Rs. 25. The *tilak* is sent to the bridegroom on some auspicious day through the Pandit and the barber, who each get as a reward some money and a full dress, the value of which depends upon the means of the bridegroom's guardian.

The next ceremony is that of introduction called *lagan*. The bridegroom is dressed in a pale yellow *dhotī* and goes to the bride at her own house. They are set together. A handful of rice with some silver ornament is put into their hands, and married women touch them from the feet upward, throwing some rice over their heads. Then follows the *matkar* ceremony. Earth is brought from a field and put in the court-yard; over it is placed a pitcher of water, covered with mango leaves; one pice and some sweetmeats are put inside, and rice or barley is deposited on the lid. Above this is set the marriage lamp, containing four wicks and hence called the *chaumukh*. The *matkar* is succeeded by the *mando* ceremony. A *mandwā* or *shamiāna* is erected and hung with mango leaves, and the beam of the plough is set up hard by. Beneath the *shamiāna* is placed an earthen elephant, three to seven holes are dug near the plough beam, and an image of Ganesh is made of cowdung and worshipped. The bride or the bridegroom sits near it and is painted with *haldī* by the near relatives. This ceremony is called *haldī charhāna*, and continues till the marriage day. But the preliminary ceremonies do not end even here. On an auspicious day fixed by the Brāhman, *manki pūjā* is observed. This is the worship of all the family gods conducted by the Pandit in conjunction with the bride's guardian. The lowest cost to the bride's guardian of this ceremony is Re. 1-4 and it may rise to Rs. 1,125. The ryot expends about Rs. 50.

At length, the day for the *barāt* or marriage procession arrives. The bridegroom is carried with much display to the bride's house, and on arrival is honoured by the bride's guardian. A garland is thrown round his neck and a *tīkā* or mark of curd and rice is put on his forehead, while some *achhar* or *mantra* is recited over him. At the same time, he is given a present, the value of which varies from Re. 1-4 to Rs. 125, according to the means of the bride's guardian. This ceremony is called the *duār pūjā*. On its completion, the *barāt* retires for a rest and refreshments. Then there is a *shāstrārtha* (a competition in reciting Shāstras) between Brāhman guests and *bahas* (discussion) between the Kāyasth guests of either party. When finished, the bride's guests retire from the presence of the *barātis*.

The next function is the presentation of presents to the bride, consisting usually of gold and silver ornaments, dresses and sweetmeats. The bridegroom's elder brother, accompanied by other relations, takes the presents to the *shamiāna* and places them in the outstretched hands of the bride, who is brought there for the purpose by the barber's wife. This done, the men retire. The bridegroom is then brought into the *shamiāna* wearing a *dhotī*, and is seated by the side of the wife's guardian. The Pandit now recites the *mantra* consecrating the marriage, and the guardian bestows the hand of the bride on the bridegroom. This final ceremony is called *kanyādān*. The bridegroom's party is then given a big feast, which often costs more than the means of the bride's guardian allow. A few years later, when the bride is of mature age, she for the first time goes to the house of her husband. The technical term for this is *gauna*, but no particular ceremony is observed. Force of custom, however, compels her guardian to give her a dowry of ornaments, furniture, cattle and dress, the cost of which he often can very ill afford.

Funeral ceremonies. When a Hindu is at the point of death, his family, if rich, give a calf, and, if poor, some pice to the Brāhman, and certain passages are read out from the Vedas. The dead body is covered with new cloth and borne to the burning ground on a bed or a bamboo *ranthi*. The heir puts the fire into the mouth. When the corpse is reduced to ashes, the mourners retire to the deceased's house, and are fed with plain rice, *urid* pulse, and cow's milk. A pitcher filled with water, and having a small hole in the bottom, is hung from a *pīpal* tree, the idea being that the departed soul of the deceased can drink, if so disposed. For 10 days thereafter food (*pīnda*) is placed near a river bank as an offering to the deceased. All the relatives assemble on the 10th day, called *daswan*, and are shaven. *Pinda* is again offered on the 11th day, and Mahāpātra Brāhmans are fed in accordance with the means of the family. A calf is then branded and let loose. The Brāhman gets a gift of all the personal effects of the deceased, new clothing, bedding, and some brass utensils. The Mahāpātras avail themselves of this opportunity to squeeze out of the family as much as they can by refusing to eat unless they are amply paid. On the twelfth day the Purohit Brāhmans are fed, and they get as charity 1 pice to 2 annas each. Finally, on the following day the relatives of the deceased are entertained to dinner.

The dead body of a Muhammadan is bathed with water in which a little camphor has been dissolved, and is then clothed in the *kaffan*; after this, it is borne to the burial-ground, where the funeral prayer (*nimāz*) is said and the body is interred. Some silver or copper is distributed to beggars. The services of a Hāfiz are secured to recite the Korān every day on the spot where the deceased breathed his last. This continues for 40 days. On the third or fourth day after the death, the relatives and friends of the family assemble and read the Korān. This ceremony, which is called *hal*, is again observed on the twentieth and fortieth days. On each occasion food and pice are distributed to the beggars. Well-to-do men give a dinner on each of these three days, but those of humbler condition are content with one on the last, *i.e.*, the fortieth day, when the closing ceremony called *chehlum* takes place. The Hāfiz gets all the personal effects of the deceased, some copper utensils and some money. Beggars also get clothing on this day, if the family can afford it.

CHAPTER IV.

PUBLIC HEALTH.

CLIMATE.

THE rainfall in Champāran is heavier than in other Bihār districts, and the moisture of the atmosphere, the presence of numerous stagnant lakes formed in old river-beds, and the proximity of the hills combine to give the district a more unhealthy climate than any other part of Bihār. The physique of the Champāran peasants generally is notoriously below that of residents of other districts in this part of the Province; in nearly every village there are a certain number of people who look most miserable specimens of humanity, and in the district, as a whole, the proportion of chronic invalids strikes one as unusually large. This is more particularly the case in the submontane tract to the north, where malarial fever is rife. The mortuary returns, however, fail to show clearly the actual state of things, as those who have their health broken down by residence in the Tarai leave it and die elsewhere. The ravages made by the climate are more unmistakably shown by deserted sites of villages, mango groves at a distance from any present dwellings, and other signs that the country once supported a population much larger than it does at present. The most unhealthy season in this part of the district is after the end of the rains, when the north wind blows off the hills, its advent being invariably signalized by an outbreak of malarial fever.

It is stated that, owing to the progress made in clearing the forests and extending cultivation, the district is becoming healthier. Thus, Mr. Stevenson-Moore, in his Settlement Report published in 1901, says:—"The question whether the district is growing healthier can be decisively answered in the affirmative; as cultivation, accompanied by the eradication of noxious growth and by improved drainage, spreads further north, it steadily but slowly drives fever back before it. The European planters who live in this area are, I believe, unanimous in the opinion that the improvement in its general healthiness during the last 20 years is quite extraordinary."

VITAL STATISTICS.

A comparison of vital statistics for a longer period than this is rendered impossible by the changes in the system of registering births and deaths which have taken place from time to time. In

1869 the duty of reporting deaths was imposed on the village *chaukīdārs*, and in 1876 the system was extended to births; but the returns received were so incomplete that they were soon discontinued, and, except in towns, deaths alone were registered until 1892, when the collection of statistics of births as well as of deaths was ordered, and the system now in vogue was introduced. Under this system vital occurrences are reported by the *chaukīdārs* to the police, and the latter submit monthly returns to the Civil Surgeon, by whom statistics for the whole district are prepared.

It was reported in 1891 that the district was gradually losing its reputation for unhealthiness, but the returns submitted since that year seem to show that the improvement has not been maintained. The census of 1901 showed a decrease of 69,002 persons or 3·7 per cent., this result being directly attributable to the short crops and unhealthiness from which the district suffered. During these 9 years fever was very prevalent, there were frequent epidemics of cholera, and there was a succession of bad seasons, which culminated in the famine of 1897. The efforts of Government to save the people from starvation appear to have been successful, and the number of deaths returned was lower than the average of the 3 preceding years. The birth-rate fell in the same proportion, but a low birth-rate is a necessary sequel of a famine. Low as the death-rate was in 1897, it was still lower in 1898, but on the other hand more births were reported in 1899 than in any other year since the registration of births was introduced. It was not until the end of 1900 that the prosperity of the people was fully restored, and in five of the nine years in question the number of deaths reported exceeded the births.

Since 1901 there has been a marked increase in the number of births, the average birth-rate up to the end of 1906 being 41·85 per mille, as compared with 34·31 per mille in the preceding 9 years. The result has been that, whereas the number of deaths in the latter period exceeded the births by 1,059, there has been an excess of 85,708 births in the 6 years ending in 1906. The highest birth-rate recorded since the present system of registering vital occurrences was introduced is 43·65 per mille in 1902, and the lowest birth-rate is 25·57 per mille in 1892. The highest death-rate was returned in 1894 when the mortality was 43·22 per mille, and the lowest death-rate is 23·04 per mille recorded in 1891.

PRINCIPAL DISEASES. Fevers. The greatest mortality is caused by fever, which has never been known to cause a death-rate of less than 17 per mille since the introduction of the present system of mortuary returns, while in two years the death-rate has risen above 27 per mille. Regarding the types of fever prevalent, Major B. H. Deare, I.M.S., formerly Civil Surgeon of Champāran, has furnished the following note:—

"The whole district lies in a corner of Bengal bounded by the Gandak river to the west and south-west, and by the Nepāl Tarai and mountains to the east and north-east; and these boundaries have a marked effect on the types and prevalence of fever. While a great part of the whole district is more or less water-logged at certain times, and natural drainage is defective, one has added to this predisposing factor the existence of a very large number of very large lakes and *nazis* which have been formed by the vagaries of rivers like the Sikrāna and Dhanauti, which have changed their course and left behind these fruitful sources for the production of malaria; and to this is added the existence, along the whole north-east and east border, of a Tarai country, in which malarial fevers of all types are very rife. Another and very important factor in the fever problem of this district is the existence of the tortuous river Dhanauti. Years back flourishing villages existed along its banks, and the land on either side was under cultivation. Gradually, the river-bed became silted up, and fever of a most malignant type broke out in these villages, the well water became unfit for use, the population was decimated and those surviving fled, fields went out of cultivation, until at the present time, the Dhanauti lands are void of villages and cultivation, and are shunned by human beings entirely.

"Malarial fevers are very common throughout the district, all types being noticed. In the towns, such as Motīhāri, Bettiah and Kesariyā, and in the southern part of the district, fever is less prevalent owing to better drainage and better perflation, through absence of jungle and forests, and a greater distance from the Tarai. The majority of cases met with in the towns and this rural area are of the benign tertian type, which readily yield to quinine, but malignant tertians are also met with, though rarely. In the rural areas, especially in the north and those parts adjoining the Nepāl Tarai, the type of fever met with is much more severe, malignant tertians and quartans being more common than in other parts of the district. Pernicious types of malaria are also seen, and some cases of black water fever have been reported. The Raxaul, Shikārpur, Rāmnagar and Bagahā thānas are especially notorious, so much so that the police in those places are provided with mosquito curtains, have prophylactic quinine, and are transferred frequently. Yet they suffer in a most marked degree; while the fever rate among the cooly population on the Tribenī canal work in the Bagahā, Rāmnagar and Shikārpur thānas, has been so heavy (in spite of medical aid and unlimited quinine) as to make the labour problem a most difficult one, and on occasions the work has almost come to a standstill.

"Thus it will be seen that there is a marked difference in the malarial type in the Tarai areas of this district, as compared with the flatter alluvial tracts, and I think it is no hyperbole to say that 75 per cent. of the residents of the Champāran Tarai are malaria-sodden. Another common type of disease, the result of malaria, is seen in all parts of the district. I refer to the so-called malarial cachexia cases with sallow countenance, pigmented tongue, huge abdomen containing chiefly a huge spleen, and attenuated extremities. These cases are not so commonly seen here, however, as in other districts, such as the Eastern Bengal ones."

Cholera.

Next to fever the greatest mortality due to any specific disease is caused by cholera, which breaks out nearly every other year in epidemic form. The worst epidemics on record occurred in 1894, 1900 and 1903, when the disease caused a mortality of 8·25, 11·74 and 7·60 per mille respectively. In 1903 over nearly 14,000 persons succumbed to its ravages, the most terrible outbreak occurring in the Dhāka and Adāpur thānas, where over 5,000 people were stricken down in July and August. Motīhāri suffered especially severely, 18·71 per mille of its population being carried off.

Other diseases.

Small-pox rarely occurs in a severe epidemic form, the death-rate due to it never having been as high as 0·50 per mille. Plague has not yet obtained a footing, only 17 persons having died of it in 1903, 34 in 1905, and 260 in 1906.

Deaf-mutism.

Deaf-mutism is more prevalent than in any other district in Bengal, the proportion of deaf-mutes returned in the census of 1901 being 275 per 100,000 males and 173 per 100,000 females. This affliction is most prevalent in the south and south-west of the district, which is watered both by the Great and Little Gandak, but is worst in Motīhāri, which does not touch the Great Gandak, but is bisected by the Sikrāna and its tributary, the Dhanauti river. The Dhanauti river has a specially bad reputation for its poisonous qualities and its tendency to cause goitre, and the two worst circles in the Motīhāri thāna are on its banks; but even so the average number of deaf-mutes per circle is highest in the circles watered by the Sikrāna or Burh Gandak river. Popular belief has it that not only human beings but also animals and birds get goitre from drinking the water of some of the rivers, and that while certain streams and wells produce the disease, the water of other wells, sometimes in the same village, cure it.

Many deaf-mutes are also cretins, and the number of the latter is remarkable. It is a common sight to see them going out with village children to tend cattle, and sometimes deaf-mute idiots tend cattle alone.

Insanity.

Insanity is not so common as in other districts in Bihār, only 9 per 100,000 males and 6 per 100,000 females being returned as insane at the census of 1901; but the common belief is that it is very prevalent. This belief finds expression in popular proverbs regarding the Majhawā *pargana*, which is regarded as the home of the feeble minded, *e.g.*, *kahān kā Majhāwā* is a delicate way of insinuating to a man that he is an idiot.

Other infirmities.

Blindness also is rarer than in the adjoining districts, but 94 per 100,000 males and 86 per 100,000 females were returned as blind in 1901. Leprosy is also less common than in any other district in Bihār, the proportion of lepers being only 33 males and 4 females per 100,000 of either sex.

VACCINATION.

Vaccination is only compulsory within municipal limits, and is not so popular as in other parts of the Province. In 1905-06 the number of persons successfully vaccinated was 51,000, representing 29·09 per mille of the population, as compared with 26·61 per mille in the preceding five years. In the same year protection was afforded to 298·67 per mille of the infant population, and only 4 other districts in Bengal had a worse record in this respect. Formerly inoculation was commonly practised, but it has now died out.

MEDICAL INSTITUTIONS.

There are 7 charitable medical institutions in the district, viz., hospitals at Motīhāri and Bettiah and dispensaries at Bagahā, Barharwā, Dhāka and Kesariyā, and a Lady Dufferin Zanāna Hospital at Bettiah. The hospital at Motihāri provides accommodation for 14 (8 male and 6 female) in-patients, and that at Bettiah for 29 (19 male and 10 female) in-patients, and the dispensary at Bagahā for 2 in-patients. The other dispensaries give outdoor relief only. The railway also maintains dispensaries at Raxaul and Shikārpur, and the Public Works Department at Bhainsalotan and Rāmnagar. A new hospital is being erected at Motihāri, which, when completed, will be one of the finest hospitals in the Province outside Calcutta.

Native practitioners.

The people generally favour native physicians rather than the European methods of treatment. Both *hakīms* and *baidyas* are numerous, the former treating patients according to the Persian system, while the latter adopt the Hindu mode of treatment. Neither class, as a rule, perform any surgical operations except bleeding; but barbers sometimes perform more serious operations, such as the removal of tumours, and also attempt the reduction of dislocations and setting of fractures. The remedies used by native physicians are not known, but they very frequently administer mercury for the purpose of causing salivation. They also apply cupping instruments in the shape of a horn (*singhi*), with which blood is withdrawn by suction with the mouth applied to the small end of the horn, the skin having been previously incised. There is also another cupping instrument, called *tumbi*, made of earthenware from which the air is exhausted by burning some grass inside, the skin being incised after the blood has been drawn to the surface by the action of the instrument. They also use leeches for abstracting blood. Cautery is applied generally in cases of enlarged spleen, either by means of hot irons or red-hot charcoal. Occasionally quicklime is used as a caustic. Wandering physicians, called *sattia*, sometimes come from other districts, generally from the United Provinces, and operate for cataract with rude instruments.

CHAPTER V.

AGRICULTURE.

GENERAL CONDITIONS.

THE greater part of Champāran is a flat cultivated expanse, but its northern and western thānas contain a large proportion of hill and jungle. It has many of the characteristics of a sub-Himālayan tract. The climate is humid, rivers and streams abound, and the normal rainfall is higher than that of any other district in the Patna Division. Chains of lakes and swamps are found lying from north-west to south-east, marking the beds of old rivers and indicating the line of natural drainage; numerous streams run into the district from Nepāl and discharge themselves into these lakes or into the larger rivers; and extensive tracts in centre and east are not infrequently inundated by floods from these rivers and their tributaries.

The Gandak bounds the district on the west, and there is an alluvial tract of great natural fertility in the vicinity of its course. The most important river, however, is the Sikrāna, also known as the Burh Gandak in its lower reaches, which flows in a south-easterly direction through the centre of the district and divides it into two distinct parts. Generally speaking, the northern part is a great rice-producing area, while the southern portion grows millets, pulses, cereals and oil-seeds; and another marked distinction is that indigo cultivation is almost entirely confined to the latter tract. In the northern area, a considerable proportion of the land receives artificial irrigation from the streams which traverse it, but away from them the cultivators are mostly dependent for their crops on seasonable rainfall. The southern tract, on the other hand, receives practically no artificial irrigation, but is comparatively safe owing to its rich fertile soil and the variety of its crops; but here again, owing to the absence of irrigation, there is widespread failure when the seasons are unfavourable. The rainfall to the north is heavier than in the south; but it is in the former tract that the effects of drought are most severely felt, owing to the fact that rice is more exclusively cultivated, while further south other produce is raised requiring less water.

Northern tract.

The country to the north of the Sikrāna is intersected by a number of streams debouching from Nepāl or the Sumeswar range, and flowing from north to south till they join that river. The soil of this tract is mainly clay, and is especially adapted for rice cultivation; but in a year of deficient or unfavourably distributed rainfall this crop is liable to extensive failure, except where resort can be had to artificial irrigation from the small streams flowing southwards. From the Sikrāna itself, except in its higher reaches, there is no irrigation in ordinary years; and even in years of great drought it is very difficult to throw weirs across it in time to be of much use in saving the winter or *aghani* rice, which is the principal crop in this portion of the district. Nearly one-third of the rice area is, however, sown with early or *bhadoi* rice, and an oil-seed or pulse crop can generally be raised after it is gathered. Where winter rice is grown, it is the only crop of the year, except in very favourable seasons, when a catch-crop of coarse pulses, ripening in spring, may be sown broadcast among the stubble.

Southern tract.

To the south of the Sikrāna the general slope is parallel to that of the river, *i.e.*, from north-west to south-east; but there are only two other streams of any size, and these have tortuous courses and a sluggish current, except in the rains. The soil consists of fine light sand and clay, which when not so low as to get water-logged in the rains, or too high to be devoid of moisture, is capable of producing double crops in the year, viz., maize and inferior millets harvested in September, wheat, barley, pulses, oil-seeds and opium reaped in March and April, and *chīna* millet (Panicum miliaceum) reaped in June. An important crop, also gathered in the rains, is indigo, but another crop cannot be taken off the ground in the same year. The spring crops on the higher lands, with the exception of *rahar* pulse (Cajanus indicus), are poor, the soil being very light and containing little moisture in the dry season of the year. Irrigation is seldom, if ever, practised in these loam soils, even where water can be had at a convenient level from wells or other sources. Clay soils are only found in limited areas near Gobindganj and Kesariyā, where the predominant crop is rice, but there are no means for irrigating it in a year of drought.

Soils.

North of the Sikrāna hard clay soils, locally called *bāngar*, predominate; these require irrigation and are particularly suitable for rice cultivation. In this northern tract a thin reddish loam called *babhni* is also found, which will not grow rice, but bears crops of maize, barley, gram, other pulses and oil-seeds. The least fertile soil is *baldhūs*, a light loose sandy soil, fit only for maize and inferior millets.

South of the Sikrāna, uplands, called *bhīth*, predominate, except in thānas Kesariyā and Gobindganj, where rice is grown in large marshes (*chaurs*) and in low land suitable for the crop and hence known as *dhanhar*. The soil in the uplands is generally a light loam and grows millets, pulses, cereals, oil-seeds and indigo. It is often impregnated with saline matter, more particularly towards the west, where a fair amount of trade in saltpetre is still carried on. The subsoil is generally a tenacious clay, often quite black ; and below this, again, sand is struck. The upland or *uparwār*, as it is also termed by the inhabitants, is divided into the following sub-classes: (1) *Dhobini*, a word meaning bleached, is a soil which corresponds to the *babhni* of the northern tract, and produces autumn and spring crops. (2) *Goenra* is the upland close to village sites, which is especially manured with cow-dung for special crops, like wheat and opium; when tending to exhaustion from continuous cultivation, it is left fallow for four months during the rains, and is then called *chaumās*. The *goenra* lands are by far the most productive in the district, and are much sought after by the Opium Department and indigo-planters. They are usually parcelled out into small plots, and almost every holding will be found to contain a portion of them. (3) *Bhāth* is a name given to land periodically visited by flood, which is enriched by a fertilizing deposit of silt and is very retentive of moisture. Sugarcane and root-crops, such as yams and potatoes, grow abundantly on it. (4) *Baldhūs* is a light loose soil, in which sand predominates, as its name denotes. (5) *Dūb* are low sandy lands on the riverside, which stagnant flood-water converts into marsh. In these a kind of coarse paddy, called *boro dhān*, is grown, which is harvested in June or July.

Rainfall.

For the *bhadoi* and late rice harvests the distribution most favourable to agriculture—the husbandman's ideal year—is when premonitory showers, falling in May or early in June, facilitate that spade husbandry which, to secure a really good crop, must precede ploughing operations. The rain in the end of June and in July should be heavy: then should come an interval of comparatively fair weather, in which weeding operations may be successfully prosecuted. The September rains must be heavy, shading off into fine weather with October showers. On the sufficiency of the September rains, more than of any other month, depends the character of the winter rice crop. Finally, periodic showers from December to February inclusive are essential to a good *rabi* harvest.*

* A. P. McDonnell, *Food-grain Supply of Bihār and Bengal*, Calcutta, 1876.

Owing to the absence of artificial irrigation, the cultivators of Champāran are at a disadvantage, as compared with other parts of Bihār. Usually, the district is blessed with sufficient natural moisture, for the rainfall is heavy in normal years. Unfortunately, however, it is exceedingly capricious, extreme variations occurring, with the result that even when the total amount reaches the normal, it may be so unfavourably distributed as to cause a failure of the crops. The most critical months of the year are June to October; and the rainfall in the *Hathiyā* asterism at the end of September is the most important in the year, for not only is it required to bring the winter rice to maturity but also to provide moisture for the sowing of the *rabi* crops.

IRRIGATION.

Owing to the heavy rainfall and the natural moisture of the soil, irrigation is very little practised; and at the last settlement it was found that only 2 per cent. of the cultivated area was irrigated. The cultivators generally are content to trust to the rainfall, which is copious in ordinary years, and have not the enterprise to guard against the evil effects which may be caused any year by its failure or unfavourable distribution. An exception to this indifference is found in the north of the district, where irrigation is most essential for successful harvests. Here the water of the hill streams is utilized to a certain extent by means of *pains* or channels leading off from them, and in dry years a weir is thrown across their beds, but full advantage has not yet been taken of the facilities which they afford. An extension of the system of *pains* has, however, been carried out in the last 20 years, and a great system of canals is under construction; and when these have been completed, this tract will be well irrigated. The following is an account of the three systems of irrigation practised, viz., from canals, *pains* and wells.

Tiar or Madhuban canal.

The oldest State irrigation work is the Tiar canal in the north-east of the district. This canal has a length of 6½ miles 5 furlongs and has one distributary, the Lakhaurā distributary, with a length of 6 miles. It derives its supply from the Tiar (Teur) river, across which a weir has been constructed near the Chauradāno police outpost north of Motīhāri. It is capable of irrigating 6,000 acres, but has not yet been fully utilized, the average area irrigated annually being 4,100 acres, of which 2,700 acres are under *kharīf* or winter rice. This canal, which was completed in 1879, is more usually known as the Madhuban canal, as it was constructed almost entirely at the cost of Rai Bahādur Durgā Parsād Singh, the zamīndār of Madhuban. It was acquired in 1886 by Government, which has since maintained it.

The Dhāka canal is the most recent addition to the canals of the district. It is a small canal designed to carry off the water of the Lāl Bakyā river to the south of the Dhāka thāna; the main canal is only 3½ miles long, but it has two branches, each 7½ miles long, called, the Sirāha and Patāhi branches. It depends for its supply on the Lāl Bakyā river, and the irrigable area is 13,500 acres, viz., 8,500 acres of rice and 5,000 acres of *rabi*. The canal has recently been completed at a cost of 4½ lakhs. **Dhāka canal.**

A far more important work than either of the two canals mentioned above is now in progress, viz., the construction of the Tribenī canal. This canal obtains its water supply from the Gandak at the point where it enters the district and has its head sluice at Bhainsalotan near the village of Tribenī, from which it derives its name. The length of the canal is to be 60 miles, and it will run parallel to the foot of the hills in a south-easterly direction to within 10 miles of Adāpur, irrigating from its right bank the country lying between it and the Sikrāna river. The area commanded, which is bounded on the north by the canal, on the south by the Sikrāna river, on the west by the Gandak, and on the east by the Thatharia river, will be 427 square miles. It is designed for a discharge of 2,170 cubic feet per second, and the area to be irrigated each year is estimated at 114,000 acres. As it will cut directly across all the numerous torrents which flow from the Nepāl hills south to the Sikrāna, the work is expensive, and progress in construction is impeded by the unhealthy climate in this part of the district and the difficulty of obtaining labour. **Tribenī canal.**

Pending the completion of the Tribenī canal, the northern portion of the district is dependant on artificial water channels, called *pains*, led off from the hill streams which feed the Sikrāna river. The area commanded by these *pains* is, however, generally small, as the supply from the hill streams is uncertain and fails altogether when the rain in the neighbouring hills ceases Many of the streams, being fed by local rain, can in favourable years protect the crops on only a small area; while in a year when the rainfall ceases prematurely, they are useless, except for irrigating a small area of indigo and *rabi*. Frequently there is not sufficient rain to bring down more water than is carried off by the channels made to take the cold weather discharge; and at times these run dry until there is heavy rain, when all the dams (*bāndhs*) are liable to be washed away. These *pains* are made by the landlords or cultivators, and as they have no means of controlling the supply in them, they sometimes do more harm than good, while disputes about the right to use the water often lead to serious quarrels among the cultivators. ***Pains.***

The most extensive system of *pains* has been carried out by the Sāthi Indigo Concern, which commenced laying down a series of channels about 20 years ago, steadily increasing them year by year until there are now nearly 105 miles of these distributaries running through the property. The rivers drawn from are the Pandāl, Maniāra, Katahā and Rāmrekhā. Starting at Harditerha the principal *pain* covers a distance of some 53 miles, crossing the railway at Shikārpur (Narkatiāganj station), and terminating at Basantpur. One offshoot of this *pain* runs to Barharwā and is 22 miles long; another taking off from the Maniāra flows through some 20 miles of country. The Rāmrekhā *pain* is close on 7 miles, and the Katahā *pain* is 6 miles long; and there are other minor distributary channels covering some 18 miles. The proprietors of the Sāthi concern give their own ryots the free use of water, and also allow the same privilege to the cultivators of other villages after their own tenants are supplied. Any surplus water is run into the village tanks for the benefit of the villagers and their cattle. It is estimated that about 20,000 acres were irrigated from this source in 1906-07.*

The only other *pain* calling for mention is the Masān *pain*, a channel 16 miles long dug in the famine of 1897, which derives its supply from a dam built across the Masān stream to the north of Rāmnagar, and conducts water to the fields for many miles south. Unfortunately, this *pain* is now largely silted up, and its utility is consequently impaired.

Wells.

There is a prejudice against irrigating loam soils, as the cultivators believe that where the soil is saliferous—as much of the loam soil is—it produces inferior salts; that the land loses its capacity for retaining moisture; and that consequently irrigation once started must be continued. Well irrigation is, therefore, seldom employed in loam soils, even where water can be had at a convenient level; and it is noticeable that during the famine of 1897 the efforts made to encourage the people to dig temporary wells had but little effect. Irrigation from wells is, however, commonly employed for poppy cultivation.

PRINCIPAL CROPS.

According to the statistics obtained at the settlement of 1899, the total cropped area is 3,157 square miles, of which 895 square miles bear more than one crop in the year. The net cropped area is thus 2,262 square miles or 64 per cent. of the entire area of the district. In Champāran, as elsewhere in Bihār, the

---

* A fuller description of these *pains* will be found in an article "Irrigation in Bihār and the Sāthi enterprise" published in the Indian Planters' Gazette, March 2nd, 1907.

crops are grouped in three great divisions—*aghani*, *bhadoi* and *rabi*. The *aghani* crops consist of the winter rice crop, which is cut in the month of Aghan (November-December), and of sugarcane; the *bhadoi* crops are the early or autumn crops reaped in the month of Bhādo (August-September), consisting of 60-days (*sāthi*) rice, *maruā*, Indian corn, indigo and various millets; while the *rabi* crop, which is so called because it is harvested in the spring (*rabi*), includes such cold-weather crops as wheat, barley, oats, pulses, and poppy. The *bhadoi* crops were found to occupy 46 per cent., *aghani* 58 per cent., and *rabi* 55 per cent. of the net cropped area, 39 per cent. being twice cropped. It would thus appear, at first sight, that Champāran is a great *rabi*-producing area, but this is far from being the case, for most of the area growing *rabi* crops is occupied by gram, *khesāri* and other cheap crops, such as only the poorest classes will eat. This is particularly the case in the Bettiah subdivision, where the *rabi* is usually of a poor kind grown after winter rice; and valuable *rabi* crops are practically confined to the headquarters subdivision. The *aghani* area, again, is comparatively small, and it might therefore be supposed that rice was not grown extensively; but Champāran is one of the great rice-growing tracts of Bengal. This apparent anomaly is due to the fact that Champāran being liable to inundation, a large proportion of its rice crop consists of autumn rice. The extent to which autumn rice is grown in this district is very marked, and this accounts for the large area occupied by the *bhadoi* harvest.

FOOD-CROPS. Altogether 2,594 square miles or 82 per cent. of the total cropped area were returned as under food-crops, a percentage smaller than in any of the adjoining districts, where the population is more dense. Among these crops rice occupies the most prominent position, and the next largest percentage is returned by food-grains of minor importance, such as *kodo*, *khesāri*, *arhar*, *chīna*, etc. Barley is the next food-grain of importance, and then maize, wheat and gram.

Rice. Rice, occupying 1,223 square miles or 54 per cent. of the net cropped area, is the all-important crop of Champāran; and the greater part consists of *aghani* rice, grown on 36 per cent. of the net cropped area, while 18 per cent. is *bhadoi*. It is cultivated most extensively in the Bettiah subdivision, where the area under the crop is no less than 62 per cent. (41 per cent. *aghani* and 21 per cent. *bhadoi*) of the net cropped area; the proportion (80 per cent.) being especially high in the Shikārpur thāna. In the headquarters subdivision 47 per cent. (32 per cent. *aghani* and 15 per cent. *bhadoi*) of the net cropped area is under rice, and here the

Adāpur thāna takes the lead with the return of 84 per cent. From these figures it will be seen that winter rice predominates in the Bettiah subdivision, and autumn rice is also more extensively grown there; the largest rice-growing tract is comprised within the Adāpur, Shikārpur, Dhāka, Bagahā and Bettiah thānas, where over one-third of the crop consists of autumn rice. In the Tarai tract to the north of the district rice is almost the only crop grown by the aboriginal Thārus, who make from it an intoxicating liquor, drunk at marriage and other ceremonies.

One special feature of rice cultivation in Champāran may be mentioned here, viz., the growth in low marshy tracts of long-stemmed rice which rises with the flood-level. As soon as the low ground has nearly dried up in February, it is ploughed, and the seed is sown broadcast. When the regular rains begin, the plant gradually rises with the water, often attaining a height of 20 feet, and being very rarely, if ever, drowned by inundation. No matter how high the water rises, the plants grow with it; and it is a common sight to see it being reaped from boats.

Miscellaneous food-grains.

After rice, the largest area is occupied by miscellaneous food-grains (excluding wheat, barley, *maruā*, maize and gram), which are grown on 561 square miles or 25 per cent. of the net cropped area. The most noticeable among these is *khesāri* (Lathyrus sativus), which is often grown as a second crop to rice. *Kodo* (Paspalum scrobiculatum) comes next in the group, accounting for no less than 7 per cent. of the net cropped area. It is eaten to a considerable extent, the grain being either boiled or ground to flour and made into bread. *Arhar* (Cajanus indicus) is another important crop in this group, as it does not require irrigation and flourishes in time of drought when other crops are parched and dying. The *chīna* millet (Panicum miliaceum) is another variety classified under this heading, which attracted a good deal of attention during the famine of 1897, as it is a crop which can be raised in a shorter time than any other, 6 weeks only being required for its growth. The grain is fried and eaten, under the name of *mārhā*, and is much used both by rich and poor; it is especially a feature of marriage and funeral ceremonies, when *mārhā* mixed with curds is served out to the servants, *pālki*-bearers and other followers. *Sāwān* (Panicum frumentaceum), another of the crops grouped under this head, is a cereal, the grain of which is cleaned, boiled and eaten as rice. Sometimes also it is consumed in the form of *khīr*, *i.e.*, it is boiled in milk, and a little sugar is added; this preparation forms one of the favourite dishes of the poorer classes. The other minor crops of the group, viz., peas, oats, *masurī*, *keonī* and *kurthī*, are mainly grown along with other crops for the subsistence of the poor, and are cultivated to a small extent only.

The single crop most extensively grown after rice is barley, which occupies 335 square miles or 15 per cent. of the net cropped area. It is very generally consumed, and is taken either fried or in the form of bread, or as flour (*sattu*) mixed with water and a little salt; barley *sattu* is much appreciated even by those who can afford more expensive food. This crop covers 19 per cent. of the cultivated area in the headquarters subdivision, as compared with 10 per cent. in the Bettiah subdivision, Motīhārī being the thāna with the largest area under it (25 per cent.). **Barley.**

After barley comes maize or Indian corn (*makai*), covering 187 square miles or 8 per cent. of the area under cultivation. It is very extensively grown in the south, where it is one of the chief staple food-crops of the poor; even those who can afford three meals usually take it in some form or other. It is eaten fried for breakfast, boiled as *bhāt* for dinner, and made into bread for supper. It keeps the ryot going usually for at least four months in the year. When still only half ripe, it is rubbed with oil and lemon, sprinkled with salt and pepper, and after being slightly fried, is eaten by the well-to-do with much relish. **Maize.**

Wheat covers 164 square miles or 7 per cent. of the net cropped area, and is the most valuable of all the *rabi* food-crops. So highly it is esteemed, that it is called *Devānna* or the food of the gods. The poor agriculturist, however, grows it only for sale, as he cannot afford to consume it. It is a crop requiring special land and good cultivation, and is usually grown on land in the vicinity of rivers or on land from which paddy has been washed away by flood. **Wheat.**

Gram covers 58 square miles or 2½ per cent. only of the cultivated area. It is eaten in the form of *sattu*, and is also used as a fodder for horses, but it is not a crop of much importance, its growth being mainly confined to the three thānas of Adāpur, Dhāka and Shikārpur, where it is sown broadcast as a second crop to paddy. **Gram.**

The area under *maruā* (Eleusine Coracana) (1·20 per cent.) is small; so, too, is that under yams and potatoes (1·67 per cent.) *Aluā* and *suthni* are grown mainly on the banks of the Sikrāna river in the south of the district, and are eaten chiefly by the poor. **Other crops.**

At the last settlement it was found that non-food crops were grown on 563 square miles or 18 per cent. of the total cropped area. This is a larger proportion than in any of the adjoining districts and is due to the fact that the pressure of the population on the soil is still light. **NON-FOOD CROPS.**

Indigo. Among these crops the most important is indigo, which at that time was grown on 96,000 acres or 6·6 per cent. of the net cropped area. A description of the cultivation of indigo will be found in Chapter IX, and it will suffice here to say that, owing to the competition of the synthetic dye, the area under the plant had fallen to 47,800 acres in 1905 and, according to the final forecast, had been reduced to 38,600 acres in 1906. The cultivation of indigo is now almost confined to the tract south of the Sikrāna river.

Oil-seeds. Oil-seeds rank next in importance, occupying 94,000 acres or 6·5 per cent. of the net cropped area. They are cultivated most extensively in the Bettiah subdivision, where they are an important source of income to the agriculturist, a brisk export trade being carried on.

Poppy. The only other single crop of great importance and value is poppy, which at the time of the settlement was found to be grown on 54,000 acres or nearly 4 per cent. of the net cropped area. Of the total area 40,000 acres were in the headquarters subdivision and only 14,000 acres in the Bettiah subdivision; in other words, the area under this crop in the former was 2½ times as great as in the latter subdivision. In 1905-06 the area under this crop had fallen to 47,000 acres, owing largely to the competition of more paying crops; but the cultivation is still more extensive than in any other district in Bihār, except Gayā. On the other hand, it is said that the crop is cultivated with less care than elsewhere and the outturn is consequently small. Here, as elsewhere in Bihār, poppy is grown on a system of Government advances, all the opium produced being delivered up to and paid for by Government.

Sugarcane. Sugarcane is grown only to a small extent, the area under the crop at the time of the last settlement being only 11,000 acres. Formerly the cultivation of sugarcane was very considerable, and many of the indigo concerns were originally started as sugar factories. The manufacture of sugar was given up when indigo proved to be more profitable, but the reverse process is now taking place, as indigo is being replaced by sugarcane. Owing to this and other causes, the area under the plant had increased in 1906 to 13,000 acres. Sugarcane is grown for the most part in the Bettiah subdivision, where the cultivation and manufacture of sugar on advanced lines is being carried on by the Parsā factory. A fuller account of the development of the sugar industry will be found in Chapter VIII.

Fibres. At the last settlement fibre crops were grown on 7,000 acres or 0·5 per cent. of the net cropped area. Since that time there has been a marked increase in the area under jute, 5,000 acres being planted with that crop in 1907, as compared with 1,500 acres in 1906.

Other crops.

Of other non-food crops *kharhaul* or thatching grass is most important, particularly in the northern thānas, for it grows naturally on land left continuously fallow for some years, and in those thānas much of the land has not yet been reclaimed. It is, in fact, a more valuable crop than many inferior crops, the production of which requires much labour. The cultivation of tobacco is almost confined to the Bettiah thāna; it is grown for local consumption and is not exported.

AGRICULTURAL STATISTICS.

In the preceding account the statistics obtained at the settlement of 1899 have been given, but in some cases the cropped area has extended or been reduced considerably. The following table is therefore given to show the normal acreage of each crop and its percentage on the normal net cropped area:—

NAME OF CROP.	Normal acreage.	Percentage on normal net cropped area.	NAME OF CROP.	Normal acreage.	Percentage on normal net cropped area.
Winter rice	615,500	39	Wheat	108,000	7
Sugarcane	12,800	1	Barley	217,000	14
			Gram	35,000	2
Total *aghani* crops ...	628,300	40	Other *rabi* cereals and pulses.	235,000	15
Autumn rice	276,000	17	Other *rabi* food-crops	38,000	2
Jowār	7,000	..	Linseed	72,000	5
Bājra	4,500	...	Rape and mustard ...	23,000	1
Maruā	20,000	1	Other oil-seeds ...	1,200	...
Indian corn	160,000	10	Tobacco	2,400	...
Other *bhadoi* cereals and pulses.	152,000	10	Opium	41,400	3
			Late cotton	2,000	...
Other *bhadoi* food-crops.	1,100	...	Other *rabi* non-food crops.	19,200	1
Indigo	38,600	2			
Til (*bhadoi*)	6,500	...	Total *rabi* crops ...	794,200	50
Other *bhadoi* non-food crops.	3,600	...			
Total *bhadoi* crops ...	669,300	42	Orchard and garden produce.	56,000	4

According to the statistics for 1905-06, the total acreage of the crops was 2,985 square miles, of which 2,484 square miles were cropped with cereals and pulses, while 146 square miles were under oil-seeds and 86 square miles under indigo. Altogether, 843 square miles were twice cropped, and the net area cropped was thus 2,142 square miles. The area not available for cultivation was returned as 596 square miles or 16·9 per cent. of the district area, while the area of waste available for cultivation (excluding current fallows, which extended over 197 square miles) was no less than 596 square miles or 16·9 per cent. of the entire area of the district.

EXTENSION OF CULTIVATION.

A large portion of the district has been brought under cultivation within comparatively recent times. In the time of Akbar not even one-twentieth of the district came under assessment, the area assessed by Todar Mal in 1582 being only 155 square miles, a fact which clearly indicates that large wastes were still unreclaimed. Within the next two centuries there was great progress, and by 1790 the assessed area had grown to 1,041 square miles. Large areas still awaited the plough, however, and in 1794 the Collector reported "*Sarkār* Champāran is not above one-fourth cultivated. This *Sarkār* has very extensive forests. It abounds with *sāl, sisū, tūn*; and I believe it would be utterly impossible to proceed to clear away with any effect to promote advantage or improvement." The era of development now set in, for the Collector, only 7 years later, reported that "where 60 *bīghas* in 100 were in cultivation formerly, 80 or more are now in that state;" and fifty years later Mr. Wyatt, the Revenue Surveyor, observed that whereas the *pargana* of Majhawā (which covers the greater portion of the district) was chiefly waste at the time of the perpetual settlement, and the northern parts were covered with forest, "they are now inhabited and under beautiful cultivation."

From the time of the permanent settlement up to the revenue survey of 1845, the progress of agricultural development was undoubtedly very rapid, but since that time it has proceeded at a much slower rate. In 1874 it was estimated that 67 per cent. of the district was cultivated and 33 per cent. was uncultivated, whereas the present proportions are 70 and 30 per cent. respectively. The increase of cultivation through the last 30 years has not apparently been very marked, but taking the whole period of British rule, the extent of cultivation has certainly doubled and perhaps trebled itself. There are still, however, 600 square miles available for cultivation, and Champāran is the only district in Bihār which has such a large area of culturable waste. In the Bettiah subdivision nearly 38 per cent. of the area is still uncultivated, mainly in the Bagahā and Shikārpur thānas, but the reclamation of this tract is proceeding rapidly, in spite of the prevalence of malaria, which saps the energy of the cultivators. Regarding the possibility of further advance, Mr. Stevenson-Moore remarks: "Allowing for the relative unfertility of the cultivable area, I should say there is still room for the district to augment its population by 12 per cent., or, say, 2 lakhs of souls, without causing the least inconvenience to its present inhabitants, but to attract the surplus population to North Champāran, the northern part of which is liable to famine owing to a precarious rainfall and is still very unhealthy, requires special measures on the part of the administration, measures which, I believe, are on a fair road to fulfilment. The Tribenī canal, if constructed, will place a very large area in the northern tract in a position secure from calamities of season. The country requires opening out, and the contemplated railways from Bettiah to Bagahā, and from Bairagniā to the same place *viâ* Rāmnagar, if constructed, are sure to give agricultural development a most marked impetus. Finally the Bettiah and Rāmnagar estates should adopt liberal rules for the settlement of waste." To this it may be added that these hopes promise to be fulfilled as the Tribenī canal and the line from Bagahā are now under construction.

Improved methods of cultivation. Cultivation is still extremely backward, partly because the vitality of the cultivators is undermined by malaria, and also because rents are comparatively low and there is ample waste land available for cultivation. There is no pressure on the soil, the cultivators are too indifferent and apathetic to learn new methods, and they see no necessity for doing so, because they can in normal years raise more than sufficient for their needs with but little exertion.

FRUITS AND VEGETABLES. The most distinctive fruit of Champāran is the mango. Mango groves occupy an area of no less than 50,000 acres, and are especially numerous in the Bettiah thāna ; here the Mahārājās of Bettiah have always evinced a keen interest in planting mango trees, which, according to the Hindu creed, is an act of religious merit ; and their example has been followed by their servants and tenantry. Among other fruits may be mentioned the *līchī* (Nephelium Litchi), plantain, peach, lime, *papaya*, guava, custard-apple, jack-fruit and *bel*. Among vegetables, potatoes, yams (*aluā*) and *suthni* are prominent, especially in the south along the banks of the Sikrāna river. A large number of other vegetables are raised in garden plots for house-hold use and for sale, such as the egg plant or *baigun* (Solanum melongena), ground-nut, pumpkins, gourds, radishes, melons, onions and carrots. The favourite condiment is the chilli, which is cultivated extensively.

CATTLE. There is abundant pasture in Bagahā and Shikārpur, which attracts great herds of cattle from the southern thānas and also from the adjoining districts of Sāran, Muzaffarpur, and to a great extent, Gorakhpur. Cattle are consequently numerous, and every family in the district owns three head of cattle on the average. Milch kine are particularly numerous in the north, and even in the headquarters subdivision there are 12 milch kine for every 100 persons, *i.e.*, more than one to supply milk and *ghī* to 10 persons. Draught cattle are also numerous owing to the deficiency of railway communications, the large demand for carts by the indigo factories, and the trade to and from Nepāl, which is carried on by bullock carts. Buffaloes are less common than in the districts south of the Ganges, and the soil being generally light, they are not required to draw the plough. Sheep are more numerous in the north, but goats are fairly distributed over the whole of the district. Donkeys are kept by *dhobis*, and pigs are to be seen in many villages. Veterinary relief is afforded at a veterinary dispensary at Motīhāri; and large cattle fairs are held annually at Madhuban and Bettiah.

CHAPTER VI.

NATURAL CALAMITIES.

LIABILITY TO FAMINE.

DURING the 40 years which have elapsed since Champāran was constituted a district, it has thrice been visited by famine, in 1866, in 1874 and in 1897, and once by scarcity, in 1889. It is, in fact, a district particularly liable to the visitations of famine owing to its dependence on the rice crop and the absence of irrigation. The normal acreage of the rice crop is no less than 891,500 acres or 56 per cent. of the normal net cropped area, winter rice occupying 615,500 acres or 39 per cent.; and according to the statistics obtained at the last settlement only 2 per cent. of the cultivated area receives irrigation. The dependence of the rice crop on the vicissitudes of the season and the gravity of its failure will thus be readily understood. A generally deficient monsoon is more disastrous to rice than any other crop; for the prospects of the early rice are seriously prejudiced by a scanty rainfall at its beginning, while a premature termination is fatal to the winter crop. If there is a total failure of both these crops, the people have nothing to subsist on until the harvesting of the *rabi* crops in the latter part of March, except maize and inferior millet crops, such as *kodo* and *sāwān*. The latter, again, are grown on a comparatively small area; and in such a year the *rabi* crops also are usually deficient both in yield and area, owing to want of moisture at the time of sowing.

The result is that, if the rice crop fails, distress inevitably ensues, and its intensity is aggravated by the general want of resource and condition among the people. For the Champāran ryots, inhabiting a district in which copious rain is in normal years a certainty, where land is comparatively plentiful and rents are low, have not acquired the resource, energy and adaptibility which are the attributes of their fellows in Sāran, and in parts of Muzaffarpur and Darbhangā; while the humidity of the climate and the greater prevalence of malaria have lowered their physique and reduced their general condition to an extent which is very marked in many parts of the district.

The following is an account of the famines which have occurred since Champāran was made a separate district.

FAMINE OF 1866.

In 1865 the rainfall was deficient and stopped early, none falling in October, with the result that the winter rice was almost a total failure. The previous autumn crops had been fair, but had been largely exported owing to the prevalence of high prices in neighbouring districts; and consequently, when the rice crop was lost, distress became general. As early as October 1865, the commonest kind of rice could not be procured at less than 9 seers a rupee—three times the rate at which it was sold at the beginning of the same year,—and the price of all other food-grains had risen in a similar proportion. The *rabi* crops were also poor owing to want of moisture, and *chīna*, a grain which is largely grown in the early summer, withered completely.

No relief measures were undertaken till June, when road-works were started and relief-centres established at Motīhāri and Bettiah for the distribution of gratuitous relief in the shape of one daily meal of soaked grain. No system seems, however, to have regulated the distribution of food, the quantity which each applicant obtained depending on the numbers present; thus, at Motīhāri the sum allotted for relief was so small, that each applicant out of 1,500 received only four chittacks, or half a pound of food per diem. To add to the general distress, the main embankment on the Gandak gave way in August, and the flood-water, passing over the district till it joined the Little Gandak, swept away the crops over a large area. The maize harvest, however, was good; prices fell in September, and all relief-centres were closed by the 1st October. In the meantime, the mortality from actual starvation and disease accelerated by want of food was very great; the total number of deaths reported being no less than 56,000, or 6 per cent. on an estimated population of 850,000. The appalling mortality that accompanied this famine is still fresh in the memory of the older inhabitants.

FAMINE OF 1874.

In Champāran, as in other Bihār districts, the year 1871 was marked by excessive rainfall, the excess varying from 12 inches in the Bettiah to 18·50 inches in the headquarters subdivision. This surplus rain fell chiefly in September and was followed by inundations, which caused great damage to the bulk of the autumn crops. The alluvial deposits brought down by the floods seem, however, to have benefited both the rice and the spring crops, and the outturn of these harvests was satisfactory. The year 1872 was on the whole favourable from an agricultural point of view, and were it not that in March 1873 violent hailstorms in the north of the district caused serious injury to the spring crops in isolated tracts of country, the harvests would have been decidedly good. As things happened, it may be said that the year preceding the year of failure was a fairly prosperous year,—neither above the average nor below it—and during the latter part of 1872 and in the early part of 1873 the grain market recovered in a great measure its normal tone.

The rains of 1873 were deficient all over the district, the deficiency being much more marked in the Bettiah subdivision than in Motīhāri. During June, July and August, *i.e.*, the months in which the autumn crop is sown and matures, the rainfall in the headquarters subdivision was somewhat in excess, while in the Bettiah subdivision it fell short of the normal quantity. The *bhadoi* crops suffered much from this capriciousness in the rainfall, and in particular maize, which is more largely grown than any other *bhadoi* crop except autumn rice, not more than five-eighths of an average crop being harvested. In September the rain practically ceased, only a third of an inch falling in the whole month, and this entailed the almost complete destruction of the winter rice crop. By the middle of January rice was quoted in Bagahā at 9 seers a rupee, and as the shopkeepers refused to sell even at that price, sales of Government rice were authorized.

Rain fell in the beginning of the next month and immensely improved the prospects of the spring crops. In the meantime, arrangements had been made for opening relief-works, and for importing over 1,000,000 maunds of grain. Incendiarism, robberies, and other crimes prevalent in times of scarcity were becoming rife along the northern borders. In February Government relief was fairly established; relief-works, in the shape of tank-digging and road-making, were opened, and the extension of the Gandak embankment was taken in hand. Early in June, the rivers rose in the north of the district and flooded about 200 square miles, destroying all the Indian corn in the thānas of Motīhāri and Dhāka. The autumn crops, however, were fair, the outturn in the north-west and the centre of the district being exceptionally large, while in the east the yield was equal to the average. In the beginning of September, favourable accounts were received from all parts of the district except the east of Gobindganj, where half of the late rice was said to have been totally lost. Before the end of that month, however, from 12 to 15 inches of rain had fallen, ensuring the winter harvest and spring sowings everywhere ; and relief operations were closed at the end of September.

In the relief of famine in 1874 Government distributed 1,190 tons of rice in charitable relief, sold 11,081 tons for cash, paid away 7,294 tons as wages on relief works, and advanced 8,012 tons on recoverable loans. It also distributed Rs. 36,950 in charity, paid Rs. 6,43,808 as wages on relief works, and advanced Rs. 3,00,430 in loans. During January 11,631 persons were daily employed on relief works; in February, 25,361; in March, 52,758; in April, 83,917; in May, 159,668; in June, 79,752; in July, 73,007; in August, 8,938, and in September, 1,849.

SCARCITY OF 1889. Owing to the deficiency of the rainfall in 1888 and the consequent injury to the winter rice crop, there was scarcity in 1889 in the north of the district, in a tract of country forming the Dhāka thāna and parts of the Motihāri thāna and Madhuban outpost. Relief operations were commenced in December, and distress became acute in March, owing to the partial loss of the *rabi* harvest. Relief works were closed at the end of June owing to the fall of abundant rain, which ensured full employment for the people on agricultural labour. The unusually heavy rain which fell in the latter part of July caused floods, and thus added to the sufferings of the poorer classes, about 2,000 of whom were in receipt of gratuitous relief during the months from July to September. The average daily attendance on relief works was greatest in May, when it aggregated 11,000.

FAMINE OF 1897. The greatest famine of the century occurred 8 years later and was caused by deficient and unfavourably distributed rainfall in 1895 and 1896, the effects of which were intensified by extraordinarily high prices consequent on famine prevailing over a great part of India. Although the rainfall of 1895-96 was above the normal it was badly distributed. It was, on the whole, favourable for the crops until August, but it ceased prematurely, none falling after the 21st September, not even in the *Hathiyā* asterism, when good rain is considered essential for the *aghani* rice crop and for providing moisture for the *rabi* and indigo crops. There was, moreover, practically no rain at all throughout the cold weather, the total fall from October to March inclusive amounting to only half an inch.

This was unfortunately followed by much more unfavourable conditions during 1896-97. In May 1896 the showers which facilitate the early sowings of the *bhadoi* crops were much scantier than usual, and the monsoon rains began late, not breaking till the 25th June, and then only feebly, the fall for June being less than half the average. The rainfall was capriciously distributed to different localities and remained in persistent defect throughout the rainy season, being 75 per cent. below the normal in September; while not a drop fell after the 18th of that month until Christmas, with the exception of a shower on the 23rd

November. There was a prolonged break of four weeks' duration from the 21st July to the 17th August, which did the greatest possible damage to the *aghani* rice and the *bhadoi* crops, and after the 1st September there was practically no rain at all that could be of any material benefit to the *aghani* rice crop. The total defect from May to October inclusive was 19·2 inches, or 40 per cent. Throughout the cold weather of 1896-97 occasional light showers fell, but in February there was a defect of 66 per cent.

The result was a very inferior *bhadoi* crop and an almost total failure of the winter rice, the outturn being only 8 and 3½ annas respectively. These two crops account for nearly three-fourths of the harvests of the district; and as the outturn of the *rabi* was only 12 annas, the distress in Champāran was more general and widespread than in any other district of the Division except Darbhangā. Moreover, Champāran shared in the general rise of prices, and felt it the more acutely because in ordinary years it produces more than it needs, and exports its produce largely to Sāran and elsewhere; consequently its dealers, and its population generally, had to submit to a complete change of normal conditions, from easy prices to famine rates, and from large exportations to the importation of food for actual subsistence.

In these circumstances, during the months of greatest distress the whole district was severely affected, except four tracts, all of which owed their comparative prosperity to irrigation, viz., (1) thāna Adāpur on the northern boundary of the district where the streams issuing from the hills were dammed, (2) a tract round Sāthi factory in Bettiah, which was irrigated from a channel from one of these streams, (3) a tract round Bettiah watered from the Sikrāna, and (4) a smaller patch in Dhāka thāna protected by the Tiar canal. Two main areas in the district were always worse than the remainder. and in one of them works remained open when they had been closed in all other parts of the Division. The first was a tract corresponding roughly to the Dhāka thāna, where the failure of the rains was more complete than elsewhere, and where rice is the principal crop. The second was a large tract to the north-west of Bettiah, of which Rāmnagar was the centre, and which included the thānas of Bagahā and Shikārpur. Here many causes combined to render distress severe and the relief of it difficult; the climate is unhealthy, the population scanty, the soil poor; the cultivators are inert, ignorant and unthrifty; there is little *bhadoi* and less *rabi*, and the prosperity of the whole tract depends on its rice crop, which in 1896 was an almost total failure. When a plentiful *bhadoi* crop restored prosperity to the rest of Champāran in August 1897, the Rāmnagar tract remained unrelieved, first, because it has little or no *bhadoi*, secondly, because up to a very late date the rainfall there was much in deficit, and, thirdly, because from its climate and its northerly position the crops in this area are always from a fortnight to three weeks later than they are in the south of the district.

The following account of the course of the famine is quoted, with some slight abbreviation, from the final report of the Collector, Mr. D. J. Macpherson, C.I.E.:—

"Although the whole of the Champāran district was at one time affected by famine, the duration and degree of distress varied considerably in different parts of it. The failure of the crops was not very serious in the portion of the district comprising the Dhanahā outpost lying to the west of the Gandak river, nor in the vicinity of that river in most of its course where, it forms the boundary of the district; nor along the north of the eastern half of the district marching with Nepāl, where much was done to save the rice crop and provide moisture for sowing the spring crops by damming the small streams that come down from that country. Serious distress was likewise staved off by similar means in the broken jungle tracts skirting the foot of the hills in the north of Bettiah subdivision: these are inhabited by a race of aborigines of Mongolian type, called Thārus, who are good husbandmen. In a limited area in the north-eastern portion of Dhāka thāna, also, a considerable area of winter rice was saved, and of spring crops sown, with the aid of water taken from the Lāl Bakyā river, across which a temporary dam was thrown by the exertions of the people interested.

"Generally speaking, in those portions of the district in which a fair *bhadoi* harvest was gathered or irrigation was available, the distress was never acute. But even throughout the more favoured areas all classes of the population, except the more substantial cultivators, who managed to raise sufficient food for their own consumption, suffered, in common with the rest of the district, from the high level which prices reached unprecedentedly early in the season and maintained with extraordinary persistency almost throughout the whole 12 months. And in the tracts which were saved for the most part by irrigation, there were always certain villages and cultivators' holdings which this benefit failed to reach. Every portion of the district had thus to be embraced in the organization for relief.

"The most severely affected area was the Rāmnagar tract in Hardi (now Shikārpur) thāna in the north of the Bettiah subdivision, where both the early and late rice, practically the only crop it yields, failed completely. Here relief measures began earlier and ended later than anywhere else, lasting altogether for 11 months from the 8th of November 1896 to the 8th of October 1897. The tract first affected there covered an area of about 445 square miles with a population of 163,000. Almost simultaneously two other rice areas began to suffer severely, one in the south of Gobindganj and the other in the south of Dhāka thāna. By the middle of December, as the *bhadoi* grain began to get exhausted, the distress had extended to considerable tracts which were not largely rice-producing; and by the close of that month not only was the greater part of Bagahā and Hardi (now Shikārpur) thānas affected, but also a large tract extending from Bettiah down the southern part of the district in Bettiah and Gobindganj thānas and the northern part of Kesariyā; while a great part of the eastern portion of the district was also suffering severely. During January and February the famine-stricken area widened somewhat in the neighbourhood of these tracts, and by the middle of March it extended over 1,865 square miles of country with a population of about 1,134,000. At the same time, there was much distress occasioned by the general pressure of very high prices and hard times in an area of about 728 square miles, with a population of about 420,000, classed as 'slightly affected.'

"The middle of March marked the end of the first stage of the famine, the period during which the necessity for relief gradually expanded, in the absence of employment for the people, until the commencement of the spring harvest. After that, the cultivators who had *rabi* crops began to be able for a time to fall back again on their own resources, and the attendance at relief works decreased until the middle of April. This period of about six weeks may be regarded as forming the second stage of the famine.

"During May the severity of the distress again deepened, and the area severely affected extended. By the latter part of that month the whole of the district had become affected, as one stratum of the population after another came to the end of their resources; and the severely affected area extended to 2,100 square miles with a population of 1,275,000, and that slightly affected to 967 square miles with a population of 584,465. This, the third stage of the famine, ended about the middle of June, when the monsoon rain reached the district, as it did on the 16th.

"The fourth stage of the famine was contemporaneous with the rainy season, and was characterized by a gradual mitigation of distress, as employment became generally available and money-lenders began to open their purse-strings, when a new crop was seen to be coming up well. The *chīna* millet, which was gathered in June, was also a help. During this period, however, there was on several occasions grave cause for the most gloomy forebodings owing to scanty rainfall and untimely and prolonged breaks, especially in the part of the district which had all along been suffering most acutely. The classes who were being relieved gratuitously continued to suffer as greatly as ever for a good while after those who could work were able to shift for themselves, as private charity could not be relied on to come to their rescue until the *bhadoi* harvest was assured, while prices were higher than ever until after the middle of August. About the beginning of September, when a decided fall in prices came about, an area of 1,400 square miles with an estimated population of one million was removed from the category of severe to that of slight distress, but the total 'affected' area remained the same as before. At this time 700 square miles with a population of 275,000 was still classed as severely affected, and 2,367 square miles, with a population of 1,584,000, as slightly affected. By the 25th of September all relief in the latter area was closed, but some works remained open until the 8th of October in the former tract, *i.e.*, the Rāmnagar part of the district, which had been the first to suffer nearly a year before."

As regards the number of those relieved, the whole population of the district was affected by the middle of May, relief in some form or other having to be given, and this continued to be the case until the *bhadoi* harvest began to come in in the middle of September. Taking this, then, as the population affected, and 10 months as the period of famine, the daily average of 59,336 relieved on works, and of 44,960 relieved gratuitously, represents a percentage of 3·19 and 2·42, respectively, on the population affected. The time when the numbers in receipt of Government relief of all kinds was largest of all was in the second week of June, when it reached a daily average of 219,005 persons, or 11·77 per cent. of the affected population, of whom 123,007, or 6·61 per cent. were relieved on works, and 95,998, or 5·16 per cent. gratuitously. The number relieved on works, reckoned in terms of one day, was a little over 18 millions as compared with 15 millions in 1874, and the aggregate number receiving gratuitous relief was over 31 millions. The total expenditure by Government amounted to nearly 25 lakhs, of which one-half was spent in wages and a quarter in gratuitous relief, while 3 lakhs were advanced as loans. Owing to the extent and adequacy of the relief measures, no deaths occurred from starvation.

PROTECTIVE MEASURES.

The two most important protective measures are the construction of the Tribenī Canal and the extension of the railway through the north of the district by a line between Bagahā and Bairagniā. Both works are now in progress, and their completion will, it is expected, revolutionize conditions in the north of the district, the former by providing the cultivators with an unfailing supply of water, and the latter by developing trade and enabling supplies to be imported quickly and cheaply when required. This tract has indeed already been tapped by the extension of the railway to Bhikhnā Thorī since the famine of 1897, when the railway ended at Bettiah and fears were entertained that the supply of grain to the Rāmnagar tract might break down. The addition of another railway traversing it from east to west should render such a possibility a remote contingency.

Among minor protective measures may be mentioned the construction of the Dhāka Canal, which has recently been opened. A number of other projects have also been proposed, mainly in the direction of utilizing the water of the streams that issue from the lower Nepāl hills. Some of these schemes are open to the objection that the Nepalese have it in their power to dam up the channels and use the water for their own purpose; and this being the case, it is only the larger streams, which they cannot stop entirely, that are worth examining for irrigation purposes. Of these there are three in Champāran, viz., the Tilāri, Pūsa and Bakyā rivers, and projects for the utilization of their water have been put forward. Regarding the possibility of carrying out these schemes, the Indian Irrigation Commission (1901-03) remarked as follows :—"These streams were said to have a minimum discharge in October of 200, 150 and 200 cusecs respectively. But gauge observations, taken in 1901 and 1902, show that throughout September in the first of these years the discharges were so low as to be practically valueless, and that they were little better in the following year. Here, as on the Son Canals, the crucial time for irrigation is the *Hathiyā* in October; and if a certain supply cannot be guaranteed at this period, it is no use proceeding with these projects. Mr. Bernard, the Collector, bears testimony to the value that these irrigation schemes would be to the district; to the urgent need of artificial irrigation owing to the irregularity of the rainfall in October; and to the eagerness of the ryots to obtain water. But in view of the liability of the supply to fail utterly when it is most wanted, we cannot regard these projects as sound. It is, however, possible that relief labour might be usefully employed in excavating channels or *pains* taking off from these rivers."

LIABILITY TO FLOODS. The configuration of Champāran, a sub-Himālayan tract traversed by numerous streams, renders it peculiarly liable to inundation. On the west it is bounded by the Great Gandak, a snow-fed river, and next to the east is the Sikrāna, which, rising in the Sumeswar range, runs south-east through the centre of the district, receiving on its left bank numerous streams and torrents from the same line of hills. Next, further east, the Bāghmati, rising near Kātmāndu pierces the hills, and after being joined by many tributaries in the Tarai, forms the boundary between Champāran and Muzaffapur. It will thus be understood that sudden heavy rain over the northern portion of Champāran, the Nepāl Tarai and the range of hills to the north of it, some 150 miles in length, may easily cause these narrow drainage channels to overflow their banks.

No portion of the district can claim absolute immunity from floods. The north is liable to inundation from the inability of the hill torrents to carry off the drainage; and in the south the beds of the rivers, raised by the silt they bring down, are elevated above the level of the surrounding country, and the water thus spreads out far and wide when they come down in flood. Extensive tracts in the centre and east of the district are specially liable to be flooded by the overflow of the Sikrāna, Lāl Bakyā and Bāghmati rivers and their tributaries; and though flooding from the Gandak is prevented by an embankment along the greater part of its course, the protection it affords is not complete.

Such floods result in much damage to the *bhadoi* crops and often to the rice crops, and cause a good deal of temporary suffering. But the distress they cause soon passes away; the dwellings which are swept away are quickly replaced, as the cost of erecting mud-walled huts is small; and the cultivators are compensated, in large measure, for the losses they sustain by the fertilizing silt left by the receding waters, which increases the productiveness of the soil and ensures rich *rabi* crops. The following account of the most serious floods which have occurred in the last 10 years will show how short-lived are their injurious effects.

FLOOD OF 1898. The highest flood on record in Champāran was that which occurred in September 1898, when over 20 inches of rain fell at Motihāri, from the 4th to the 10th. The tract most seriously affected extended over 350 square miles, or about one-tenth of the district, lying chiefly in a strip about 4 miles broad on either bank of the Sikrāna between Sugauli and Mehsī; but the inundations were also of considerable extent in the south, where the floods of the Bāghmati met those of the Sikrāna. The loss of life was very slight, only 16 persons being drowned, but about 220 cattle and over 1,000 sheep and goats were swept away, and not less than one-third of the houses in the badly affected area collapsed. The circuit-house at Motīhāri fell, and the police stations at Sugauli, Madhuban, Chauradāno and Raxaul were destroyed. The Bengal and North-Western Railway was topped for miles and badly breached, with the result that traffic was at a standstill for over a month; while the Sugauli-Raxaul line was most severely damaged, the bank being completely washed away in many places. Both these lines run across a strong line of drainage; and the waterway being insufficient, the flood was given an accumulated volume and velocity, which greatly increased its power for destruction.

Most of the *bhadoi* crops in the affected area were destroyed, the loss being estimated at about two-thirds of the outturn. On the other hand, the winter rice was not damaged to any considerable extent, and in fact was benefited by the heavy rain except in the tract close to the Sikrāna. The cultivators were also compensated by the rich deposit of silt, in some places 3 inches thick, which was left on the land submerged by the flood; and no sooner did the water recede than they began to prepare their fields for the cold weather crops. The labouring classes were not in any distress, as there was employment for all willing to work, houses being rebuilt, lands prepared for the *rabi* crops, and roads repaired on all sides. Agricultural loans were granted on a large scale, but no other relief measures were necessary.

FLOOD OF 1906.

The last serious flood occurred in August 1906, owing to the overflow of the Sikrāna river and its tributaries, and also, in a less degree, to the temporary rise of the Great Gandak, by which some damage was caused in the Bettiah and Gobindganj thānas. The whole of the Motīhāri and Madhuban thānas, a portion of the Dhāka thāna, and small tracts in the east of the Kesariyā thāna, the north of the Gobindganj thāna, and the east of the Bettiah thāna were affected, the worst damage being in the area between Sirahā and Mehsī in the Madhuban thāna. The area affected was roughly 400 square miles, and here the maize crop was almost entirely swept away, while the *bhadoi* and *aghani* rice crops were seriously damaged. Considerable distress was caused by the flood, and it was found necessary to open kitchens for granting gratuitous relief and to advance a large sum in loans. Test works were opened, but failed to attract labour and soon after the floods evidence of the marvellous recuperative power of the people was forthcoming, for scarcely had the flood subsided when they began to sow and transplant the paddy seedlings.

EMBANKMENTS. Government maintains an embankment along the left bank of the Great Gandak, which protects an area of 2,677 square miles. This embankment, which is 62 miles long (including 20 miles of retired lines), extends from near Bagahā to the southern extremity of the district, but there are 4 breaks in it. It is kept up under a contract with the proprietors of the estates protected from inundation. The first contract was made in 1883, and on its expiry in 1903 it was renewed for another term of 20 years, the sum of Rs. 20,000 per annum being fixed for the maintenance of the embankment.

CHAPTER VII.

RENTS, WAGES AND PRICES.

CASH RENTS.

RENTS are, on the whole, low in Champāran, the average rate per cultivated acre being only Re. 1-13-9, as compared with Rs. 3-13-5 in Muzaffarpur. This low incidence of rents is due to the fact that the population is sparse, that the area of waste land available for cultivation is large, and that the greater part of the district is held by the Bettiah Rāj and a few other large proprietors, and not by petty landlords. There is, in fact, more competition among landlords for tenants than among tenants for holdings, and the landlords have consequently refrained from resorting to the oppressive methods of enhancing rents common among petty proprietors elsewhere. There are no recognized rent-rates for different classes of soil, a lump rental being fixed for the entire holding. Cultivators belonging to the higher castes such as Brāhmans, Bābhans, Rājputs and Kāyasths generally hold their lands at privileged rates. The almost invariable reason for this is that they have been able to resist the landlord's efforts to enhance their rent, while the Kurmi or Koeri have consented to enhancements; they have similarly refused to give their landlords what is known as *bethbegāri*, *i.e.*, a plough to till his fields for 3 days in the year and labour for about 3 to 7 days.

Rents are much higher in the headquarters than in the Bettiah subdivision, the rate of rent per acre for occupancy ryots, who hold no less than 83 of the caltivated area, being Rs. 2-0-6 in the former and Re. 1-10-2 in the latter subdivision. There is also a marked difference in the rentals paid in different parts of the headquarters subdivision, the rent to the west of the Sikrāna river, where the prevailing soil is light and sandy, being less than in the tracts to the east of that river, where there is a thick clay soil, producing rich rice crops. Occupancy ryots pay the highest rent rate (Rs. 2-11-3 per acre) in the Madhuban thāna, which is the most densely populated tract in the district and also contains a number of petty proprietors; they pay the lowest rent rate (Re. 1-9-2 per acre) in the Bagahā thāna, where the density of population is least.

The following table gives the average rent-rates per cultivated acre for each class of ryot as ascertained at the last settlement:—

CLASS OF RYOTS.	Area in acres.	Total rental.	Rate per acre.
		Rs.	Rs. A. P.
Ryots at fixed rates ...	26,803	30,632	1 2 3
Settled and occupancy ryots	1,255,967	23,63,256	1 14 1
Non-occupancy ryots ...	38,624	69,538	1 12 10
Total ...	1,321,394	24,63,426	1 13 9

It is noticeable that 24 out of 25 lakhs of the total rental is payable by settled and occupancy ryots, only a lakh being realised from ryots at fixed rates and non-occupancy ryots. Ryots at fixed rates pay at the lowest rate, viz., Re. 1-2-3 an acre, while settled and occupancy ryots pay an average of only Re. 1-14-1. This is the highest rent-rate, non-occupancy ryots paying Re. 1-12-10 per acre, or nearly 2 annas less. That this should be so is eloquent testimony of the general absence of a keen demand for land, those who are willing to reclaim being allowed settlement at privileged rates.

Enhancement of rents. "There is," says Mr. Stevenson-Moore, "one thing that a Champāran ryot, his general apathy and ignorance notwithstanding, will not submit to, and that is, an enhancement of his rent-rate. He willingly gives a large *salāmi* or an increased rent on excess area, but if his landlord tries to enhance his rent-rate, he will fight or abandon his holding and go elsewhere, and there being available land elsewhere, he is largely master of the situation." The rent-roll has mainly developed as the result of new assessment on extended cultivation, but in spite of the low rent-rates still prevailing, there has been some enhancement of rents, obtained mainly by means of *abwābs* or illegal cesses before the passing of the Bengal Tenancy Act. In 1790 the total rental of the district was Rs. 5,55,615; and in 1876, when the rental was again ascertained for the purpose of determining the road-cess, it was estimated at Rs. 26,20,942. This was further raised to Rs. 30,73,556 at the next revaluation in 1893, but, as shown above, the settlement records gave a total of Rs. 24,63,426, excluding the rent of land in the direct cultivation of landlords. The last revaluation, completed in 1906, gave a gross rental of Rs. 32,54,697.

PRODUCE RENTS. Produce rents are of little importance in this district, as they are paid for a very small proportion of the land under cultivation.

They are paid, it is true, for 22 per cent. of the area held by non-occupancy ryots and for 65 per cent. of that held by under-ryots; but the proportion of the cultivated area held by these two classes is very inconsiderable, and less than 4½ per cent. of the area held by settled and occupancy ryots, who absorb more than four-fifths of the land under cultivation, pays rent in kind. There appear to be several reasons for the rarity of produce rents. In the first place, most of the district is owned by big zamīndārs, and they are naturally averse to any system of produce rent, for it requires constant supervision and entails the employment of an expensive staff: in extensive properties the system is costly and never works satisfactorily. The second reason is the influence of indigo-planters, who hold a considerable area in the district, as they favour a stable and enlightened rent system. Lastly, there is a tendency for produce rents to be more prevalent where there are a number of petty proprietors and the population is dense; for where there is a keen competition for land, the cultivators are tempted to take up land on terms which they would decline in less congested areas and to pay produce rents for fields of which the crops are precarious. Champāran is a district of large proprietors and sparse population, and the system of payment of rents in kind is therefore not general.

Batāi system. There are several ways in which produce rents are paid. Under the *batāi* system the actual produce is divided between the landlord and tenant. The crop is either divided on the field, in which case the practice is known as *bojh-batāi*, because the landlord and tenant each get a fixed share of the sheaves (*bojhā*), or the division of the produce takes place on the threshing floor and is called *agor-batāi*, because the crop has to be carefully watched (*agornā*) to prevent pilfering.

There is a further variety characteristic of this district, called *batāi tekuli*, under which two-thirds of the crop is taken by the ryot and one-third by the landlord. This arrangement is usually resorted to where land has to be reclaimed, and sometimes when it is infertile and therefore unremunerative on other terms.

Batāi kankut system. Under the *batāi kankut* system the crop is appraised in the field before it is reaped, and the value of the landlord's share is paid by the tenant either in grain or cash; grain is usually given in payment of the current demand and cash in payment of arrears. This system, which is not so common as the *batāi*, is generally more advantageous to the landlord, both because there is no pilfering and because he can bring pressure to bear on the cultivator to secure a favourable appraisement.

Mankhap system. The *mankhap* system of rent payment is a peculiar system, under which the tenant binds himself to pay annually so many maunds of grain either on specified plots or a certain proportion of his holding. It differs from the ordinary system of payment of rent in kind, in that the demand does not adjust itself to good or bad seasons; and it is in this respect that it is so inequitable, as whether his crop is a bumper one or an utter failure, the tenant has to pay the amount agreed upon. It is thus rigid and oppressive, and naturally unpopular among the tenants. It is met with mainly in *zirāat* lands let to tenants for short periods.

Hundā system. The last system of produce rents is known as the *hundā* system, which is prevalent in a large estate, called the Bhopatpur estate or Mahāl Narkatiā in thāna Adāpur, which now forms part of the Bettiah Rāj. Here the practice is for almost every tenant to pay *hundā* rents for a portion of his holding, *i.e.*, he stipulates to pay a certain amount of paddy, usually 10 to 20 maunds per *bīgha*, to his landlord, on a specified portion of the holding. This system is also found in the Adāpur thāna, where it is employed by *mahājans* and traders of Motīhāri, who like to obtain land there, because its soil produces the kind of rice of which they are particularly fond.

Rents for trees. The rights owned by landlords and tenants in trees are of a somewhat complicated character, and almost peculiar to Champāran. They fall, generally speaking, into two broad divisions, *gayāri* and *anthrop*. The former, which belong solely to the landlord, include trees standing on the *mālik's* waste land, or on holdings surrendered to the landlord, or taken possession of by him on being abandoned by the ryot. The *anthrop* trees (literally trees whose *anthi*, or seed, was *rop*, *i.e.*, sown by the ryot) are those planted by a ryot in a holding for which he pays a cash rent. The landlord claims half the value of the timber when the tree is cut down, but the tenant gets the whole of the fruit; the latter is precluded from felling such trees without his landlord's consent. Fruit-producing *gayāri* trees are generally let out by the landlord on the *batāi*, usually the *batāi kankut* system, or for a certain stipulated money rent described as *sair* in the rent-roll. In re-settling abandoned holdings, the landlord invariably settles the trees separately on a *batāi* or cash rent and keeps them *gayāri*.

WAGES. The wages of skilled labour have risen considerably during the last 30 years. In 1870 masons received a daily wage of 2½ to 3½ annas, blacksmiths got only 2 annas a day and carpenters the same; whereas a mason now obtains 3½ to 4 annas a day according to his skill, a common blacksmith 3 annas and a skilled blacksmith 4 annas a day, while a common carpenter gets a daily wage of 4 annas, and a superior carpenter of 5 annas. The wages of unskilled labour have not risen very much. In the year 1874-75 the wages of unskilled labour, *i.e.*, for a common cooly and agricultural labourer, were 2 annas for a man, $1\frac{1}{2}$ annas for a woman and 1 anna for a boy. These rates have continued ever since, except that a boy now receives $1\frac{1}{4}$ anna a day. In addition to the above, it is customary to add a small quantity of parched barley or maize for the midday meal, which may be taken as equivalent in value to half an anna, so that the average wage of an adult male cooly may be taken as equal to $2\frac{1}{2}$ annas.

Field labourers are, however, mostly paid in kind, and in this light, the scale of wages has risen owing to the greater market value of the grain, the quantity given as wages having remained unaltered. Ploughmen receive $3\frac{1}{2}$ seers of grain per diem if they work till noon, and for a full day's work $3\frac{1}{2}$ seers, 7 *lohiā* pice, *i.e.*, about an anna, and an allowance of one seer for food. Labourers engaged in weeding get $3\frac{1}{2}$ seers of grain a day or 7 pice and an allowance of half a seer for food; for reaping they get one *bojhā* or bundle out of every 16 bundles reaped and harvested, and in threshing and husking one maund out of every 16 maunds threshed and husked. Then come the blacksmith and carpenter, and the watchman, if any, who are given 10 *dhurs* each per *bīgha* or one-twentieth in all, if paid in kind. Generally, however, the ryot does not have a watchman, but guards the crops himself or deputes a regular servant to do so. The barber and the washerman also come in for their share in the produce, the rate depending on the size of the cultivator's family; but generally washermen get the crop of 3 to 4 *dhurs* of land per male in each family for which they wash clothes, and the barber gets the same for each man requiring the razor. The blacksmith gets 10 to 12 *dhurs* for each plough possessed by a tenant (ploughshare). The ploughman often gets no wages in cash from either the landlord or the tenant, but in return uses the plough and bullocks for his own purposes every third day; the landlord, on the other hand, is generally entitled under village custom to use in rotation the plough of each tenant for one day in each of the 3 seasons—*bhadoi*, *aghani* and *rabi*, this practice being called *harai*, *har* meaning a plough. The Pāsī gets as payment the toddy from the palm or date trees on alternate days, and receives no wages in cash from the tenant.

This system is peculiarly suitable for an agricultural district like Champāran, as the wages of the village labourers remain unaffected by any rise in the price of food-grains in the markets.

Supply of labour.

The following account of the supply of labour in Champāran is quoted from Mr. Foley's Report on Labour in Bengal, 1906:—"There is practically no emigration to the industrial centres, and this is not to be looked for. Except the south-east corner, where the richest land is, the district is sparsely populated. It attracts immigrants from the surrounding districts; but considering how cheap the land is, it is surprising that it does not attract more. This is due chiefly to the fact that it is considered unhealthy, and for this reason it has been found extremely difficult to obtain a sufficiency of labour for the Tribenī Canal. The decline of indigo has not had much effect on the labour supply, as most of the indigo was cultivated *āsāmiwār*."

PRICES.

The wages of labour have not risen as greatly as the price of food. The mean price of staple food-grains, viz., common rice, wheat, barley and gram, rose from $23\frac{1}{5}$ seers during the 4 years 1870-73 to $17\frac{2}{5}$ seers during the five years 1891—95, *i.e.*, by 30·6 per cent. The upward movement has continued since that time, as will be apparent from the marginal table, which gives the average price (in seers and chittacks per rupee) of common rice, wheat, gram and salt, during the last fortnight in March for the 15 years ending in 1905. The average of prices during the quinquennium 1896—1900, it may be explained, was inflated by the famine of 1897, and the cheapening of salt in the last quinquennium is due to the reduction of the salt tax.

YEARS.	Common rice.	Wheat.	Gram.	Salt.
	S. Ch.	S. Ch.	S. Ch.	S. Ch.
1891—1895	15 5½	13 7	17 9½	10 4
1896—1900	13 8	12 4½	15 13	10 3
1901—1905	15 3	13 14	18 2	11 5

As regards the prices of food-grains in different periods of the year, prices are easy at the end of September, when the *bhadoi* crop is in the market. They then rise slightly and remain fairly steady until December, when the *aghani* rice crop is reaped. After that, they rise steadily till the middle of March, when the highest prices in the year are obtained. Relief then comes with the ingathering of the *rabi* harvest, and prices fall till the middle of May, after which they become unsteady until the lowest point is reached about the end of June after the rains have been established. Then a rise commences once more, which continues till the early *bhadoi* crops come in, towards the end of July.

These crops are so cheap and plentiful, that the general average then falls sharply till the end of September.

As might be expected, the harvesting of each of the three great crops ushers in a distinct fluctuation in prices. Grain is, on the whole, cheapest in September, just after the *bhadoi* is in; not quite so cheap early in May, when the *rabi* has all been gathered home; and less cheap at the end of November, when the rice reaches the market. Conversely, grain is dearest just before each of these three harvests is reaped, *i.e.*, in October, February and July. It might have been thought that as rice is the largest and most important crop in the district, its advent would have had the greatest effect on the prices of food; but it must be remembered that rice is never a very cheap grain owing to the demand for exportation. The same consideration holds good in a less and still lesser degree as regards *rabi* and *bhadoi*, for this latter crop (except maize) is but little exported; in other words, and speaking generally, the influence of each crop on the prices varies inversely with the demand for it for exportation.

The marginal table shows the prices obtained for food-grains during the last two famines (1873-74 and 1896-97). The course of prices during the last famine was very different from what it usually takes. In 1896 a sharp rise to $15\frac{1}{4}$ seers took place in the early part of August, owing to the serious break in the rains and to the reserve stocks having to be trenched upon after the poor harvests of the previous year. After August prices rose steadily for several months with a sharp bound in the latter part of November, when all hope of rain for the *rabi* sowings had passed. The rise continued until the beginning of March, when the mean price reached $9\frac{15}{16}$ seers per rupee. With the advent of the spring crops and increasing importations, Famine prices.

		1873-74.		1896-97.	
		S.	Ch.	S.	Ch.
Common rice	Lowest price ...	20	0	11	4
	Highest price...	8	8	7	11
	Average of year	12	9	8	14
Wheat ...	Lowest price ..	16	0	9	4
	Highest price...	10	0	7	12
	Average of year	12	0	8	11
Barley ...	Lowest price ...	33	0	14	0
	Highest price ...	13	0	9	8
	Average of year	18	10	12	2½
Maize ...	Lowest price ..	38	0	20	0
	Highest price...	13	0	8	0
	Average of year	18	6	11	2
Gram ...	Lowest price ...	26	0	12	0
	Highest price...	12	8	9	8
	Average of year	15	10	10	12

price began s to fall in the middle of March, reaching their lowest level at the end of that month and of April, when the mean price was $10\frac{7}{8}$ seers. After April there was a steady rise until after the middle of August, *i.e.*, until the *bhadoi* crops were assured, and for the last month of this period the mean price remained at $9\frac{3}{4}$ seers per rupee. This was the highest level reached during the famine except once, in the end of December, when the same level was attained. From the end of August prices began to fall, and at the end of September were at the same level as in the middle of October of the preceding year, viz., $12\frac{1}{16}$ seers.

MATERIAL CONDITION OF THE PEOPLE.

Thirty years ago the material condition of the people of Champāran was described as follows by Sir W. W. Hunter in his Statistical Account of Bengal:—" The people of Champāran, as a rule, are badly off. The whole agricultural population is in debt to the *mahājan*, or village money-lender, who has advanced money or grain on the security of the next crop. Though rents are low, and the produce of the land good, the cultivators are in constant difficulties, partly through this system of mortgaging their future crops, and partly from improvidence. Droughts and floods render matters still worse, so that Champāran, with one of the most fertile soils in Bihār, is probably the poorest district in the Province."

The lapse of 20 years did little to improve the state of affairs, for in 1897 we find the Collector, Mr. D. J. Macpherson, C.I.E., giving the following summary in his final famine report:—" The economic condition of the people, in spite of the very moderate rents they have usually to pay, is far below the standard of adjoining districts. The small attention devoted to irrigation, a most powerful stimulus to careful cultivation, has already been noticed. Freed as he usually is by a sufficiency of natural moisture from the necessity of irrigating, the Champāran peasant is the most inert and inefficient cultivator in the Province. In the submontane tract in the north of Bettiah his inefficiency is mainly due to another cause—the prevalence of malaria, which saps his energy. The sparseness of the population there, moreover, leads him to attempt to cultivate more land than he can attend to properly. The physique of the Champāran peasant generally is notoriously below that of other districts in Bihār, and an unsightly form of goitre is very prevalent. The number of cretins is remarkable. In the low rents which prevail another potent stimulus to efficient cultivation is wanting. But whatever the causes, the people are undoubtedly very thriftless, and their extravagance has led them greatly into debt and imperilled the possession of their lands."

The information obtained during the last settlement has gone far to confirm the correctness of this opinion, and Mr. Stevenson-Moore writes :—"Optimistic views of a high degree of prosperity in Champāran receive a most emphatic contradiction from the fact that, given a failure of the rice crop, Champāran is the first district to succumb to distress. In view of its acute susceptibility to famine, general statements of its internal prosperity are either valueless or misleading. Where a district with land plentiful and population sparse has one-third of its people compelled to eke out a living by labour, that district can lay no claim to a general prosperity. Where that district has in addition $2\frac{1}{2}$ per cent. of its ryoti land transferred by sale and 1 per cent. mortgaged, or a total of $3\frac{1}{2}$ per cent. thus alienated in 10 years, with 40 per cent. of the transferees belonging to the class of professional money-lenders, its claim to this condition becomes still further diminished."

To this it may be added that the course of events in the last famine of 1897 showed that there has been a certain improvement in the staying power of the peasantry; for even in the worst months, February to March, only about 10 per cent. of the population was in receipt of relief. Here, as elsewhere, the labouring classes are most exposed to distress, and as they constitute 30 per cent. of the population, it is obvious that true agriculturists can have been affected only to a very small degree. The area of liability to famine also tends to grow narrower, and the cause must be an all-round amelioration in the material condition of the people.

As regards the labourers, who have less resources than any other class, it is estimated that the maximum earnings obtainable by a hard-working family, including two adult males and two adult females as working members, amounts to Rs. 118-2 for nine working months in the year, a sum which considerably exceeds their cost of living, viz., Rs. 75 per family. In reality, however, the two women could not work for this period, and it is unlikely that even the men would get full employment for the whole nine months, so that the margin is very slender. There appears, however, to be little doubt that in normal years a labouring family can get enough to live on in comparative comfort; if it also has some cultivation, its condition is probably still better, though the earnings from hired labour are, of course, diminished.

As regards the cultivating classes, who form the bulk of the population, it is estimated that the area of a subsistence holding, *i.e.*, a holding sufficient to support an average family in fair comfort, is 3·7 acres, or allowing for the portion necessarily left uncultivated, 4 acres. This is the district average; but the area

H

of the subsistence holding may be taken at 5 acres in the Bettiah subdivision, where the *bhadoi* and *rabi* crops are inferior and some of the rice land is not very productive, and at 4 acres in the head-quarters subdivision, where crops are more varied and secure, and profitable markets are more accessible. It is, therefore, a matter for some satisfaction that the average area of occupancy holdings, which comprise practically the whole rent-paying area, is 6 acres in the former and 4 acres in the latter subdivision, and in the district as a whole 5 acres or one acre more than the area of the subsistence holding.

Indebtedness.

It has already been noticed that enquiry has shown that as much as 3½ per cent. of the area held by tenants was alienated within 10 years, and that no less than 40 per cent. of the transferees were money-lenders. The mortgages were found to be twice as numerous as the sales of holdings. The reason for this appears to be that the ryot who has mortgaged his holding, or part of it, can always cherish the hope of being able some day to redeem it; and the money-lender also, as a rule, prefers a mortgage with possession to a sale. In the first place, it keeps the ryot in his power. The money-lender does not want to ruin the ryot outright and drive him away from the village, but to keep him there as long as possible, and make as much out of him as he can. In the second place, the transferee, who acquires a holding by sale, usually has considerable trouble before he can get himself recognized by the landlord. He either has to pay a heavy bonus (*salāmi*), or, if the landlord is an indigo planter, he may be called on to execute an agreement to grow indigo on the best land of the holding for a considerable term of years. Perhaps the landlord will not allow a person whom he considers to be a professional money-lender to acquire any occupancy rights in his villages, and in that case the transferee has to bring a suit in the Civil Court for possession. The transferee by sale is thus entirely in the hands of the landlord, who can either refuse to recognize him altogether or can exact any terms he pleases from him as a condition of recognition. On the other hand, a transferee who gets a mortgage with possession has none of these difficulties to contend with. The rent is still nominally paid by the old tenant, and the landlord, in the majority of cases, knows nothing about the transaction. Even if he gets to hear of it, it is very difficult for him to do anything, as the ryot and the *mahājan*, acting in collusion, can easily outwit him. Meanwhile, the creditor retains his hold on the debtor, and can either cultivate the land himself, or, as is more usual, let it out to the former ryot at an exorbitant produce rent.

The following account of the methods of the money-lender is quoted from Mr Stevenson-Moore's Settlement Report :—"It is generally in Jeth, *i.e.*, May-June, that the cultivator has to borrow grain from the money-lender, and the contract usually is for repayment in Kuār (September-October), just after the *bhadoi* crop is harvested, with an interest amounting to 25 per cent. of the capital. Failing that, the interest is added to the capital, and 50 per cent. of the whole is charged as interest in the following Baisākh (April-May). The ryot can never get free, and must be sold up in the end, to begin life afresh in some other village. Allowing that the ryots, with their vitality often sapped by malarial fever, will not struggle to resist the consequences of a temporary calamity, allowing that the quality of land available tempts them to habits of improvidence, it is still a puzzle why the money-lender, in a district where free transferability of tenant right does not exist, has been allowed to get such a hold on the land. The district for the most part is parcelled out amongst big zamīndārs, each of whom would be ready to assert that he considers the absence of right to transfer holdings without his consent as one of his most valuable privileges, because it enables him to keep out the money-lender. In Muzaffarpur, where transfers are freely made without the landlord's consent, the money-lenders are few; in Champāran, where the landlord's consent is required in practice as well as in theory, the money-lenders flourish."

Generally speaking, the position which Champāran at present occupies in the scale of well-being is a low one. The ryots, who form the bulk of the population, are poor agriculturists; irrigation is but little practised; and the prosperity of the people generally is dependent on the condition of the crops, and consequently, in the long run, on so uncertain an element as the weather. This dependence on the vicissitudes of the seasons is not relieved by the existence of any large industries (except indigo manufacture), affording a diversity of occupation and bringing wealth into the district; and even the ubiquitous native trader conducts his operations with but little of his usual commercial activity. While elements of prosperity doubtless exist in the fertility of the soil, the sparseness of the population and the moderate rent-roll, we have, on the other hand, still more potent factors in the comparative unhealthiness of large tracts in the north of the district, the inferior standard of cultivation, the dependence of the population upon agriculture for subsistence, the deficiency of communications, and the consequent stagnation of trade. The increase of population, the extension of the railway system, the Summary.

development of irrigation projects, a gradual improvement in communications and the establishment of agricultural banks are all factors which may be looked to for an amelioration of the circumstances of the people in the future. Already some of these reforms have become accomplished facts, while others are in course of accomplishment, so that Champāran may now be regarded as in a transitional state.

CHAPTER VIII.

OCCUPATIONS, MANUFACTURES AND TRADE.

OCCUPATIONS.

ACCORDING to the statistics obtained at the census of 1901, no less than 80·2 per cent. of the population are dependent for their livelihood on agriculture. The proportion of agriculturists is higher than in any district in Bihār, except Sāran, and is much above the general average for Bengal; 52 per cent. of them are workers, and of these, 589,000 are returned as rent-payers, 4,000 as rent-receivers and 144,000 as field labourers, including 59,000 women. The predominance of the agricultural element is very marked, and the explanation seems to be that it is usual for every one, whatever his occupation, to invest any little money he can save in land. Altogether 6 per cent. are engaged in industrial avocations, 8 per cent. are classed as general labourers, while less than one per cent. are engaged in commerce. The remainder follow other occupations. Herdsmen and dealers in dairy-produce together number 18,000, while there are 6,000 cotton weavers and 4,000 mat and basket makers. Priests number 2,000, religious mendicants 3,000, and other beggars 6,000; and there are 6,000 general servants.

MANUFACTURES.

The proportion of persons dependent for their livelihood on industries is smaller than in any Bihār district, except Muzaffarpur. The district contains no important trade centres or manufacturing towns; and the bulk of the artisans are engaged in supplying the simple needs of a rural people. This economic backwardness is the result of the dependence of the majority of the people on agriculture. They live in villages dotted among their fields, and each village constitutes, to a large extent, a self-sufficing industrial unit. The villagers grow their own food, grind their own corn, and build their own houses. In spite of the introduction of manufactured piece-goods, their cloth is still woven to some extent by the village weaver, while the rough implements needed in agriculture are invariably made and repaired by the village smith and carpenter. There are, in fact, only three industries of any importance, viz., the manufacture of indigo, sugar and saltpetre.

Indigo manufacture.

The manufacture of indigo is the premier industry of Champāran. An account of it will be found in the next chapter.

Sugar manufacture.

The manufacture of sugar is said to have been introduced by immigrants from Azamgarh and Gorakhpur about 100 years ago, and in the first half of the 19th century was the most important industry in Champāran. Many of the European indigo concerns were originally started as sugar factories, a number worked by steam being scattered through several *parganas*. The manufacture of sugar was, however, given up when indigo proved more profitable, and for the last half century the industry has been entirely in native hands. The manufacture is principally carried on in the west and north-west of the Bettiah subdivision, where there are six refineries with 24 minor *golās*. The outturn has declined considerably in recent years, and has now fallen to 14,000 maunds.

With the decline of the indigo industry caused by the competition of synthetic dye, the manufacture of sugar by more scientific methods has been taken up. A few years ago manufacturing plant was set up at Sirahā, a branch factory of the India Development Company, the headquarters of which is at Ottur in the Muzaffarpur district. More recently the manufacture of sugar with modern machinery has been started by the Parsā Indigo Concern, which has its head factory at Parsā and two outworks at Harpur and Serukahiā. A sugar factory was erected in 1906 at Pakrī, 5 miles from Parsā, and the Company has closed its first season with an outturn of 1,100 tons of sugar besides a large quantity of molasses.* Large sugar works, with improved machinery, have also been set up recently at the Bārā factory.

Saltpetre manufacture.

The only other important industry is the manufacture of saltpetre from the saliferous earth found round village homesteads, where potassium of nitrate appears on the surface as a white efflorescence. The process of manufacture is simple, and the implements employed are primitive. Manufacture is carried on in small factories situated in the towns and villages scattered over the country. Nitrous soil is collected from the vicinity of the village houses and steeped in small earthen filters. The nitrous brine is next concentrated in iron or earthen vessels with the aid of artificial heat, and saltpetre is obtained by crystallization, as the temperature of the concentrated liquid falls. The saltpetre so obtained is impure in quality, as it contains earthy matter and foreign salts (such as chloride of sodium) in mechanical

* For a detailed account of the work carried on by this factory, *see* "Sugar manufacture in Bihar," an article published in the *Empress*, No. 1, May 1907.

admixture. This impure saltpetre is collected in refineries situated at different points among the village works, is purified in them to a fair degree of refraction, and is then sent to Calcutta, whence some of it is exported, while some is purified to a higher degree of refraction in the local refineries.

The manufacture, which is in the hands of a poor but hardy caste called Nuniās, is founded on a system of advances made to them by middlemen, who again contract with the larger houses of business in Calcutta. It is controlled by the Northern India Salt Department, which grants licenses for refining salt, for making crude saltpetre, and for the manufacture of the unrefined saltpetre called *khārī*. It is a declining industry, and the outturn has steadily decreased of late years. A series of bad seasons, combined with low prices in Calcutta, has had an injurious effect on the manufacture, and many refineries have been closed. The outturn of saltpetre has accordingly fallen gradually from 70,500 maunds in 1895-96 to 25,000 maunds in 1904-05, and that of the salt educed during the manufacture has fallen in the same period from 4,000 to 2,600 maunds.

Weaving. Weaving is still carried on in the villages on a small scale, but the fabrics turned out are only coarse cotton cloths, which the poorer classes prefer to the cheaper European piece-goods on account of their greater warmth and durability. The looms used are the old-fashioned country looms, and the weavers mostly use imported thread. Weaving of the coarse carpets known as *darīs* and *satranjīs* is also carried on to a fairly large extent, especially at Mehsī and Gobindganj, where the cotton cultivators do both the spinning and weaving. Machine-made yarn is, however, more generally used, and jail-made *darīs* are preferred to those made by the local weavers. Blankets are also made, but weaving generally is not a profitable occupation, and those weavers who are strong and fit for hard labour do not weave, but cultivate the soil or earn their living by other manual labour.

Gold washing. Gold is washed in minute quantities from the Gandak river and from the Pānchnad, Harhā, Bhabsā and other hill streams. The gold-washer stands in the water up to his knees, and heaps the earth in the bed of the stream on a rude sort of cradle, allowing the force of the current to wash away the sand, leaving a dark earthy deposit behind. In this the gold is found, either in small particles or in grains about the size of a pea. No statistics of the amount of gold thus obtained are available. Formerly, it is said, the Rājā of Rāmnagar collected several thousand rupees worth of gold every year, but the amount now obtained is believed to be insignificant.

Other industries. The gold-washers are generally aboriginal Thārus, who also make strong and durable mats out of *sābe* grass (Ischœmum angustifolium), which they gather from the lower ranges of the hills. Excellent twine and rope are made from the same material; and such twine is used for the manufacture of fishing nets, nooses, and snares, for drawing water from the well, for tethering cattle, and many other purposes. They are not less skilled in making funnel-shaped baskets in which fish are caught, and in thatching the roofs of their houses. The other industries are of little importance, and consist entirely of small hand industries, such as making pottery, brassware, mats and baskets.

TRADE. The trade of Champāran, both in exports and imports, is smaller than in any other district of the Division, but it seems probable that there will be a considerable expansion in both branches, when the railway from Bagahā to Bairagniā is completed. The principal exports consist of rice, paddy, linseed, gram and pulse, other food-grains, and indigo. Rice, paddy, gram and pulse are exported to other districts in Bihār, and to a smaller extent to the United Provinces; while linseed and indigo are sent to Calcutta for shipment over seas. The principal imports are coal from the Rānīganj and Gīrīdih coal-fields, salt from the godowns in Calcutta, and kerosine oil from the depôts in the 24-Parganas.

A considerable trade is carried on with Nepāl, one of the main routes to Kātmāndu lying through this district. The principal articles of import from Nepāl are rice, paddy, gram, pulses and oil-seeds, while the chief articles of export to that country are cotton piece-goods, salt and sugar, besides considerable quantities of tobacco and kerosine oil. The bulk of this trade passes through Raxaul, the terminus of the Sugauli-Raxaul branch railway, and is registered there and also at Tribenī, Adāpur, Ghorāsahan and Chauradāno.

The railway is the main artery of commerce, but the Gandak and Sikrāna rivers are also used, as river transit is cheaper and more convenient for the river marts. Of these the principal are Gobindganj, Barharwā, Mānpur and Bagahā. The other trade centres are Bettiah, Motīhāri, Chainpatiā, Chhapkahiā, Rāmgarhwā, Kesariyā and Madhuban. The traders are mainly Mārwāris, Kalwārs and Agraharis, and to a small extent Muhammadans.

Fairs Much of the trade is carried on at the fairs held from time to time at different places. The following religious gatherings, always accompanied by small fairs, are held in Champāran:—at

Bakulahar, Tetariā, Dhekāhā, Gobindganj Ghāt, Uttar Bāhani and Rajwatiā, on the 31st October during the Kārtik Snān or bathing festival; at Mahamadā, Banwariā and Kuriā, on the 1st April, the anniversary of the Sheorāt or holy night of Siva; at Machhargāon, 10 miles west of Bettiah, on the 30th August, the Janamastamī or birthday of Krishna; and at Maināṭānr and Dhobanī, on the 26th September, the Dasaharā, another bathing festival.

The following assemblages are of a more commercial character, but religious ceremonies are not wanting to any of them. At Bettiah a fair is held annually in the month of October, and is attended by from 25,000 to 30,000 persons. It lasts for 15 days, and commemorates the story of Rāma, the son of Dasarath. Two boys dressed as Rāma and Lakshman are carried about the fair, while the crowd prostrate themselves. Rāvana and Hanumān with his monkey army are also represented, the whole ending with the destruction of Rāvana. Cloth and iron and brass utensils are largely sold. At Sirsā, 6 miles from Motihāri and at Madhubanī, 5 miles from that town, fairs are held at the same time with the same object; only 2,000 people attend each. At Sītākund, 12 miles east from Motihāri, a fair is held in April, which lasts for 3 days, and is attended by about 15,000 people. Visitors worship the images of Rāma and Lakshman, which are placed on the banks of the tank where Sita is said to have bathed when on her way to her marriage. The principal articles of commerce are cloth and metal vessels. A similar gathering, established about 60 years ago, is held at Adāpur, also in April. Here are two temples, one containing an image of Rāma, the other of Lakshman; in a third temple the spirits of departed Brāhmans are supposed to dwell. Cattle, goats, cloth and utensils of various kinds are the principal articles of trade.

At Lauriyā Ararāj, 16 miles west of Motihāri, there is a stone image of Mahādeo in a deep dry well, over which a large temple has been built. A fair is held here in March, attended by 10,000 people, and lasts 8 days. Water from the Ganges is poured over the figure of the god. Cattle, horses and cloth are largely sold. A similar fair is held in May, but it only lasts for 3 days, and is attended by fewer people. At the same time a fair, also connected with the worship of Mahādeo, is held at Lakhaurā, 6 miles north of Motihāri, attended by 10,000 people and lasting 10 days. Tribenī, in the extreme north-west point of the district, is the site of a fair held in the month of February. Three rivers unite here soon after they quit the hills; and, in accordance with a common Hindu superstition, the spot is on this account considered holy. It is also believed to be the scene of the commencement of the fight between Gaj and Garāh, the elephant and the crocodile, which is recorded in the Purānas and piously credited by good Hindus. The fair lasts three days, and is attended by 2,000 people, of whom many are Nepālis. The chief ceremony consists in bathing in the Gandak river. Cloth and grain are the principal articles sold. At Kunrwā, a mile from Motīhāri, a one-day fair is held in November. A Brāhman, Ajgaibnāth, is said to have been buried alive beneath the tank where the people now bathe. At Dewar, in the extreme north of the Bettiah subdivision, two fairs are held yearly, one on the occasion of Rām Navamī in April, and the other at the full moon of November. The object of worship is an image of Mahādeo, the shrine being known as *Sahodar āsthān*.

Coins, weights and measures.

There are two kinds of uminted copper coins current in the district, viz., the dumpy pice called *lohiā* and Gorakhpurī pice. The latter are largely composed of copper, while the former contain a larger admixture of iron; both are indifferently called *dhebuā* and are believed to be manufactured in Nepāl and the United Provinces. They have no fixed value, but generally from 104 to 128 go to the rupee, according to the demand in the market and the seasons of the year; in 1907 their value rose as high as 90 to the rupee, and this increase in purchasing value was of inestimable benefit in a year of abnormally high prices.

The use of Government copper coins is practically confined to the larger shops in towns, to payment of Government dues, and to the post office, railway booking, municipal, and other quasi-official transactions. During the famine relief operations in 1897 large quantities of these coins were introduced in the hope that the dumpy pice might be superseded, but as the *baniyās* in the villages refused to sell grain in exchange for Government pice, except at a considerable discount, this hope was not realized. Dumpy pice are still universally in use, especially in the north, where such a thing as a Government copper coin is hardly ever met with. The extent to which financial transactions are carried on by means of *lohiā* pice will be apparent from the fact that, during the recovery of costs at the last settlement, the Settlement Department, being unable to saddle itself with large quantities of uncurrent coin, found it necessary to attach to each camp a *baniyā*, who in return for a small commission gave Government pice in exchange for dumpy pice.

The unit of calculation for measures of weight and capacity is the *gandā*, which nominally is equal to 4 pice, but its value varies immensely. Thus, 121 *gandās* of *lohiā* pice have been weighed with the result that they were found to have no less than 60 values varying from 531 to 675 grains, the mean value being 600 grains. In the headquarters subdivision the standard seer is taken as equivalent to 22 *gandās* at Motihāri, and the local seer as equal to 10 *gandās* ; but in the interior there is great variety in the values assigned to the seer, as practically each bazar has its own scale of weights. These measures are also used for liquids, such as milk and oil, as the capacity of the vessels is determined by weighing the contents with *lohiā* pice of a quantity representing a seer, half seer, quarter seer, etc..

In the Bettiah subdivision the recognized seer is equal to 11 *gandās* at Bettiah, but elsewhere the divergence is very great. In the northern portion of the Dhanahā outpost and of the Bagahā thāna, Gorakhpurī pice are used, while in the rest of the subdivision the ordinary *lohiā* pice are used. Where the latter form the standard, the seer of weight varies from 8½ *gandās* to 11½ *gandās ;* where Gorakhpurī pice are in vogue, the measure of a seer varies from 24 to 30 *gandās*. The measure of capacity, as a rule, depends on the weight of unhusked rice or paddy ; in the former case the *pāthāi* is two seers and in the latter case 1½ seers. The oil measure is usually 29 *gandās* of Gorakhpurī pice or 11 *gandās* of *lohiā* pice. In bazars on the border land the measure of capacity is calculated with Gorakhpurī pice, while the measure of weight is calculated with *lohiā* pice.

1 *girah* = 2¼ inches.
1 *bitta* = 4 *girahs* or 9 inches.
1 *hāth* = 2 *bittas* or 18 inches.
1 *gaz* = 2 *hāths* or 1 yard.

The measures of length given in the marginal table are reported to be prevalent in the case of cloth, but it must be remembered that the *hāth* or cubit, which is the unit of measurement, though nominally 18 inches, is an indeterminate quantity, for it is not measured by the standard cubit, but by the forearm of some villager, generally the longest in the village. In fact, it varies from place to place, but is invariably longer than 18 inches, and is generally at least 18½ inches. For measuring land, the *laggi* is in common use, and this is supposed to be equivalent to so many *hāths*—7¾ *hāths* in Motihāri and 8 *hāths* or more in the north of the district. The actual length of the *laggi* depends on the length assigned to the *hāth*, and it varies from 17 feet 5½ inches to 10 feet 10½ inches in different parts of the district.

CHAPTER IX.

THE INDIGO INDUSTRY.

PROGRESS OF THE INDUSTRY. THE pioneer of the indigo industry in Bihār was Francois Grand, Collector of Tirhut (Muzaffarpur and Darbhangā) in the years 1782-85, who left it on record that he introduced the manufacturing of indigo after the European manner, encouraged the establishment of indigo works and plantations, and erected three at his own expense. Thirty years appear, however, to have elapsed before the cultivation of indigo by European methods was introduced into Champāran; for it was not till 1813 that the first factory was founded by Colonel Hickey at Bārā. Shortly afterwards, the Rājpur and Turkauliā concerns were started by Messrs. Moran and Hill respectively, and the cultivation then steadily extended, for in 1830 we find the Collector urging the construction of roads for the development of the country and reporting that Government would be able to avail itself of the assistance of the indigo planters spread over a large extent of country. During the first half of the century, however, indigo had to yield precedence to sugar, the manufacture of which was the premier industry of Champāran, steam sugar factories being scattered over several *parganas*. About 1850 the high prices obtained for indigo dealt a final blow at this industry, the cultivation of sugar was replaced by indigo, and the sugar factories were converted into indigo concerns.

The advance of the industry was seriously threatened in 1867-68, when there was a strong demonstration against the cultivation of indigo, accompanied in some instances by acts of violence. The causes of dissatisfaction on the part of the ryots were several. They objected to the unusual trouble and hard labour required for the successful production of the indigo plant, and felt that the rates being paid for its cultivation did not give adequate remuneration for the labour expended. There was a widespread knowledge that enormous profits were made from indigo, and they had a natural desire to obtain a larger share of them, while the high prices of food had raised the profits obtained from the cultivation of food-grains, and therefore made indigo still more unpopular than before. Further, they resented the harassment of the factory servants, who, besides committing various acts of oppression, were alleged to be in the habit of taking a large percentage of the payments made to the ryots as their own perquisites under the general name of *dasturi*. Added to all this, there was an absence, on the part of the managers of factories, of that sympathy with the ryots which used formerly to be displayed by the old proprietor planters, who paid more attention to the well-being of their tenantry.

The opposition of the ryots showed itself in a general refusal to sow indigo, and in some cases in the forcible appropriation to other crops of the lands already prepared for the cultivation of indigo. The first instance of such proceedings occurred in a village called Jaukatiā, the ryots of which, in defiance of the contract into which they had entered with the Lālsaraiyā factory, sowed their lands with cold weather crops; and this example was rapidly followed by other villagers. As the interests of the planters at stake were very considerable, and it was necessary that they should receive prompt and final decisions on their complaints, Government, at their request, established a Small Cause Court at Motīhāri, with jurisdiction over the entire district of Champāran, for the trial of all cases of breach of contract between them and the ryots. This Court was composed of two Judges, the one a Covenanted Civil Servant and the other a native gentleman; and these two officers were directed to sit together for the trial of all suits connected with the indigo question. The result of this measure was entirely satisfactory. But few suits were instituted, the mere knowledge that such a Court was at hand to enforce promptly the payment of damages for breach of contracts being apparently sufficient to deter the ryots from wantonly breaking them. At the same time, the demands of the ryots were met by concessions from the planters, whose bearing was most moderate and temperate throughout this trying period. Within 9 weeks of the establishment of the Court, the Lieutenant-Governor was able to put an end to its special constitution, leaving the native Judge only to preside over it. Before it was too late to retrieve the prospects of the indigo season, all open opposition to the cultivation had ceased.

The disputes between the ryots and planters had at one time threatened to become very serious. The local officers almost unanimously reported that the cultivation of indigo had become very unpopular, and that there was not a ryot who would not abandon the cultivation if he could; and this state of things was ascribed as much to the insufficiency of the remuneration which the ryots received, as to the exactions, oppression, and annoyance to which they were exposed at the hands of the factory servants. Government was satisfied that the time had passed when planters could hope to carry on an indigo concern profitably by forcing on the ryots a cultivation and labour which were to them unprofitable; and it was clear that in the altered circumstances of the time they must be prepared either to close their factories or to give to the ryots, in some shape or other, a remuneration which should make it worth their while to grow indigo. This necessity was recognized by the general body of planters, and they yielded to the pressure, raising the rate of remuneration from Rs. 7-8 to Rs. 12 per *bīgha.*

It was believed that this movement among the ryots was instigated by certain persons who had their own interests to serve; and this belief appeared to be borne out by the fact that the open opposition to the planters was mainly confined to the estates of the Mahārājā of Bettiah. The management of the Bettiah estate by an English gentleman was said to have given rise to much dissatisfaction among the influential natives of the Rājā's household, whose opportunities of enriching themselves at the expense of the Rājā had been restricted thereby; and the combination among the ryots was said to have been got up by them, mainly with the object of involving the manager of the estate in difficulties, so that the Rājā, disgusted with the management, might allow his affairs to revert to their former neglected condition.*

Ten years later the financial embarrassment of the same estate resulted in the indigo industry being placed on a firm footing. Hitherto the planters had been able only to secure temporary leases of land, but circumstances now arose which gave them a more permanent and secure hold on the soil. By 1876 the Bettiah Rāj, owing to the extravagance of the Mahārājā and the mismanagement of his employés, had become heavily involved in debt; and as a means of extricating it from its difficulties a European Manager, Mr. T. Gibbon, was appointed. One of the first steps of the new Manager was to ensure financial equilibrium, and the Gulliland House consented to float a sterling loan of nearly 95 lakhs, on the sole condition of substantial European security. To satisfy this condition and cover the interest on the loan, permanent leases of villages were granted to indigo planters, and the industry was thus placed on a secure basis. Permanent rights in the land being assured, the cultivation of indigo was widely extended, until by the end of the 19th century no less than

* C. E. Buckland, *Bengal under the Lieutenant-Governors,* Calcutta, 1901.

21 factories, with 48 outworks, had been established, while the area under indigo was 95,970 acres, or 6·6 per cent. of the cultivated area.

Since 1900 the industry has suffered from the competition of the artificial dye in Europe and from the high prices of food-grains and the consequent demand for land in Bihār. The price of the natural dye has fallen rapidly, and the area under cultivation has diminished, being returned at 47,800 acres in 1905, while in the final forecast of the indigo crop in Bengal for 1906 the area sown is shown as only 38,600 acres. Government has come to the aid of the planters with substantial grants for scientific research, the aim of which is to ascertain whether it is possible to increase the outturn and quality of the dye at a cheaper cost: excellent work in the chemistry, bacteriology and agriculture of indigo has been done and is still progressing; and efforts have been made to improve the quality of the plant by importing fresh seed from Java and Natal. But so far these experiments have not succeeded in arresting the decay of the industry. The price obtained for indigo is barely sufficient to cover the cost of production, and many factories are either closing altogether or are reducing the area cultivated with indigo, growing in its place sugar, cotton, and country crops. The figures given below show sufficiently clearly how greatly the outturn has decreased in consequence of these adverse conditions, though there has been a slight improvement in 1906-07—

Year.	Outturn.	Value.	Price per maund.
	Maunds.	Rs.	Rs.
1895-1900 (average)	17,734	32,95,631	186
1901-05 (average)	15,602	22,11,141	142
1905-06	8,717	12,82,618	141
1906-07	9,495	14,49,809	153

Cultivation. The land on which indigo is to be grown is prepared for sowing as soon as the *kharif* crops have been reaped, as it is of great importance that the soil should retain the moisture supplied by the rainfall in October and November. The land is ploughed and reploughed until the clods are all pulverized, and after being manured, it is levelled and smoothed with a plank roller composed of a long heavy beam on which two men stand. The seed is sown at the beginning of the hot weather, as soon as the nights begin to get warm, a special drill, with coulters about 5 or 6 inches apart, being used for the purpose; and after sowing the roller is again used to level the surface. The seedlings are very delicate until their roots are well developed, and many perish owing to dry west winds; but moist east winds after sowing, and spring showers later, are beneficial to the young plants, if they do not bring caterpillars. The plants make slow progress until the monsoon sets in, when the growth becomes rapid; and they are ready for cutting, which takes place immediately before they flower, in July or August. A second crop is obtainable in September, but usually yields less than the first crop, the outturn of which is ordinarily 80 to 120 maunds of green plant per acre. The yield of 100 maunds of good ordinary plant should be about 10 seers of indigo.

Soils and manures.

Indigo may follow indigo, but is more generally rotated with such crops as sugarcane, tobacco, poppy, cereals and oil-seeds. It is an exhausting crop, which cannot well be grown on the same land for more than three successive seasons; on the other hand, being a deep-root crop, it forms an excellent rotation crop for those which have surface roots, as is the case with many food-grains. It is usually grown on high lands beyond the reach of floods; the soils are varied in character and composition, but deep alluvium loams seem to suit the crop best. Many soils of this description are deficient in phosphoric acid and nitrogen, but are generally rich in other useful constituents; while extensive experiments have proved that superphosphate and nitrate of potash can be economically applied. The refuse indigo plant (*sīth*) is the manure most easily obtained, and is very valuable; but it is less suited for indigo itself than for rotation crops, such as those mentioned above. It produces heavy crops of indigo, but the leaf is deficient in colouring matter; and indigo grown on land heavily treated with *sīth* is liable to injury from insect-pests. Farm manure, chemical manures, such as saltpetre and lime, bone-dust and oil-cake are also used.

Seed.

The seed used in Tirhut comes for the most part from the United Provinces, as there is a general belief among the planters that the best seed is obtainable there, and that local seed does not keep good from season to season and does not germinate properly. The system of getting seed in this way, without any special selection, has however caused deterioration in the varieties commonly grown, and there is little doubt that the plant commonly cultivated does not now produce a satisfactory amount of dye matter, particularly on worn-out indigo lands. The chief cultivated form is not *Indigofera tinctoria* as was formerly supposed, but *Indigofera sumatrana*, which was introduced about 150 years ago.

Within recent years Natal indigo (*Indigofera arrecta*) has been introduced, the seed being obtained direct from Natal and also from plants acclimatized in Java. This plant has been found to give a very considerable increase of colouring matter from the unit area of land, and will produce excellent cuttings for two years in succession and mediocre plants for a third year, whereas other varieties have to be resown annually. It gives two good crops a year and has a much more vigorous habit of growth than the old variety, and the leaf contains a larger proportion of the colour-yielding principle. It appears to be eminently suited to the soils and climate of Bihār, and farms have now been established for the cultivation of its seed on an extensive scale.

Colouring matter. The colouring matter from which indigotin is derived exists almost entirely in the leaf of the plant. It increases as the plant grows, but deteriorates after a certain stage, and harvesting and steeping have therefore to be carried on expeditiously. Plants which have been cut some time and become blackened by heating in bulk contain very little dye matter, so that the green plant cannot be carted very far. A plant which is forced by manure to very active growth also gives a poor percentage of dye matter.

MANUFACTURE. Steeping. After they have been cut, the leaves are taken to the factory, and are there steeped in large vats until fermentation is complete. The old system of treating the plant requires two sets of vats, one on a lower level than the other, those on the highest level being used for steeping the plant, which is kept submerged by logs of wood or bars fixed in position. During this process active fermentation takes place through the action of soluble ferments (enzymes), and causes the formation of a compound which is easily convertible into indigotin by the action of air. The period of steeping varies with the temperature of the air and water; if the temperature of the water is 90° to 92° F., steeping for 10 hours is sufficient, but instead of varying the time, it is preferable to heat the water in the reservoir to a definite temperature. It has been shown by experiment that when the plant is steeped in water at 150° to 160° F., the colouring principle is extracted in half an hour; and indigo made in this way is superior in quality and contains about 75 per cent. of indigotin.

Oxidation or beating process. When fermentation is complete, the liquid in the steeping vats, which varies in colour from bright orange to olive green, is drained off into the lower vats, and is there subjected to a brisk beating, the effect of which is to cause oxidation and separate the particles of dye. As oxidation proceeds, dark blue particles of indigotin appear in the liquid, the colour of which consequently changes; and the beating is continued until a little of the liquid placed in a saucer readily throws a dark blue precipitate, itself remaining of a clear amber colour. If there is any delay in oxidation, there is a considerable loss of colouring matter, and the indigo produced is inferior. Oxidation was at one time accomplished by hand-beating, but in most Bihār factories it is now done by a beating wheel worked by power from a central engine.

Lime and ammonia process.

The improved method of treating the plant known as Coventry's lime and acid process, which is used in a few Bihār factories, requires a vat intermediate between the steeping and beating vat. Lime is added to the indigo liquor, and a precipitate of calcium and magnesium carbonates then forms, which also carries down various other impurities. The cleared liquor, when run off into lower vat and oxidized, yields indigo of good quality, and a substantial increase of colouring matter is obtained. An ammonia gas process, patented by Mr. Rawson in 1901, also produces a direct increase of colouring matter.

Boiling and final preparation.

Finally, the sediment (*māl*) which remains in the vat is boiled, strained and made up into cakes for the market. The first process in these final stages of manufacture is to boil the precipitate which settles after oxidation; the indigo produced from it is improved, if sulphuric acid is added. The dye matter is next placed on a cloth strainer until it becomes fairly dry. It is then carried to the press and subjected to gradually increasing pressure until it has taken the form of firm slabs, which are cut into cakes and slowly dried on racks. Good indigo should contain 60 per cent. or more of indigotin, should be bright and of a dark blue colour, with a coppery gloss, and should break with an evenly coloured fracture.

LANDED INTERESTS.

From the statistics obtained during the course of the last survey and settlement operations it has been ascertained that the indigo concerns exercise the rights of landlords in nearly half of the district, either as proprietors or tenure-holders; in the headquarters subdivision they hold no less than 58·5 per cent. of the whole area, and in the Bettiah subdivision nearly 35 per cent. in the capacity of superior landlords. In the latter subdivision the percentage (45·2 per cent.) is highest in the Bettiah thāna, over which a large number of factories are scattered, and it is lowest (30 per cent.) in the Bagahā and Shikārpur thānas, where only about one per cent. of the cultivated area grows indigo and the concerns are mainly engaged in zamīndāri. In the headquarters subdivision the highest percentage (73 per cent.) is found in the Kesariyā thāna, and the lowest (32·3 per cent.) in the Madhuban thāna, in which there are numerous petty proprietors holding small shares of estates. It is not perhaps too much to say that the indigo industry owes the strength of its position in this district to the fact that the planters possess a landlord's interest in so large an area; not the least noticeable result of which is that, most of their indigo being grown on land of which they are the landlords, they are relieved from the necessity of haggling with petty proprietors and cultivators, to which their less fortunate fellow-planters have to submit in Sāran and Tirhut.

The proportion of land held by planters as proprietors is inconsiderable, amounting to only ½ per cent. in the whole district; in the Bettiah subdivision no land is so held, as all three thānas belong to large zamīndārs, viz., the Madhuban estate, the Bettiah Rāj and the Rāmnagar Rāj. The percentage of land held in permanent tenure is 17·2 per cent.; and the largest percentage of area held by factories is under temporary leases, the district figure being 25 per cent. The percentage of area held in under-tenure is small, 3·15 per cent. being the proportion for the whole district. Generally speaking, the interest of the indigo concerns in the land is mainly that of tenure-holders, but in thānas Bettiah, Motīhāri, Gobindganj and Kesariyā, where the proportion of land held on permanent tenure varies from 23 to 45 per cent., it is practically as secure as a proprietary right.

SYSTEMS OF CULTIVATION.

The two main systems of indigo cultivation practised in Champāran are known as *zirāat*, *i.e.*, the home-farm system of direct cultivation by means of hired servants, and *asāmīwār* or cultivation through factory tenants (*asāmī*). A third system, which is uncommon in Champāran, is *khushkī* or cultivation by means of agreements with outside ryots. Roughly, one-third of the cultivation is carried on under the *zirāat* system and two-thirds under the *asāmīwār* system.

Zirāat.

The term *zirāat* is applied to any land in the direct occupation of a factory and not only to land held by a proprietor or superior tenure-holder. *Zirāat* indigo land is cultivated by the factory at its own expense and with hired labour. Over one-fourth of the area under indigo is of this class, and owing to its careful cultivation returns the best profits.

Asāmīwār.

When the system of *asāmīwār* cultivation is followed, the indigo is grown by the factory tenants, under the direction of the factory's servants, at fixed rates per *bīgha*. Generally documents called *sattas*, are executed, the ryot receiving an advance and binding himself to grow indigo on a certain specified portion of his holding, and to pay damages if he should fail to carry out his contract. All the expenses of cultivation are paid by the ryot, but the seed is given by the factory, which also cuts and carts away the indigo, the ryot being paid for the latter at fixed rates. When the contracts (*sattas*) are executed, the cultivators generally agree for a term of years to grow indigo on 3 *kathās* per *bīgha* of their holdings. This is sometimes called the *tinkathiā* system, but must be distinguished from the system, now almost extinct, under which the planters appropriated 3 *kathās* per *bīgha* out of the ryot's holding, giving him in return nothing beyond a proportionate reduction of rent.

Badlain or exchange is a prominent characteristic of the *asāmīwār* system. Lands after being cropped three and four years successively with indigo require to be sown with grain and other surface root crops. Indigo, being a plant with a deep root, forms an excellent rotation crop with them, but successive crops of indigo exhaust the soil. Hence it seems necessary to arrange for an exchange of land, and *badlain* is a practice universally followed.

Khushkī. Agreements executed by ryots who are not the tenants of the factory, are called *khushkī*, as the cultivators voluntarily agree to grow indigo. In this case the factory supplies the seed and pays for the crop when delivered at privileged rates ; it sometimes also gives an advance to the cultivators at a light rate of interest. The system is very rarely found in Champāran, as, if it is to pay, indigo requires selected lands, carefully cultivated, and rotated in an intelligent manner. These conditions are all wanting in the *khushkī* system ; the rate of remuneration has to be high in order to induce the outside ryot to grow indigo ; and in Champāran factories have such extensive tenure-holding rights that they can generally make better terms with their own ryots and have no need to enlist the services of cultivators holding land in other estates.

Kurtaulī. Under the *kurtaulī* system (sometimes also called the *shikmī* system) the factory sublets from a ryot and grows the indigo itself with its own labour, the rent agreed on being deducted from the rent due from the ryot to the factory in its capacity as landlord ; the factory is, in short, a mere under-ryot. *Kurtaulī* leases are rare in Champāran and appear to be more common in Motīhāri thāna than elsewhere.

Hiring of carts. An important feature in indigo cultivation is the hiring of carts, which is generally effected by means of agreements, as it is imperative that the indigo plant should be cut and brought into the factory directly it is ripe. In consideration of an advance, the owner of the cart agrees for a term of years to place it at the disposal of the factory, and in return receives a fixed rate of payment a little below the ordinary rate.

Regarding the advantages and disadvantages of indigo cultivation, the following remarks are quoted from the Settlement Report of Mr. Stevenson-Moore, with some slight condensation: "My conclusions are that the indigo industry in relation to Government and the administration, in relation to landowners, and in relation to labourers, confers very decided benefits on the district, but that in relation to cultivators its advantages are very much more questionable. In Champāran the utility of the indigo factory is largely connected with the management of the Bettiah Rāj. It has been seen that it was their security which rendered possible the raising of the Bettiah sterling loan. Further, while the factories, to the best of my knowledge, are good and considerate landlords to their ryots, they increase the value of property they supervise by dint of good management, and pay up their rents with punctuality. The Bettiah Rāj has not the organization requisite for the efficient management of all its estates direct. That, relying on indigo and not on zamīndāri for their profits, indigo factories have been available to share with it the responsibility of management, at a very slender rate of remuneration, has proved a decided advantage to that estate. INFLUENCE OF THE INDUSTRY.

"The benefits of the indigo industry to the labouring population are still more marked, for these are the classes in greatest need of support. The average number of labourers employed in Champāran per diem by indigo factories is 33,000, and more than half the labour is employed in the cold weather months, when these classes are most liable to destitution. It is true that the factory rates of labour are somewhat lower than those ordinarily paid, and it is often urged that factories have had a tendency to keep down labour rates. A large employer of labour naturally gets it cheaper than the man who employs a single cooly, and if factories have attempted to keep down rates, they have not invariably succeeded, as the rates differ considerably in different tracts.

"In relation to the agriculturists, its merits are more questionable. But here again, so far as ryots not called upon to grow indigo are concerned, an indigo factory as landlord is a very decided advantage. The indigo concern's best interests centre in maintaining stability of rents, and, what is of more importance, this truth is generally both recognized by them and acted upon. Again, non-indigo ryots who are tenants to factories have their accounts kept well and accurately, are given proper receipts, are not called on for additional demands to meet domestic ceremonies so common in native estates, and are protected and helped when they fall into difficulties. Pecuniarily, a cultivator loses per acre by growing indigo. This deficiency may or may not be made up by other advantages, but these are less tangible, and he does not appreciate them at their full value. He finds that if he had grown another crop, he would have made more money. He forgets that he received an advance when he required it; that the existence of indigo gives him more profits from his cart than he would otherwise obtain; and that his rent, had the village been leased to a native *thikādār* instead of to an indigo planter, would probably have been more onerous.

"The fact remains that the ryots, on the whole, do not like indigo, though I do not think they possess very active sentiments on the subject, their attitude being one of passive acquiescence. Again, the system of accounts is open to the objection that it tends to check independence of thought and action. The accounts for rents, advances and indigo are all mixed up together, and though kept no doubt well and accurately, are incomprehensible to the ordinary uneducated mind. Finally, the system of exchange (*badlain*) raises apprehension in the ryot's mind that his tenant right will be interfered with. His tenant right is, as a rule, preserved unimpaired, and the record-of-rights will afford him full protection. Moreover, indigo, as a rotation crop for food-grains, distinctly benefits the land. But a ryot may be asked to give, in *badlain* for indigo, a plot which he has liberally manured and carefully tilled in anticipation of fat profits to be realized from some other crop. Whatever the cause, the fact remains that the *badlain* system is not generally liked. My general conclusions then are that the cultivators who grow indigo on agreement receive little advantage from it, and in their own opinion the crop is generally believed to be pecuniarily disadvantageous; that, on the other hand, only two-thirds of the indigo cultivation is of this nature, that is to say, only 4 per cent. of the cultivated area in the district; and that to be set against the real and imaginary disadvantages to a comparatively small body of ryots are the great and material benefits that accrue to the administration, to landlords and to labourers from the presence in the district of the indigo concerns and their industry."

PRINCIPAL FACTORIES. Indigo factories are found for the most part in the headquarters subdivision, and are less common in the northern thānas, which consist mainly of rice lands unsuitable for the growth of indigo. This is particularly the case in Shikārpur, Bagahā and Adāpur. In the thāna last named there is but little indigo, and rice is the planter's main source of income. In the other two thānas a large number of villages are held by native *thikādārs* with a view solely to the profit to be derived from zamīndāri, and the concerns that exist ostensibly for the cultivation of indigo make their profits mainly from the cultivation of rice. The following is a list of the indigo factories at work in the district—

Factories.	Sub-factories.
MOTIHARI SUBDIVISION.	
Bārā ...	Gaundrā. Jugauliā. Manuāwā. Rasūlpur.
Belwā ...	...
Motīhāri ...	Chailaha. Harāj. Mirpur. Purnahiā. Sugāon.
Nawāda ...	Parsauni.
Padumker ...	...
Pīpra ...	Daini Math. Dhekahā. Dhobwaliā. Madhuban.
Rājpur ...	Husaini. Jamunāpur. Pakrī.
Sirahā ...	Parewā.
Telārha ...	...
Tetariā ...	Bāla. Chahuniā.
Turkauliā ...	Barbarwā. Gahiri (Bettiah subdivision). Khairwā (do.). Makhwā. Olahā. Sakhwā. Tejpurwā.
BETTIAH SUBDIVISION.	
Bairiā ...	Nautan.
Kuriā ...	Lālgarh.
Lālsaraiyā ...	Farawā. Mādhopur. Rājghāt.
Malahiā. ...	Sirsiā.
Parsā ...	Harpur.
Sāthi ...	...

CHAPTER X.

MEANS OF COMMUNICATION.

DEVELOPMENT OF COMMUNICATIONS. A century ago Champāran had not a single road worthy of the name. In 1800 the Collector of Sāran, within the jurisdiction of which Champāran was then included, was constrained to report that, as far as his local knowledge and enquiries extended, it did not appear that there were any roads in the district, except one in Sāran. Fair-weather tracks undoubtedly existed, but roads practicable for cart traffic were unknown. This state of affairs was altered within the next 30 years by the necessity of having good roads for the passage of troops during the Nepāl war and lines of communication between the cantonments along the frontier; for in 1830 we find the Collector reporting that the road passing from Sattar Ghāt *viā* Dhāka to the cantonments at Mallai in the Muzaffarpur district were in a tolerable state of repair, as well as the roads from the cantonments along the Nepāl boundary between Tirhut and Gorakhpur. He added that there were two other very good roads, the one from Bettiah to Tribenī and the other from Bettiah to Rāmnagar, for which Champāran was indebted to a visit from the Governor-General. He went on to point out that there were numerous old roads in Champāran from north to south and from east to west, but until they were repaired and opened for "land carriage" very little trade could be carried on; the little trade that existed was, he added, mainly to be attributed to the Little Gandak, which afforded communication with the Ganges.

About this time a great change was effected by the enterprise of the indigo and sugar planters, to whom good lines of communication were a vital necessity. The result of their energy was soon apparent, for in an account of the district given in the Bengal and Agra Guide and Gazetteer of 1841 we find it stated:—"In Champāran the roads are excellent and kept in good and substantial repair by the indigo planters at their own expense. From Mehsī, the most eastern part of Champāran, to within a few *kos* of Bettiah, a distance of nearly 50 miles, the roads are excellent." The same description could not be applied to other roads. The road leading to Sattar Ghāt on the Gandak, which was the high road to Champāran, was described as being hardly passable in many places for 5 or 6 months in the year; there was but little intercourse between Bettiah and Bagahā, and the road was, consequently, in many places a mere pathway covered with turf; while the cross roads from one village to another were wholly neglected, except in a few instances where they were repaired by zamīndārs. Gradually, but surely, the roads were improved and extended; and by 1876 there were 26 roads with a length of 438 miles. Within the 30 years which have since elapsed, the mileage of the roads, excluding village tracks, has been more than doubled, and they now extend over 1,081 miles.

Prior to 1883 there was no railway in Champāran, the Tirhut State Railway being extended to it from Muzaffarpur in that year; and this was the only railway line in the famine of 1897. It ended at Bettiah, nearly 50 miles from the foot of the hills and about 65 miles from the north-western extremity of the district, so that the northern portion of the Bettiah subdivision was in imminent danger of being cut off from supplies. This isolation no longer exists, for the Tirhut State Railway (now worked by the Bengal and North-Western Railway) has been extended as far as Bhikhnā Thorī. This line is joined at Sugauli by another running from Raxaul, and a third line is now under construction from Bagahā to Bairagniā, which will traverse the north of the district throughout its length. The terminus is, at present, at Bagahā, but it is expected that next year a temporary bridge will be built across the Gandak; and communication will thus be established between the great rice producing tracts in Tirhut, Champāran and Gorakhpur.

ROADS.

The District Board maintains 1,307 miles of roads, of which 15 miles are metalled and 1,066 miles are unmetalled, while village roads account for 226 miles. The small proportion of metalled roads is very marked, and is due to the fact that in the greater portion of the district good road-metal is not available, and that, rents being low, the resources of the District Board are insufficient for the construction of expensive roads. The area to be dealt with is also large, and it is already a difficult task for that body to keep up the long lines of communication with the limited funds at its disposal, especially as its resources are frequently strained severely by the occurrence of floods. At the same time, it may be said that the roads now maintained are fairly sufficient for all parts of the district except the north of the Bettiah subdivision. There are, indeed, three main roads from the railway to different points in that tract, with one road running right across the centre of it; but there is no network of subsidiary roads as in the rest of the district, and wheeled traffic is possible therefore only in the dry season. The rude tracks along which carts manage to find their way are interrupted by the numerous water-courses that flow from the hills; and for the most part produce has to be conveyed by pack-bullocks. The deficiency of communications in this part of the district will be remedied when the new railway from Bagahā to Bairagniā has been completed.

The most important roads are those which lead from the Nepāl border to the railway and the banks of the Gandak. Bridges are comparatively few in number over even the more important streams, and there is only one of any large size, a bridge, 400 feet long, over the Sikrāna at Chainpatiā, which was constructed in 1885. There was another bridge, 700 feet long, over the same river at Sugauli, but this was carried away by the floods of 1898.

Ferries. Owing to the paucity of bridges, ferries are numerous and largely used. The principal ferries are those on the Great Gandak at Sattar Ghāt (Dhekahā), Sangrāmpur, Gobindganj, Bariārpur, Pīpra, Ratwal and Bagahā; and on the Sikrāna at Lālbeghiā, Piparpānti, Jatwā and Sugauli. The number of minor ferries is very considerable, and the District Board obtains a not unimportant part of its income from their lease.

RAILWAYS. Champāran is transversed from south to north by the Muzaffarpur-Bhikhnā Thorī branch of the Bengal and North-Western Railway. Starting from Muzaffarpur, this branch line enters the district a few miles south of Mehsī, and runs south of and parallel to the general course of the Sikrāna river as far as Bettiah; it then strikes almost due north to its terminus at Bhikhnā Thorī on the Nepāl frontier. On this line there are 15 stations within the district, viz., proceeding from south to north, Mehsī, Chakiā, Pīpra, Jiudhāra, Motīhāri, Semrā, Sugauli, Majhauliā, Bettiah, Chainpatiā, Sāthi, Narkatiāganj, Amolwa, Gaunaha and Bhikhnā Thorī.

Sugauli is the junction for a short branch line, 18 miles long, running due north to Raxaul on the Nepāl frontier, with one intermediate station at Rāmgarhwā. A third line is now under construction; it will extend from Bairagniā, the present terminus of the Darbhangā-Bairagniā branch, as far as Bagahā on the western boundary of the district, and thence into Gorakhpur, having a junction with the Sugauli-Raxaul branch at Raxaul and crossing the Muzaffarpur-Bhikhnā Thorī branch at Narkatiāganj. The stations in this district proceeding from east to west will be at Kunrwā, Ghorāsahan, Chauradāno, Adāpur, Raxaul,

Bhelhai, Siktā, Gokhulā, Narkatiāganj, Rāmnagar, Khoripākar and Bagahā. This line will convey the grain traffic of Nepāl and the north of Champāran direct to Gorakhpur and the United Provinces without the present long detour through Muzaffarpur and Sāran.

Although a large number of rivers intersect the district, three only are navigable, the Great Gandak, Sikrāna and Bāghmati. The other rivers are little more than hill streams, which in the rains have a deep rapid stream, but remain almost dry for the rest of the year. The Great Gandak is navigable by boats of 1,000 maunds burden, and is used by a large number of country boats carrying timber, grain, etc., in the hot and cold weather; in the rains navigation is dangerous owing to the violence of its floods and the large number of trees swept down by its turbulent stream. The Bāghmati is navigable by boats of 400 to 500 maunds burthen, and the Sikrāna by boats of 200 to 300 maunds burden, in the southern portion of their course; in the rains there is sufficient water in the latter river to float boats of far heavier tonnage, and a number ply as far as Sugauli, returning with cargoes of timber and grain. **WATER COMMUNICATIONS.**

In postal and telegraphic communications the district is still backward, owing to the fact that its people are mainly ignorant cultivators, and that its resources have not yet been developed. Altogether 424 miles of postal communication have been opened, and there are 52 post offices, *i.e.*, one post office for every 68 square miles. The number of postal articles delivered in 1906-07 was 1,754,532, including letters, post cards, packets, newspapers and parcels; while the value of money orders paid was Rs. 5,51,184 and of those issued Rs. 11,42,682; the large amount accounted for by the latter is due to the work in progress on the railways and the Tribenī Canal, the labourers employed using this means of transmitting money to send their savings home. The number of Savings Bank deposits in the same year was 3,359, the amount deposited being Rs. 96,455. There are 10 postal telegraph offices, from which 13,586 messages were issued; these offices are situated at Motīhāri, Bārā (Chakiā), Bettiah, Kesariyā, Pīpra Factory, Rāmnagar, Raxaul, Sirahā, Sugauli and Turkauliā. **POSTAL COMMUNICATIONS.**

CHAPTER XI.

LAND REVENUE ADMINISTRATION.

REVENUE HISTORY. Early settlements.

THE records of the earlier settlements made in Champāran, before it came into the possession of the British, are not sufficiently detailed to give any clear idea of its progress. In the settlement made by Todar Mal, in the time of the Emperor Akbar, 99,424 acres, or 155 square miles, are said to have been assessed to a revenue of Rs. 1,37,835; but it seems uncertain that this area included even all the cultivated land of the district, and it is probable that isolated stretches of cultivation escaped assessment. However this may be, it is noticeable that the assessment was based on the high incidence of Re. 1-6 per acre. About a century later the revenue was raised to Rs. 2,10,150 by an assessment made in 1685 by Shāh Jahān in the reign of Aurangzib; but in 1750 it was reduced by nearly Rs. 10,000 by Alī Vardi Khān. It is difficult to ascertain what the actually assessed revenue of the district was when the British took it over in 1765, but it appears to have stood at about 2 lakhs.

At this time *Sarkār* Champāran was in the possession of the Bettiah Rāj family, the head of which, Rājā Jugal Keshwar Singh, fell into arrears of revenue and defied the authority of the British Government. The estate was thereupon seized and brought under the direct management of the East India Company, and annual settlements were made until 1772; but the revenue dwindled year by year, until it was only Rs. 1,39,389 in 1773, *i.e.*, very little more than the amount assessed by Todar Mal two centuries before. This state of affairs was due not only to the troubles with the Bettiah Rāj, but also to the famine of 1770. According to Hamilton's Description of Hindostan (1820)—"*Sarkār* Champāran or Bettiah suffered severely during the great famine of 1770, when almost half the inhabitants are supposed to have perished. Besides this, the zamīndārs of Champāran having for many years been deprived of their lands, which were leased to ignorant and rapacious farmers of the revenue, they experienced such oppression that the majority of the population which survived the famine were obliged to abscond, leaving the country almost a desert. Since that melancholy epoch the zamīndārs have been re-established by the decennial settlement, many of the ancient inhabitants have returned, and cultivation has been prosecuted."

Permanent Settlement.

In the meantime, various disastrous experiments in land revenue administration had been embarked upon. In 1772 a quinquennial settlement, under the control of European Supervisors, was attempted, but it proved a failure. Annual settlements were then made with farmers and were also largely unsuccessful; and in 1786 the Directors, tired of these fruitless experiments, expressed a desire for a durable assessment on the basis of actual collections for a term of years. The decennial settlement of 1790 was the result. This settlement was made with the zamīndārs, farmers being introduced only in case of recusancy; and the revenue assessed was settled at Rs. 3,98,253, or, excluding *pargana* Babra, which was transferred to Tirhut in 1865, at Rs. 3,51,427. When this settlement was concluded, Champāran was divided into 6 estates, the largest of which comprised the two *parganas* of Majhawā and Simrāon and was charged with a revenue of over 2 lakhs, while the smallest consisted of one village, Harpur Rai, assessed at Rs. 300. Majhawā and Simrāon were held by Bīr Keshwar Singh of the Bettiah Rāj, Mehsī and Babra with a revenue of Rs. 1,25,350 by the Sheohar Rāj family, *tappā* Duho Suho by the founder of the Madhuban family, and *tappās* Rāmgīr, Jamhaulī and Chigwān by the Rāmnagar Rājā. In other words, four of the proprietors were the founders of the four great families of the district.

At the Permanent Settlement concluded 3 years later, in 1793, this settlement, with some slight modifications, was confirmed in perpetuity, the revenue assessed being Rs. 3,85,587. Its result was not, as elsewhere in Bengal, to secure in possession men who had been mere rent collectors, but to recognize as proprietors the local Rājās, whose ancestors had for generations past exercised the powers of semi-independent chiefs ruling over a large extent of territory.

Growth of revenue and estates.

During the next century the demand of land revenue was largely increased owing to the resumption between 1834 and 1841 of lands held without payment of revenue under invalid titles; and at the last settlement concluded in 1899 the revenue of the district was Rs. 5,15,803, assessed upon a cultivated area of 1,447,874 acres. Since that time, it has fallen slightly, and in 1905-06 the revenue demand was Rs. 5,15,469, the number of estates borne on the revenue roll in that year being 1,260, as compared with 879 in 1870-71, and 1,101 in 1888-89. The increase in the number of estates since the Permanent Settlement is due partly to the disintegration of the Sheohar estate, which fell into arrears at the close of the 18th century, and was sold up from time to time in small parcels, until it was left with only one-fourth of its former area; it is partly due also to the addition of resumed estates to the revenue roll, and it has been caused in a minor degree only by partitions, which have never been very numerous.

Incidence of revenue. Comparing the incidence of land revenue with what it was 300 years ago in Akbar's time, we find that it has decreased from Re. 1-6 to annas 3-11 per acre, and that while the cultivated area has increased fifteen-fold, viz., from 155 square miles to 2,262 square miles, the revenue has risen from Rs. 1,38,000 to Rs. 5,16,000, or nearly four-fold. This disproportion is a sufficiently striking proof of the loss sustained by Government owing to the Permanent Settlement. The revenue, instead of being nine-tenths of the rent, according to the proportion sanctioned by the Permanent Settlement, is now only one-fifth; for the total rental of the district is nearly 25 lakhs,* while the revenue is only a little over 5 lakhs. Comparing the rates per acre, we find that the average rent-rate is Re. 1-13-9, while the incidence of revenue is nearly 4 annas per acre, *i.e.*, the rate of rent is 7 times that of revenue. To this it may be added that Champāran returns only 6 per cent. of the land revenue demand of the Patna Division, though it accounts for nearly one-sixth of its total area.

SURVEYS AND SETTLEMENTS. The first survey undertaken in Champāran was the revenue survey of 1845, the object of which was to map out the boundaries of villages and estates, in order to put a stop to the constant boundary disputes, which formed a serious administrative difficulty. This was followed in 1865 by a *diāra* survey carried out for the purpose of assessing to revenue all alluvial formations outside the area of the permanently settled estates as mapped at the time of the revenue survey. In this survey the riparian lands on the Gandak were measured, the total area surveyed being 548 square miles; and the result was that Rs. 700 were added to the revenue roll.

By far the most interesting event in the revenue history of Champāran since the Permanent Settlement has been the survey and settlement carried out between 1892 and 1899. This was a work of great magnitude; for the whole district, with the exception of a hilly tract in the north, was cadastrally surveyed

---

* This is the figure ascertained at the last settlement. According to the revaluation concluded in 1906, the gross rental of the district is 32½ lakhs, *i.e.*, the land revenue is less than one-sixth of the total rental.

on the scale of 16 inches to the mile, and 400,592 holdings, with an average size of 5·19 acres, and 2,807,976 plots, with an average size of 0·74 acres, were recorded. A complete record of rights was also prepared for the whole district; and this has enormously strengthened the position of the cultivators, and done much to protect them in the peaceful occupation of their holdings and from oppressive enhancement of their rents.

Champāran is a district owned mainly by a few big proprietors, with a small number of petty revenue-free properties, and with but few subordinate tenures. The disintegration of property, which is such a marked feature in Muzaffarpur, has not proceeded to any extent in this district, and the greater part is still held by 3 great estates—the Bettiah Rāj, the Madhuban estate and the Rāmnagar Rāj. Petty proprietors are fairly numerous in the Madhuban, Dhāka and Kesariyā thānas, but everywhere else the Bettiah Rāj and a few big zamīndārs predominate. Though the area of Champāran is 3,531 square miles or over one-seventh of the area of the Patna Division, there are only 1,260 estates borne on the revenue roll, or less than 2 per cent. of the number returned for the whole Division. Of these 1,260 estates all but six are permanently settled. The six temporarily settled estates, which are all very small properties, are Malkauli Patkhauli in *tappā* Chigwān Batsarā, Charki Diara and Khutwaniā in *tappā* Patjirwā, Gopālpur Masānthān in *tappā* Daulatā, Serukahiā in *tappā* Sugāon, and Ghormarwā in *tappā* Mānpur. The estate last named is the only Government estate in the district; it has been held by Government since 1831, and is now in lease to the Bettiah Rāj. ESTATES.

Nearly the whole of the area comprised within the different estates is in the occupation of tenants; and the area held as proprietors' *zirāat* or private land is inconsiderable, amounting only to 0·3 per cent. of the total occupied area. Besides this, 2 per cent. is in the direct cultivation of proprietors, but is not true *zirāat*. Only 36,212 acres are cultivated by the proprietors, for in Champāran the competition is mainly for tenants to occupy land, and the landlords have no incentive to reserve land for their own cultivation.

A large number of the tenures found in the district are held by indigo concerns, which are in possession of 357,000 acres or 17·17 per cent. of the district area as permanent tenure-holders (*mukararidārs*) and of 524,000 acres or 25·20 per cent. as temporary tenure-holders (*thikādārs*). Altogether, the tenures held by indigo concerns account for 1,377 square miles or 42·37 per cent. of the entire area of the district. The large proportion held TENURES.

under temporary tenures is due to the fact that, Champāran being a backward district split up into a few extensive zamindāris, the *thikādāri* or farming system prevailed from the early days of the industry; and this naturally was the tenure under which the European planters first acquired an interest in the land. The permanent tenures are mainly those obtained 30 years ago, when, as stated in Chapter IX, the Bettiah Rāj granted permanent leases of large areas to the important factories in order to cover the interest on the English sterling loan. A large portion of this estate and of the Rāmnagar Rāj and the Madhuban estate have been farmed out on short leases (*thikā*) to middlemen; as a rule, petty native *thikādārs* are most numerous in the south of the district, and the majority of rent-free holders are found in the same tract. Other tenures are the rent-free grants held by *biritdārs*, which are largely sublet.

Indigo factories also hold 65,000 acres as under-tenure-holders, but otherwise under-tenures are comparatively rare; among them may be mentioned the sub-leases, known as *katkanās*, held by factories either from native *thikādārs* or from one another. Altogether 17,000 acres, or 7½ per cent. of the occupied area, are in the direct occupation of tenure-holders, the average size of the holdings being 12 acres.

TENANTS. Ryots holding at fixed rates (*sharamoyan*) are very few in number and account for only 26,800 acres or 2 per cent. of the occupied area. The average size of a holding, however, is large, viz., 8 acres; and no less than 13 per cent. of the area of these holdings is uncultivated. There appear to be several reasons for this state of affairs. The ryots at fixed rates, being the earliest settlers in the village, have homesteads above the average size. They hold at a low rate of rent, and can therefore afford to have more land under mango groves or to reserve some for private grazing. Finally, inherent lethargy is a very important factor, for they do not require to cultivate all their lands for their subsistence, and so they leave part fallow to save themselves trouble.

Settled or occupancy ryots hold no less than 1,314,465 acres or 83 per cent. of the cultivated area, and nearly 86 per cent. of the total number of holdings; the average size of an occupancy holding is slightly under 4 acres. These occupancy rights have been transferred to a remarkable extent. From statistics compiled for the 10 years preceding the last settlement it appears that, whereas in Muzaffarpur in an area of 850,000 acres the transfers numbered 14,500 only, nearly 36,000 transfers in a million acres were recorded in Champāran; and while in Muzaffarpur 79 per cent. of the transfers were made to fellow-ryots and not more than 13 per cent. to money-lenders, only 55 per cent. of the transfers in Champāran were made to fellow-ryots, and no fewer than 41 per cent. to money-lenders.

Non-occupancy ryots hold only 3·1 per cent. of the cultivated area, the average size of the holding being under 2 acres. Non-occupancy rights are generally held in *diāra* lands; they are most common in the Bettiah subdivision, where such holdings are held for the most part by agricultural labourers, who take settlements for a little land as a supplementary source of income.

Rent-free holders are also an unimportant class, as rent-free grants of any magnitude are largely sublet and therefore come under the category of tenures. The average size of the rent-free holdings is only 2·4 acres, and they account for 2·1 per cent. of the cultivated area.

Under-ryots occupy 2 per cent., and the average size of their holdings is only one acre, a fact which seems to indicate that when lands are taken on sub-leases, it is mainly with the object of obtaining a supplementary source of income.

RELATIONS OF LANDLORDS AND TENANTS.

The position of the tenants 30 years ago was described as follows by Sir W. W. Hunter in the Statistical Account of Champāran:—"Hardly any land in Champāran is held by tenants with a right of occupancy under Act X of 1859. The principal cause of this is the almost universal custom of letting villages in farm for short terms. Very few landlords let their lands to the ryots direct, but farm them out to *thikādārs* (lease-holders) for five or seven years. When the term expires, the landlord, as a rule, demands an enhanced rental from the lease-holder; and the increase falls ultimately on the ryots, either in the shape of a higher rent per acre, or by the addition of waste lands to their cultivation, for which rent is charged; or where there is no waste, by exacting rent for some fictitious land, commonly known as *kāghazi zamin*, i.e., paper land. It thus happens that few ryots are able to hold their lands uninterruptedly for 12 years at the same rates. Only ryots of a superior class receive *pattās*, which when given are generally the pretext for exacting *salāmis*. There are other reasons, however, to account for this unusual state of things. Champāran ryots for the most part are extremely careless and ignorant of their legal rights. The zamīndār is looked up to with unusual deference, and his demands are rarely disputed. Most of the district belongs to one or two proprietors, whose influence among their tenants is enormous, and who can eject and dispossess at pleasure."

The change which has taken place since the time when Sir W. W. Hunter wrote will be sufficiently apparent from the fact that no less than 83 per cent. of the cultivated area has now been secured to occupancy ryots. That occupancy rights should now be enjoyed by the cultivating classes to such an extent shows how much the Bengal Tenancy Act and the preparation of a record of rights have done to establish the rights of the tenantry. The other features noticed by Sir W. W. Hunter still exist—the landlords are powerful, and the tenants are ignorant, apathetic and improvident, and have not been compelled by circumstances to appreciate the value of tenant rights.

On the other hand, the population is sparse, rents are low, culturable land is available in large quantities; and if the landlord is oppressive or endeavours to enhance his rent rate, the tenant throws up his land and goes elsewhere. Another very important factor in the agricultural economy of the district is that the indigo factories are landlords in more than half the occupied area; and the cultivator derives very considerable advantages from the regularity in the payments made to him for indigo, from the excellent management of their estates and tenures by the planters, and from the fact that rents have been kept down to a great extent by the lease of considerable areas by the Bettiah Rāj to the planting community. Not only is there this numerous body of considerate landlords, but a very large tract is under the management of the Court of Wards; and, last but not least, there is more demand for ryots than for land. The result of these combined influences is that, on the whole, there is comparatively little friction between landlords and tenants, though instances of oppressive landlords and of truculent, and even savage, tenantry are not unknown.

REVENUE DIVISIONS. For the purposes of revenue administration the district is divided into 3 *parganas* or fiscal divisions, known as Mehsī, Simrāon and Majhawā. *Parganas* Mehsī and Simrāon are almost co-extensive with thānas Madhuban and Dhāka respectively, and cover a long narrow strip of land, running from the confines of Nepāl on the north to the borders of Tirhut on the south, and separated from the latter on the east by the Bāghmati and from the neighbouring *pargana* of Majhawā on the west by the Tiar and Burh Gandak rivers. In density of population, fertility of soil, abundance of rice fields, and absence of uncultivated wastes, they are similar to the adjoining tract of Tirhut. These two *parganas* account for the area of only two rather small thānas, and the rest of the district is contained in the immense *pargana* of Majhawā; its northern and north-western boundaries march with Nepāl, and the Gandak separates it from Rāj Butwal in that State, and from the districts of

Gorakhpur and Sāran on the south-west and south. It extends over an area of nearly 1½ million acres, and includes the Bettiah Rāj, the Rāmnagar estate and the greater part of the Madhuban estate. This enormous *pargana* can be divided into two portions, marked by a different degree of fertility; the portion on the east comprises the thānas of Adāpur, Motīhāri, Kesariyā, Gobindganj and Bettiah with small portions of Bagahā and Shikārpur, while the greater portion of the two extensive thānas last named comprise the portion to the west. These *parganas* are divided into 32 *tappās* or minor divisions, of which a list is given below:—

MAJHAWA PARGANA.	MAJHAWA PARGANA. *contd.*	MAJHAWA PARGANA. *concld.*
Bahās.	Harnātānr.	Sāthi.
Balthar.	Jāfarābād.	Sonwal.
Baluā Gondaulī.	Jāmhaulī.	Sugāon.
Belwā.	Khadā.	MEHSI PARGANA.
Bhabta.	Madhwal.	Hariharā.
Chānkī.	Māndo.	Haveli.
Chigwan Batsarā.	Mānpur Chaudānd.	Salempur Hādiābād.
Chigwan Nisf.	Olahā.	Siraunā.
Daulatā.	Patjirwā.	SIMRAON PARGANA.
Deorāj.	Rājpur Sihoriā.	Nonaur.
Duho Suho.	Rāmgīr.	
Gopālā.	Sakhwā.	

CHAPTER XII.

GENERAL ADMINISTRATION.

ADMINISTRATIVE CHARGES AND STAFF.

FOR administrative purposes the district is divided into two subdivisions, viz., Motīhāri and Bettiah. The Motīhāri or headquarters subdivision is under the direct supervision of the Collector, while the other subdivison is in charge of a Subdivisional Officer. At Motīhāri the Collector is assisted by a staff of Deputy Collectors, consisting generally of three officers in the regular line, besides a Deputy Collector in charge of Excise and Income-tax; there are also occasionally an Assistant Magistrate and one or two Sub-Deputy Collectors. The Subdivisional Officer of Bettiah is usually assisted by a Sub-Deputy Collector. Champāran also forms a separate division of the Public Works Department, under the control of an Executive Engineer, who is in charge of the embankments and the canal system; owing to the construction of the Tribenī Canal, this officer is at present assisted by a large staff of Assistant Engineers. For the administration of the Opium Department the district was formerly divided into 2 sub-agencies, Motīhāri and Bettiah, each under the supervision of a Sub-Deputy Opium Agent, assisted by an Assistant Opium Agent; but owing to the reduction of the area under poppy cultivation, these two charges were amalgamated in 1907. Under the provisions of Act XIII of 1857, the Collector is *ex-officio* Deputy Opium Agent, but in practice he takes no part in the administration of the Department.

REVENUE.

The revenue of the district under the main heads rose from Rs. 8,80,000 in 1880-81 (when the income-tax had not been imposed) to Rs. 10,31,000 in 1890-91, and to Rs. 10,84,000 in 1900-01. In 1905-06 it amounted to Rs. 11,77,000, of which Rs. 5,15,500 were derived from land revenue, Rs. 3,08,000 from excise, Rs. 1,84,500 from cesses, Rs. 1,18,000 from stamps and Rs. 51,000 from income-tax.

Land revenue.

The collections of land revenue aggregated Rs. 5,13,000 in 1880-81, Rs. 5,14,000 in 1890-91, and Rs. 5,17,000 in 1900-01; but fell to Rs. 5,15,500 in 1905-06, when they accounted for nearly half of the total revenue of the district. In the year last named the current demand was Rs. 5,15,469 payable by 1,260 estates, Rs. 5,14,583 being due from 1,254 permanently-settled estates and Rs. 886 from 5 temporarily-settled estates.

The excise revenue decreased from Rs. 2,16,496 in 1892-93 to Rs. 2,13,300 in 1900-01. Since that year there has been a steady growth in the receipts, and in 1904-05 they amounted to Rs. 2,82,835, the increase during the quinquennium being 32·5 per cent. The incidence of the excise revenue during this period was, however, less than in any other district in the Patna Division except Muzaffarpur and Darbhangā, averaging annas 2-3 per head of the population as compared with annas 3-3 for the whole Division. In 1905-06 the receipts from this source increased still further to Rs. 3,08,187, but this total is lower than that for any district in the Division. The net excise revenue was only Rs. 1,622 per 10,000 of the population or a little over 2½ annas a head, as compared with the Provincial average of Rs. 2,876 per 10,000. **Excise.**

The greater portion of the excise revenue is derived from the sale of the country spirit prepared by distillation from molasses and the flower of the *mahuā* tree (*Bassia latifolia*). The receipts from this source amounted in 1905-06 to Rs. 1,65,716 or nearly half of the total excise revenue. The manufacture and sale of country spirit are carried on under what is known as the dual system, *i.e.*, there is a central distillery, which serves Bettiah, and there are outstills for the supply of the rest of the district. There are 9 shops for the sale of distillery liquor and 97 selling outstill liquor, *i.e.*, one retail shop for the sale of country spirit to every 16,891 persons; the average consumption of the former liquor is 80 proof gallons and of the latter 33 proof gallons per 1,000 of the population. The consumption of the fermented liquor known as *tāri* is not so great, and in 1905-06 its sale brought in only Rs. 29,763. Imported liquors have found no favour with the mass of the population, both because they are unable to afford them, and also because they prefer the country spirit and *tāri* they have drunk for generations past. The receipts from both the latter represent an expenditure of Rs. 1,096 per 10,000 of the population, a figure lower than that returned by any district in the Patna Division except Darbhangā.

The receipts from hemp drugs and opium account for practically all the remainder of the excise revenue. The greater part (Rs. 1,09,425) is derived from the duty and license fees on *gānja*, *i.e.*, the dried flowering tops of the cultivated female hemp plant (*Cannabis sativa*) and the resinous exudation on them. The consumption of hemp drugs is, in fact, greater than in any other district in the Division except Shāhābād, the expenditure being Rs. 611 per 10,000 of the population, as compared with the Divisional average of Rs. 482. On the other hand, opium is not much used; in 1905-06 the duty and license fees on this drug brought in only Rs. 2,000, and the incidence was not more than Rs. 11 per 10,000 of the population, as compared with the Divisional average of Rs. 41 per 10,000.

Cesses. Road and public works cesses are, as usual, levied at the maximum rate of one anna in the rupee. The current demand in 1905-06 was Rs. 1,75,565, the greater part of which (Rs. 1,73,445) was payable by 1,808 revenue-paying estates, while Rs. 1,569 were due from 65 revenue-free estates. The number of tenures assessed to cesses was 10,908 or 6 times the number of estates, while the number of recorded shareholders of estates and tenures was 6,647 and 15,816 respectively.

Stamps. The revenue from stamps ranks next in importance as a source of income to that derived from cesses. The receipts from this source fell from Rs. 1,39,236 in 1896-97 to Rs. 1,18,364 in 1905-06 or by 15 per cent. The decrease is, however, fictitious, being due to the retransfer of the Subordinate Judge's Court to Sāran, where all the important original and appellate civil work of Champāran is carried on. The sale of court-fee stamps, which in 1905-06 realized Rs. 74,142, is by far the most important item in the receipts from judicial stamps. Among non-judicial stamps, impressed stamps account for Rs. 33,611 or nearly the whole of the receipts under this head.

Income-tax. In 1901-02 the income-tax yielded altogether Rs. 54,875 paid by 1,744 assessees, of whom 1,096 paying Rs. 12,361 had incomes of Rs. 500 to Rs. 1,000. At that time the minimum income assessable was Rs. 500, but this was raised in 1903, by the Income-Tax Amendment Act of that year, to Rs. 1,000 per annum, thereby affording relief to a number of petty traders, money-lenders and clerks; and the number of assessees consequently fell in 1903-04 to 620, the net collections being Rs. 48,027. In 1905-06 the amount collected was Rs. 50,739 paid by 709 assessees. The realizations are chiefly on account of grain and money lending, the renting of houses and trade.

Registration. There are 4 offices for the registration of assurances under Act III of 1877. At the headquarters station (Motihāri) the District Sub-Registrar deals, as usual, with the documents presented there, and assists the District Magistrate, who is *ex-officio* District Registrar, in supervising the proceedings of the Sub-Registrars in charge of the other registration offices. The average number of documents registered annually during the quinquennium 1900-04 was 10,443 as against 14,266 in the preceding 5 years, the decrease amounting to 26·7 per cent. This decrease was due to the fact that the years of famine and distress in the first quinquennium led to the registration of an exceptionally large number of documents, and was also partly caused by the practice followed by many zamīndārs, in the earlier stages of the settlement operations, of taking *kabuliyats* from their ryots to secure proof of the rents payable by them. The marginal statement shows the number of documents registered, and the receipts and expenditure, at each office in 1906.

NAME.	Documents registered.	Receipts.	Expenditure.
		Rs.	Rs.
Motīhāri ...	4,862	6,838	4,852
Bettiah ...	4,242	4,282	2,226
Dhāka ...	4,670	4,285	1,505
Kesariyā ...	3,500	3,197	1,530
Total ...	17,274	8,602	10,113

ADMINISTRATION OF JUSTICE.

Civil Justice.

In 1906 the district was included within the limits of the Muzaffarpur Sessions Division and placed under the jurisdiction of the District Judge of Muzaffarpur. The Civil Courts are those of the District Judge and of a Munsif stationed at Motīhāri. Statistics of the civil work will be found in the Statistical Appendix, and it will be sufficient to state that of late years there has been a considerable increase in the number of suits under the rent laws. The growth of litigation about title is attributed to the fact that the settlement operations brought disputes to a head, and made it necessary for the person who lost his case before the Revenue Officer to apply to the Civil Court or forfeit his claim permanently. The reasons for the increase in rent suits are that the record of rights, which has now been prepared, affords facilities to landlords for the recovery of their rents through the Courts, and that their possession of a title-deed in the record of rights has strengthened the position of the tenants and enabled them to withstand any illegal coercion which may be practised by the landlords. Thus, the zamīndārs now have a record of rights on which they can safely rely in order to prove their claims, whereas previously they were deterred from litigation by the fear that the papers filed by them would not be accepted by the Courts; and on the other hand, the tenants, relying on the same record, will not pay rents for which there is no legal liability, and therefore compel the landlords to resort to the Courts to prove their claims.

Criminal Justice.

Criminal justice is administered by the District and Sessions Judge of Muzaffarpur, who holds a Court of Sessions at Motīhāri for the trial of cases committed from Champāran, by the District Magistrate, and by the magistrates subordinate to him. The sanctioned staff at Motīhāri consists, in addition to the District Magistrate, of two Deputy Magistrates of the first class and one Deputy Magistrate of the second or third class. Besides these officers, an Assistant Magistrate and one or two Sub-Deputy Magistrates exercising second or third class powers are sometimes posted there. The Subdivisional Officer at Bettiah is almost invariably an officer vested with first class powers, and is usually assisted by a Sub-Deputy Magistrate of the second class. There are also Benches of Honorary Magistrates at Motīhāri and Bettiah, which exercise second class powers, and one Honorary Magistrate with first class powers.

Crime. The commonest crimes are burglary, theft, cattle lifting and rioting. In the quinquennium ending in 1904 there were more cases of rioting than in any other of the North Gangetic districts of the Patna Division, the average being 55 per annum. The majority of these cases, however, are of a petty nature; they are generally connected with land disputes or with disputes arising out of cattle trespass or questions of irrigation. Burglaries are not so frequent as in other districts of the Patna Division, and in the same quinquennium Champāran returned fewer cases than any other district; the average number per annum was, however, 675. Dacoities and robberies, on the other hand, are more common than in any of the North Gangetic districts. They are mainly the work of criminals who make raids into this district from across the border of Nepāl. To prevent the inroads of such bands of robbers, a small number of *chaukīdārs* are organised into a special frontier patrol.

Criminal classes. Champāran is the home of a criminal tribe known as Magahiyā Doms or Maghaya Doms, of whom a full and excellent account is given in a monograph entitled *The Outcasts* (Calcutta, 1903), by Geoffrey R. Clarke, I.C.S., from which the following extracts are quoted. " The Maghaya has made little or no advance since we first knew him. He is still a nomad and a thief. In the words of Mr. J. Kennedy, late Collector of Gorakhpur, " He is born in an *arhar* field and schooled to theft from his infancy. He wanders an outcast from the beginning. He lives without shelter and without food for the morrow, perpetually moving from encampment to encampment, chased by the police and execrated by the villagers. His greatest pride is a successful burglary and a prolonged drinking bout his most coveted reward. Hinduism has failed to reach him, its great gods are unknown to him ; even the local divinities are seldom the object of his reverence. An apotheosized Domra is his principal deity, and his gods are other than those of the country. The advance of civilisation has only thrust him into deeper degradation. He has laid aside his horror of the burglar's iron and has added robbery to his other resources. Beyond this, I do not know that civilisation has touched him."

"This eloquent and graphic description of the Maghaya Dom will appeal to all those officers of Government who have ever had any intimate dealings with him. He is a thief by nature and looks on work in any form as a punishment. He cannot appreciate the benefits arising from earning an honest livelihood. To the Dom such money is earned with far greater toil and far poorer results than a successful burglary would give.... Jail offers no terror to the Dom. It is with him the inevitable result of being a bungler at his trade. He has come to regard it as part of his education, much the same as we regard the time spent at school. His greatest terror is the lash ; ... and I have no doubt that this is the sole form of punishment which acts as a real deterrent.

"Despite the fact that Government has provided agricultural settlements for him in Gorakhpur and Bihār, the Dom is still a nomad. The settlements serve as houses for the women and children, but the men are seldom to be found in them. The women are all prostitutes, and are of exceptionally fine and handsome appearance.... There is no doubt that the Dom women act as spies for the men. They enter the villages on the pretext of begging, and find out the persons who have property worth stealing and where they keep it. They have a much readier wit than their masters and always act as spokesmen when an official visits any of their settlements. The older women, who have passed their prime and lost their personal attractions, become hawkers of stolen property, which they dispose of among the inhabitants of distant villages at a half or even one-third of its value.

"On the whole the Dom, under the present regime, has not an altogether unpleasant life. When he has become *au fait* at his profession, he can practise it with comparative impunity. The so-called agricultural settlements always provide him with an asylum if the house of a friendly zamīndār is not near at hand. He goes about armed with a sharp pointed knife, which he uses for all purposes and which forms a very efficient weapon for either attack or defence. To give him his due, the Dom will only use his knife when in a very tight corner, but when he does use it, the result is often fatal. The Maghaya is extraordinarily fearless in committing a burglary, and, in this respect, appears to be somewhat of a fatalist. On effecting an entry into a house, he will usually strike a light and march boldly about seeing what he can lay hands on. He is always provided with a box of matches for this purpose . . . . When the Dom has secured his booty without causing an alarm, he will probably make his way into the house next door and repeat the performance . . . . When detected, they disappear like jackals and have a wonderful faculty for escaping their pursuers. . . .

"In fine, the life of the Dom is one of perpetual excitement. He has a handsome wife, if not two, and so long as she brings grist to the mill, he is not particular about the favours which she confers upon others. If he makes a good haul, he has a splendid feast and is drunk for a week; if he is caught, it means a cessation of work for two or more years, only to begin his old career with a renewed energy on release. Surely such a life, though perhaps degrading, is full of a certain romance, and at present there are no signs that the Maghaya is being won from his ancient ways and is being induced to adopt the humdrum existence of an honest cultivator."

The first systematic attempt to reclaim the Magahiyā Doms in this district was made in 1882 by Mr. (now Sir E.) Henry, then District Magistrate of Champāran. He found that the greater number of the adult members of the tribe were in jail; that scattered gangs consisting of females and some males, had taken up their quarters at various places on the other side of the frontier and in the Madanpur jungle in the Bettiah subdivision, whence they periodically made incursions, committing on the occasion of each visit numerous burglaries and thefts. The villagers hated them as much as they dreaded them; and cases had occurred of Doms caught thieving being mobbed to death by the exasperated villagers. Every police officer was held responsible if any Doms were found located in his jurisdiction, the result being that unless a Dom upon release from jail effected his escape to some safe asylum, he was liable to be arrested and sent back to jail on conviction under the bad-livelihood sections of the Criminal Procedure Code, no *locus pœnitentiæ* very often being given to him. The treatment they experienced and the course of life which necessity almost compelled them to adopt were a blot upon the criminal administration of the district. Mr. Henry came to the conclusion that the only scheme which offered any chance of ultimate success was to establish agricultural settlements; and his recommendations were accepted by Government. One of the leaders of the tribe was induced, through the intervention of some women, who were being hunted from village to village while their husbands were in jail, to settle with the Doms in a locality assigned to them; and settlements were made at Chautarwā in the village of Bargāon and at Fatehpur, where they were given land to cultivate, huts to live in and agricultural implements and farm stock. The community was divided into gangs, each of which was composed, as far as possible, of one family, under a gangsman who was its acknowledged head. Land was allotted to each gang according to its strength, and the gangsman was responsible for the cultivation being properly carried on. When the crop was ripe, it was the property of each gang, who divided it among themselves as they pleased.

From the first they were made to understand that the position taken up by the authorities is not that of favouring them unduly with the object of inducing them to abstain from theft and crime generally, but that of removing to some extent the disabilities under which they formerly laboured in the struggle for life. The main object kept in view in making and maintaining these settlements has been to make a resting place for the Magahiyā Doms, and to provide them with employment, and thereby to enable them to live honestly on the proceeds of their own earnings. At present, there are two Dom settlements situated at Chautarwā and Rāmnagar containing nearly 400 Doms; they were formerly settlements at Ekdari and Fatehpur, but these have been abandoned, as it was considered that concentration of the Doms in fewer settlements might facilitate their supervision. In these settlements the Doms are given lands to cultivate, and attempts have also been made to train them in different handicrafts, such as the weaving of *newar* and *darīs*; there are schools for the children, while the women have been taught basket-making and encouraged to breed and sell fowls. They are by nature thieves, but a few yield to treatment when circumstances are favourable. Some have taken to settled cultivation, but many still leave the settlements occasionally and undertake thieving expeditions.

POLICE. The police of each subdivision are in charge of an Inspector, under the general control of the Superintendent of Police. The police force in 1905 consisted of a District Superintendent of Police, 3 Inspectors, 36 Sub-Inspectors, 1 Sergeant, 27 Head-constables and 328 constables. The total strength of the regular police was therefore 396 men, representing one policeman to every 8·9 square miles and to every 4,521 persons. There is also a small body of town police; and the rural force for the watch and ward of villages in the interior consists of 138 *dafadārs* and 2,405 *chaukīdārs*. The chaukīdāri union system was for the first time introduced in the headquarters subdivision and in two outposts of the Bettiah subdivision in 1902-03, and was extended to the rest of the district in the following year.

Motihari Subdivision.		Bettiah Subdivision.	
Thana.	Outpost.	Thana.	Outpost.
Motihāri ...	Sugauli.	Bettiah ...	Majhauliā.
Kesariyā ...	Pīpra.		Bhaurā.
Gobindganj...	...		Jogāpati.
Dhāka ...	Ghorāsahan.	Shikārpur ...	Rāmnagar.
Adāpur ...	Raxaul,		Lauriyā.
	Chauradāno.		Mainātānr.
	Madhuban.	Bagahā ...	Dhanahā.

The marginal statement shows the different thānas and police outposts in Champāran.

JAILS.

There is a district jail at Motīhāri and a subsidiary jail at Bettiah. The sub-jail at Bettiah has accommodation for 23 male and 3 female prisoners. The jail at Motīhāri has accommodation for 349 (318 male and 31 female) prisoners distributed as follows:—barracks without separate sleeping accommodation are provided for 256 convicts, 20 female convicts, 6 under-trial prisoners, and 6 civil prisoners; the hospital holds 43 prisoners; and there are separate cells for 13 male, 3 juvenile, and 2 European convicts. The principal industries are mustard-oil pressing, the weaving of the coarse carpets called *darīs*, net making, and the manufacture of string money-bags. The mustard-oil, *darīs* and nets are sold locally, and the money-bags are supplied to Government treasuries in Bengal.

CHAPTER XIII.

LOCAL SELF-GOVERNMENT.

DISTRICT BOARD.

OUTSIDE the municipalities of Motihāri and Bettiah, local affairs are managed by the District Board, the Local Board system not having been introduced. The District Board, which was established in 1886, consists of 17 members. The District Magistrate is *ex-officio* a member of the Board and is invariably its Chairman ; there are 4 other *ex-officio* members ; and 12 members are nominated by Government. Government servants and planters predominate among the members, the former representing, in 1905-06, 35 per cent. and the latter 59 per cent. of the total number, while the landholding class accounted for 6 per cent.

Income.

The average annual income of the District Board during the 10 years ending in 1901-02 was Rs. 1,41,000, of which Rs. 87,000 were derived from rates ; and during the quinquennium ending in 1904-05 it amounted to Rs. 1,48,000. In 1905-06 the opening balance was Rs. 60,000, and the receipts of the year aggregated Rs. 2,28,000, including Rs. 87,000 obtained from Provincial rates, Rs. 13,500 contributed from Provincial revenues, and Rs. 11,000 realized from tolls on ferries and Rs. 10,000 from pounds. In Champāran, as in other districts, the road cess is the principal source of income ; the incidence of taxation is light, being only 9 pies per head of the population—a proportion lower than in any other district of the Division. The income both from pounds and ferries is a fluctuating one. In the quinquennium ending in 1899-1900 the average annual receipts from pounds were Rs. 12,100 ; in the next quinquennium they were Rs. 10,100, and in 1905-06 altogether Rs. 10,000 were obtained from 98 pounds leased out by the Board. Similarly, as regards ferries, the receipts averaged Rs. 12,000 per annum in the first quinquennium, and Rs. 11,800 in the five years ending in 1904-05, but fell to Rs. 11,000 in 1905-06.

Expenditure.

The average annual expenditure during the decade ending in 1901-02 was Rs. 1,39,000, of which Rs. 82,000 were expended on civil works, Rs. 5,000 on medical relief and Rs. 19,000 on education. During the quinquennium ending in 1904-05 the expenditure averaged Rs. 1,44,000 per annum, and in 1905-06 it amounted to Rs. 1,80,000, leaving the large balance of Rs. 1,09,000. By far the largest portion of the income of the District Board is spent on civil works, *i.e.*, the extension and maintenance of communications, the upkeep of staging bungalows, the construction of buildings, the provision of a proper water-supply, etc. Over Rs. 1,27,000 were spent on these objects in 1905-06, and of this sum Rs. 1,01,000 were allotted to the extension and maintenance of communications. The District Board maintains 15 miles of metalled roads and 1,066 miles of unmetalled roads, besides a number of village tracks with an aggregate length of 226 miles; the cost of maintaining these roads in 1905-06 was Rs 244, Rs. 25 and Rs. 6 per mile respectively. After civil works, education constitutes the heaviest charge on the resources of the Board, entailing in 1905-06 an expenditure of Rs. 28,000 or nearly one-sixth of its total expenditure. It maintains 3 Middle schools and gives grants-in-aid to 4 Middle schools, 25 Upper Primary schools and 569 Lower Primary schools.

For the relief of sickness the Board maintains 2 dispensaries, and aids 5 others; and when cholera breaks out in the interior, it despatches native doctors with medicines to the affected villages. During 1905-06 the Board spent 5·9 per cent. of its ordinary income on medical relief and sanitation, a percentage higher than in any other district of the Division except Patna and Gayā. An itinerant Veterinary Assistant is also employed by the District Board, and a stipend is given to a student sent to the Veterinary College at Belgāchia.

As regards the general position of the District Board, it may be pointed out that it is the poorest District Board in the Patna Division, though Champāran is one of its largest districts and needs development more than any other. Rents being low, the funds at the disposal of the Board are limited, and this is the chief obstacle to progress. Improvement in the means of communication, improvements in the arrangements for providing medical aid, and the extension of primary and female education are the principal needs of the district. Something has been done and is being done in all these directions, but very much still remains unaccomplished, and for all the great need is more money.

MUNICIPALITIES.

There are 2 municipalities in the district, viz., Motīhāri and Bettiah. The number of rate-payers in 1905-06 was 6,706, representing 17·4 per cent. of the total number (38,426) of persons residing within municipal limits, as compared with the average of

18 per cent. for the whole Division. The average incidence of taxation in that year was annas 11-7 per head of the population, as against the Divisional average of annas 12-11, and varied from 12 annas in Bettiah to annas 10-10 in Motīhāri.

Motīhāri. The Motīhāri Municipality, which was established in 1869, is administered by a Municipal Board consisting of 13 Commissioners, of whom 8 are elected, 4 are nominated, and one is an *ex-officio* member. The area within municipal limits is 6½ square miles, and the number of rate-payers is 1,730, representing 12·6 per cent. of the population. The average income of the municipality during the 5 years 1895-96 to 1899-1900 was Rs. 16,200 and the expenditure was Rs. 13,600; in the quinquennium ending in 1904-05 they were Rs. 20,400 and Rs. 16,600, respectively. In 1905-06 the income aggregated Rs. 24,000, besides an opening balance of Rs. 4,900. The chief source of income is a rate on holdings assessed at 7½ per cent. on their annual value, which in that year brought in Rs. 8,250; and next in importance come the fees from markets, which realized Rs. 4,000; the total incidence of taxation is annas 10-10 per head of the population. The expenditure in the same year was Rs. 21,500, excluding Rs. 2,500 expended in advances, deposits and the repayment of the loans, and the closing balance was Rs. 4,900. The principal items of expenditure are medical relief, public works and conservancy, which accounted for 37, 14·1 and 12·6 per cent. respectively of the disbursements.

Bettiah. Bettiah was constituted a municipality in 1869 and has a Municipal Board consisting of 13 Commissioners, of whom 12 are nominated and one is an *ex-officio* member. The area within municipal limits is 8½ square miles, and the number of rate-payers is 4,976 or 20·1 per cent. of the population. The average annual income during the 5 years ending in 1899-1900 was Rs. 16,600, and the expenditure was Rs. 15,700; and in the quinquennium ending in 1904-05 they were Rs. 21,600 and Rs. 19,200 respectively. In 1905-06 the income of the municipality was Rs. 25,000, of which Rs. 11,100 were obtained from a personal tax levied according to the circumstances and property of the rate-payers. Other taxes are a rate on holdings, assessed at 7½ per cent. on their annual value, which brought in Rs. 4,300, and a latrine rate, which realized Rs. 1,000; the incidence of taxation was 12 annas per head of the population. The expenditure in the same year was Rs. 24,400, the principal items being conservancy, which accounted for 24·9 per cent. of the disbursements, public works (21·9 per cent.) and medical relief (28·5 per cent.).

CHAPTER XIV.

EDUCATION.

PROGRESS OF EDUCATION.

WHEN Champāran was constituted a district, education was in a very backward condition; and even as late as 1870-71 there were only 2 schools under Government inspection, attended by 51 pupils and almost entirely supported by a Government grant. Within the next two years there was a great development owing to the introduction of Sir George Campbell's scheme for the advancement of vernacular education, by which the grant-in-aid rules were extended to village *pāthsālās*. The result was that in 1872-73 there were altogether 72 schools maintained or aided by Government, attended by 1,121 pupils, besides 6 unaided schools with 101 pupils. Considerable difficulties were, however, encountered in the extension of primary education, owing to the ignorance and prejudices of the people, an idea of which may be gathered from a report regarding the progress made in the Bettiah subdivision. "In this subdivision," it was said, "only 5 original *pāthsālās* were discovered; and the Assistant Magistrate reports that he has had the greatest difficulty in inducing the people to send their children to the new schools, and in obtaining qualified *gurus*. Anything like systematic education is quite unknown in these parts; and the new system has not only not been viewed with favour by the people, but has been passively resisted as much as possible. The *patwāri* class oppose it especially, because they fear that an extended system of education will afford too great facilities to aspirants for their particular business. The zamīndār class has also failed to give that assistance which in other and more enlightened districts has been willingly afforded. This arises very much from the fact that there are very few resident members of this class, who are themselves sufficiently intelligent to comprehend the utility of an extended system of education among the masses, and to take an active interest in its promotion."

During the next 20 years progress was rapid and sustained, and in 1892-93 altogether 1,036 schools were in existence, and the number of pupils under instruction was 21,803. In the course of the next 10 years there was a falling off in the number both of schools and pupils, the former decreasing in 1901-02 to 810 and the latter to 19,974; this was due largely to the famine of 1896-97, for the number of educational institutions fell from 1,136 in 1895-96 to 773 in that year and the aggregate of scholars from 25,723 to 17,696. The last quinquennium has not witnessed any recovery, in consequence of a series of bad years in which disease has been prevalent and crops have been short; the number of educational institutions on the 31st March 1907 standing at 798 and the number of pupils on the rolls at 17,770.

STATISTICS OF EDUCATION. Of the total number of schools now in existence, 717 are public institutions, including 11 secondary schools, 699 primary schools, 3 training schools and 4 other schools, and 81 are private institutions. Of the total number receiving instruction, 16,582 study at public institutions and 1,188 at private institutions; altogether 14,192 are Hindus, 730 are Muhammadans, and 60 belong to other religions. The number of girls at school is 1,109, and of boys 16,661, representing only 12·5 per cent. of the boys of school-going age. The inspecting staff consists of a Deputy Inspector of Schools, 5 Sub-Inspectors of Schools and 11 Guru Instructors. According to the statistics obtained at the census of 1901, only 2·3 per cent. of the population (4·5 males and 0·1 females) are literate, *i.e.*, are able to read and write.

SECONDARY EDUCATION There is no college in the district. There are altogether 11 secondary schools, including 2 High schools, 7 Middle English schools and 2 Middle Vernacular schools, and the number of pupils on the rolls is 1,124. One of the High schools, the Motihāri Zilā school, which is attended by 283 boys, is maintained by Government; the other, the Bettiah Rāj school, at which 230 boys receive instruction, is unaided. Two of the Middle English schools are maintained by Government, and five receive grants-in-aid; these schools, which are situated at Motihāri, Bettiah, Bagahā, Barharwā, Kesariyā, Madhuban, and Turkauliā, have an aggregate attendance of 531 pupils, while the Middle Vernacular schools at Mehsī and Sangrāmpur, which are maintained by Government, are attended by 130 pupils.

PRIMARY EDUCATION. In 1906-07 there were 31 Upper Primary schools for boys attended by 1,332 pupils, and 645 Lower Primary boys' schools with an attendance of 13,420. Of the Upper Primary schools two are maintained by Government, 28 are aided by the District Board, and one is unaided; of the Lower Primary schools two are maintained by Government, 598 are aided by the District or Municipal Boards, and 45 are unaided. Comparing these figures with those for 1891-92, we find that the aided Upper Primary schools, of which there were 16 in that year, have increased by 100 per cent., while the number of Lower Primary schools has fallen from 682, all of which were aided. There has been, however, an increase in the total number of Primary schools since 1901-02, when there were 673, but the number of pupils has fallen from 17,097 to 14,752; this decline is attributed to the hard times the peasantry have had to pass through. The two Lower Primary schools maintained by Government are intended for the education of Dom children in the Dom settlements at Chautarwā and Rāmnagar. Efforts are also being made to educate the aboriginal Thārus and several schools have been opened for their benefit, but only 60 Thārus study at them. Night schools, to the number of 16, have been started for the education of labourers and cultivators after their day's work.

SPECIAL SCHOOLS.

There are 3 Training schools, viz., a second grade Training school at Motīhāri, and Guru Training schools at Bettiah and Dariyāpur for the training of Primary school teachers. Among other special schools may be mentioned 30 Sanskrit *Tols* (4 public and 26 private institutions), of which the most important is the Dharma Samāj school at Motīhāri, supported largely by the Bettiah Rāj, 17 Arabic schools and 22 Korān schools; a Muhammadan *madrasa* has also been opened recently at Dhāka.

FEMALE EDUCATION.

For the education of girls, one Upper Primary and 22 Lower Primary schools have been established, at which 555 girls receive instruction, as compared with 10 Primary schools with 215 girls on the rolls in 1901-02; there are also 554 girls reading in boys' schools. Besides these Primary schools, three model girls' schools, attended by 77 girls, have been started, one of which, the Bettiah model girls' school, is maintained by the Bettiah Municipality, the other two being aided by Government. Efforts have also been made since 1902-03 to convey education to zanāna ladies by means of a lady teacher. At first, such instruction was regarded with great suspicion, and only women of the lower classes would agree to be taught; but *pardānashīn* ladies belonging to respectable families now consent to receive visits.

MUHAMMADAN EDUCATION.

The Muhammadans of Champāran are described as being backward, but the number of Musalmān pupils in all classes of schools is 3,284 or 18·4 per cent. of the pupils of all denominations. According to the statistics of the census of 1901, Muhammadans only form 14·7 per cent. of the population; the total number of boys of all creeds receiving instruction is 12·5 per cent. of the number of boys of school-going age; and it would appear therefore that Muhammadans take a more active interest in education, at least in elementary education, than the

Hindus. Progress has been most marked in primary education, the number reading in public primary schools rising from 1,863 in 1891-92 to 2,453 in 1906-07. They have, however, shewn but little advance as regards secondary education, the number of Muhammadan pupils in secondary schools falling from 150 to 113 during that period.

There are 6 boarding houses, attached to the Training schools at Motīhāri, Bettiah and Dariyāpur, to the Zilā school at Motīhārī, and to the Middle English schools at Kesariyā and Madhuban. BOARDING HOUSES.

CHAPTER XV.

GAZETTEER.

Ararāj.—See Lauriyā Ararāj.

Bagahā.—A village in the Bettiah subdivision, situated on the eastern bank of the Great Gandak, 35 miles north-east of Bettiah. It is one of the largest villages in the subdivision, is the headquarters of a thāna, and contains a dispensary in charge of a Civil Hospital Assistant; an ayurvedic dispensary, which is very popular with the people, is also maintained by an Indian gentleman. Bagahā is the headquarters of Messrs. Dear & Co., the timber merchants who hold a lease of the Rāmnagar forests, and also contains the office of the Rājpur Sihoria Circle Officer of the Bettiah Rāj. The village of Chakhnī, situated two miles south-east from Bagahā, is an outstation of the Prefecture Apostolic of Bettiah and Nepāl, and contains a Roman Catholic church and the monastic-like quarters of the priests. The church is an imposing edifice, designed and built under the supervision of the priests themselves. Further along the same road, at a distance of 5 miles from Bagahā, is the Dom settlement of Chautarwā in the village of Bargāon.

Bārā.—An indigo factory in the headquarters subdivision, situated within a few hundred yards of Chakiā station on the Tirhut State Railway. The station was formerly known as Bārā, but its name has been recently changed to Chakiā. This is the oldest factory in the district, having been established by Colonel Hickey in 1813; large sugar works, with improved machinery, have lately been put up.

Bāwangarhi.—A name, meaning 52 forts, given to the remains of some old fortifications near Darwābāri, in the extreme north-western corner of the district, about 5 miles from Tribenī; the place is also called Tirpan Bazar or the 53 bazars, and the name Darwābāri appears to mean the door of the palace. Darwābāri itself is a small village on the edge of the forest, with swamps to the east. The remains of the 52 forts and 53 bazars are a short distance to the north, and include some ruins known as the *kachahri*, close to which are an old tank and a curious well on the edge of which there are rude stone representations of alligators. To the north-west across the swamp are remains of massive embankments, which may perhaps have been intended to serve as lines of circumvallation or as reservoirs.

No trustworthy information can be obtained as to the history of Bāwangarhi, though Mr. Vincent Smith hazards the opinion that it is perhaps just possible that it is identical with Rāmagrāma, the ancient city visited by the Chinese pilgrims Fa Hian and Hiuen Tsiang.* It forms the subject of various traditions, one of which connects it with the lives of the Pāndavas, who are said to have spent the weary years of their exile in the neighbouring forest. According to another legend, it was the residence of a chief called Bāorā, who is said to have been contemporaneous with the Simrāon dynasty; it has been conjectured that the forts were erected by this Rājā as a retreat for himself and his followers from the invasion or depredations of his more powerful neighbours to the south and the hill tribes of Nepāl to the north. Another tradition is that there was a chain of 52 forts erected by immigrants from South Bihār, who came here under a leader called Bhīm Singh, and continued to hold this tract under a number of petty chieftains. The general belief is that the surrounding country was once thickly populated, and this belief is confirmed by the remains of walls, with tanks and wells inside them, as well as by the deserted villages, plantations and mango groves found in this part of the district.

The following legend regarding Bāwangarhi, which forms one of the favourite songs of the Nats, was discovered by Mr. W. R. Bright, C.S.I., when Subdivisional Officer of Bettiah. At one time, the Rājās of Bāwangarhi were two brothers, Jāsor (the elder) and Torar, the former of whom had two sons, Allaha and Rūddal, and the latter two sons, named Jhagru and Jāman. Disputes arose between them, which ended in their agreeing to divide their kingdom, but when they came to divide a mango orchard containing 5 trees on the banks of the Gandak, a quarrel broke out in which Torar was killed by Jāsor. Torar's son, Jhagru, avenged his father's death and would probably have also killed Jāsor's widow and her sons, had she not escaped with them to Sāgarpokhrā at Bettiah. Thence she went to various friends, only to be expelled by them as soon as Jhagru heard that they were giving her shelter, until at last in despair she wandered out with her two sons into the forest hoping that they would be killed

---

* V. A. Smith, Prefatory Note, Report on Tour of Exploration of the Antiquities in the Nepal Tarai, Calcutta, 1901.

by wild beasts. It happened, however, that the Benāres Rājā passed through the forest on a hunting expedition, and, having found the mother and her children, had compassion on her and took them to Benāres. For two years they lived there, until Jhagru heard of it and once more demanded their expulsion. From Benāres she wandered to Kālinjer, where Allāha attained his majority, and having shown some skill in war was given the fortress of Mahuāgarh. Having learnt his history, he travelled off in the garb of a *fakir* to Bāwangarhi, and while sitting by the great *jhīl* which is still a prominent feature of the place, saw his father's corpse hanging on a tree and being daily scourged by Jhagru. When he went up to the tree to take the corpse down, his father's spirit told him that he must win it by force of arms and not by theft. He was afterwards recognized by Jhagru, but managed to escape on an old horse, which recognized him, to Mahuāgarh. Having collected a large force there, he attacked Bāwangarhi, only to meet with a decisive defeat at the hands of Jhagru and to become his prisoner. The tables were, however, turned by the skill in witchcraft possessed by his wife, who overcame the spell cast by Jhagru's mother and released her husband and other captives. A battle ensued, in which Jhagru was defeated, taken prisoner, and then killed; and Allāha, after dividing the Rāj between his aunt and a female servant of his, left the place and returned home.

Bediban.—A village situated in the south-east of the headquarters subdivision, about half a mile north-east of the Pipra railway station and about a mile to the south of Sītākund. The village contains the remains of an old fort, 925 feet long from north to south and 670 feet broad, with an average height of 12 feet above the surrounding country. The ramparts, which appear to be of earth only, are covered with trees and surrounded by a broad shallow ditch. Close to the northern end of the enclosure there is a lofty terrace, 20 feet high, surrounded by a brick wall, with two long flights of steps on the north and the east. On the western half of this terrace stands a Hindu temple, a domed building with a verandah or portico on the entrance side, which faces the east. The only object of worship in this shrine is a stone with a Muhammadan inscription, which is called *Bhagwān-kā-charan-pad*, or the footprints of Bhagwān. The stone is 2 feet square and one foot thick, with seven lines of Arabic writing in the usual raised letters. Unfortunately the daily libations of *ghī* and water have injured the letters so much that the record is not very legible; but General Cunningham was able to decipher the name of Mahmūd Shāh, whom he identified with Mahmūd Sharki, King of Jaunpur (1450 A.D.). He was of opinion that not only was this Arabic inscription adopted as an object of Hindu worship, but that the temple itself had originally been a Muhammadan tomb which the Hindus appropriated. This, if true, would be a remarkable fact, as the reverse has generally been the case; but the style of the temple is not unusual in Bihār and does not point to a Muhammadan origin. [Reports, Archæological Survey, India, Vol. XVI; Report, Archæological Survey, Bengal Circle, 1901-02.]

Bettiah Rāj.—A great estate extending over 1,824 square miles, mainly in the subdivision of the same name. It belongs to a Bābhan family over 250 years old, which traces its descent from one Ujjain Singh, whose son, Gaj Singh, received the title of Rājā from the Emperor Shāh Jahān (1628-58). The family came into prominence in the 18th century during the time of the downfall of the Mughal Empire, when we find frequent references made by Muhammadan historians to the Rājās of Bettiah as independent chiefs. Thus, in the Riyazu-s-Salātin, the Rājā is described as a refractory and turbulent chief, whose territory had never been entered by the armies of former Nāzims, and who had never acknowledged the dominion of any of the Sūbahdārs. In order to subdue this chief, Alī Vardi Khān led an expedition against him in 1729, and brought him and his territory under subjection. Subsequently, in 1748, the Rājā seems to have entered into an alliance with the Afghān rebel chiefs of Darbhangā and gave shelter to their families during their war against the Bengal Viceroy; when the Afghāns were defeated by Alī Vardi Khān, he offered to purge his contumacy with a contribution of 3 lakhs of rupees. In 1759 Caillaud advanced against the fort of Bettiah, and compelled the Rājā to submit; in 1762 another expedition was sent against him by Mīr Kāsim Alī Khān, and his fort was again captured; and in 1766 a third expedition under Sir Robert Barker was necessary to establish British authority. A more detailed account of these transactions will be found in Chapter II.

At the time when *Sarkār* Champāran passed under British rule, it was in the possession of Rājā Jugal Keshwar Singh, who succeeded Rājā Dhurup Singh in 1763. This Rājā soon came into conflict with the East India Company. He fell into arrears of revenue, and in the words of the Judges of the *Dīwāni Adālat* "rebelled and fought with the forces of the British Government, was defeated and fled to Bundelkhand for safety, and his *Rājgi* was seized upon and brought under the direct management of the

Company." The attempt to manage the estate proved, however, a complete failure; and the Company, finding that its revenue grew less and less, persuaded Jugal Keshwar Singh to return. Then they settled with him *parganas* Majhawā and Simrāon, the remainder of the district being given to his cousins, Srī Kishan Singh and Abdhūt Singh and forming the Sheohar Rāj. The same two *parganas* of Majhawā and Simrāon were settled with Bīr Keshwar Singh, the son of Jugal Keshwar Singh, at the Decennial Settlement in 1791, and still constitute the greater part of the Bettiah Rāj estate. Bīr Keshwar Singh played a prominent part in the disputes which, as related in Chapter II, led to the Nepalese war, and was succeeded in 1816 by Anand Keshwar Singh, on whom Lord William Bentinck conferred the title of Mahārājā Bahādur as a reward for services rendered. On the death of his successor, Newāl Keshwar Singh, in 1855, the estate passed to Rājendra Keshwar Singh, who, in the words of the Lieutenant-Governor, gave at the time of the Mutiny "praiseworthy aid and support to Government during the whole progress of the rebellion." The title of Mahārājā Bahādur was also given to this Rājā and to his son, Harendra Keshwar Singh, the last Mahārājā of Bettiah, who was subsequently made a K.C.I.E. and died in 1893. He left no children and was succeeded by his senior widow, who died in 1896. The estate which has been under the management of the Court of Wards, since 1897, is at present held by the Mahārājā's junior widow, Mahārānī Jānki Kuar, who is styled Mahārānī by courtesy. Her title to the estate has been contested on three occasions. Bābu Rāmnandan Singh and Bābu Girijānandan Singh of Sheohar each in turn laid claim to the estate, but their claims were disallowed by the Privy Council in 1902. It is reported that it is now being claimed by Bābu Bishun Prakāsh Singh of Madhuban.

Besides the property in this district, the estate also possesses landed property in the districts of Muzaffarpur, Patna, Sāran, Mirzāpur, Allahābād, Basti, Gorakhpur, Fyzabād and Benāres; the property in the six districts last mentioned is now under the management of the Court of Wards, United Provinces. The land revenue and cesses due from the estate amount to 5 lakhs, and the collections of rent and cesses to nearly 18 lakhs; a great portion of the estate is held on permanent leases by European indigo planters. In 1885, in order to pay off heavy debts, a loan of £2,45,000 was negotiated in London, bearing interest of 5 per cent. on a sinking fund; a sum of £28,000 is paid annually to the loan trustees in liquidation of this debt, which will be paid off by 1925. The estate maintains at its exclusive cost a large female hospital in Bettiah under the Countess of Dufferin's Fund.

Bettiah Subdivision.—Northern subdivision of the district, lying between 26° 36′ and 27° 31′ N., and 83° 50′ and 84° 46′ E., with an area of 2,013 square miles. The southern portion of the subdivision is a level alluvial plain, but towards the north-west the surface is more undulating and rises gradually as the Nepāl frontier is approached. From the north-western corner a range of low hills extends in a south-easterly direction for a distance of some 20 miles; and between this and the Sumeswar range, which extends along the whole of the northern frontier, lies the Dūn Valley. There is a marked difference between the crops grown in different parts of the subdivision. In the northern and eastern portions the chief, and in many places, the only crop is rice, while in the south and west a great variety of crops are grown, including indigo and sugar. The population of the subdivision was 749,864 in 1901, as compared with 759,865 in 1891; the slight decrease was due to unhealthiness and a series of lean years culminating in the famine of 1897. The density is only 373 persons to the square mile, as compared with 507 for the whole district. The headquarters are at Bettiah (population 24,696), and there are 1,319 villages. The bulk of the subdivision is included in the Bettiah Rāj estate, much of which is held by European indigo planters on permanent leases.

Bettiah Town.—The headquarters of the subdivision of the same name, situated in 26° 48′ N. and 84° 30′ E. Its population in 1901 was 24,696, of whom 15,795 were Hindus, 7,599 Muhammadans and 1,302 Christians.

Bettiah, which has been the headquarters of the Bettiah Rājās for the last two centuries, has an eventful history, being more than once attacked and taken in the closing days of Muhammadan rule; an account of its fortunes during this period has already been given in Chapter II. Even as late as the close of the 18th century Bettiah was a place of considerable importance; and Father Tieffenthaler, the great Jesuit Missionary and author of Descriptio Indiæ, one of the first Gazetteers of India, which was published in 1786, describes it as "a populous city defended by a great castle surrounded by walls, and fortified by towers; near it are the temple and convent, where dwell the missionaries of the Franciscan order." The castle referred to by Tieffenthaler appears to have been erected by Dhurup Singh, Rājā of Bettiah, and remains of the fortifications are still traceable. Though it has lost something of its old importance, Bettiah is the principal trade centre in Champāran, and there are several houses which carry on a considerable business with Patna, Muzaffarpur and Chaprā. The site of the town from a sanitary point of view is unsatisfactory, as it is bordered to the north and east by swampy land, and to the south by the Chandrāwat river, which stagnates in the hot weather. It is, however, a good specimen of a native town, for the streets are in most cases fairly wide and clear. The name Bettiah (properly Betiā) is said to be derived from the fact that the place was once famous for its cane (*bent*) jungle. Even now cane of a superior quality is found on the banks of the Chandrāwat and other streams.

Leaving the railway station, a picturesque avenue leads through a mango grove to the residence of the Subdivisional Officer; and close by are the court house, other Government buildings, and the jail. Just beyond the jail a road branches off to the south from the road leading from the railway station to the town; to the left of this road are the dāk bungalow and the bungalow of the Assistant Manager of the Bettiah Rāj, while to the right may be seen the pinnacles of some temples and the substantial bungalow of the Manager with its well laid-out lawn and garden. In front, appearing among the trees, is the graceful spire of a small Anglican church, completed in 1905, and opposite it are a temple of the Mahārājās of Bettiah and the guest house where Lieutenant-Governors and other distinguished guests are entertained by the estate. At this point the road turns east to Barwat, where the opium godowns and the Sub-Deputy Opium Agent's house are situated, and to the west is a road leading to the town. The whole of this portion of the town is beautifully wooded, the portion between the station and the Barwat road being known as Hazāribāgh or the wood of a thousand trees; each tree is planted so that from whatever point one looks an avenue is seen stretching away into the distance. On the south of the Barwat road, where the trees are less regularly planted, the wood is known as the jungle and is the home of hundreds of grey monkeys, which are often fed by the people of the town.

After leaving the jail, the road from the station to the town passes by the post office, and a little further on is a bridge over the old moat of the Mahārājā's palace, which is now used as a municipal drain. This point marks the commencement of the quarter of the town known as the Christian Tolā, because it is inhabited by the Christian converts. They are said to be the best carpenters and smiths in the district, they own the finest carts and bullocks, and their standard of living is considerably above that of their Hindu and Muhammadan neighbours. In this quarter of the town is the Mission church, an imposing edifice in the Italian style of architecture; it has a lofty belfry, containing an excellent set of bells recently sent out from Europe. Close to it is situated two orphanages maintained by the Capuchin Fathers and the main Mission building, containing a printing press, which turns out excellent work; these neat white-washed buildings, with their shady colonnades, remind one strongly of the monastic buildings in Italy. The Christian Tolā is sharply divided from the Hindu quarter by a narrow alley, to the south of which is the Bettiah Rāj palace occupying a large area in the centre of the town. Much of the old palace has recently been removed, and large modern additions have been made by the Court of Wards. Within the open space surrounding the palace is the office of the Manager. Not far from the palace walls the quarter known as Lāl Bazar runs north and south; this contains the residences of the richest men of the town, several of whom have reputed incomes of over a lakh a year. The bazar is well lighted by a succession of lamps erected at the expense of two Mārwāris of the town. At the southern end of the Lāl Bazar, the Ramna, a large open common, opens out. The northern end of this common, known as the Chota Ramna, is the site of a bazar, where on Saturdays thousands of people congregate from the neighbouring villages. The southern end is occupied by what is said to be the best polo ground in Bihār, to the west of which is the main building of the Dufferin Hospital, with a Lady Doctor's and Matron's quarters and cottage wards attached; there is also a public library close by.

To the south of the polo ground is the Chandrāwat river, which for many months of the year is a succession of stagnant pools. There is a proposal to make a cutting in the north of the district, so as to enable the water of the Harhā, which at present flows into the Gandak, to be diverted into the Chandrāwat and thus give the town a good supply of fresh running water. Following the river bed towards the east we come to the hospital situated on the high northern bank. The buildings have lately been much improved and include medical and surgical wards for men, a Jubilee ward for women and children, an operating room, a large dispensary, and out-buildings with infectious and moribund wards. A little further to the east is a deep pool over which the District Board road is carried by a wooden bridge, while on the other side are the temples and bathing *ghāts* of Sant Ghāt presenting a picturesque scene.

Bettiah is the headquarters of a Capuchin Mission, which has an exceedingly interesting history, as it is the lineal descendant of the great Capuchin Mission, which penetrated to Lhāsa and Nepāl at the beginning of the 18th century. The Mission was established at Bettiah in December 1745 by the Revd. Father Joseph Mary dei Bernini, an Italian Capuchin Father. He came to India in 1739 and was first stationed for two years in Patna, where he made the acquaintance of Dhurup Singh, Rājā of Bettiah, and treated him medically. The Rājā invited him several times to visit Bettiah when there was sickness in his palace, and on one of these visits Father Joseph Mary succeeded in curing the Rānī of a serious illness. Impressed by his skill and knowledge, Dhurup Singh wanted him to stay in Bettiah; but the Father refused to do so, unless sanction was obtained from Rome. He was transferred in 1742 to Lhāsa, and in the meantime both the Rājā and the Superior of the Mission wrote to Rome for permission to establish a station at Bettiah, the Rājā asking the Pope to send two Capuchin Fathers there. Eventually the Superior of the Mission at Lhāsa received a letter from Rome granting him permission to open a Mission in Bettiah. In 1745 the Capuchin Fathers had to abandon Lhāsa on account of the persecution of the Tibetans and took refuge in Nepāl, whence Father Joseph Mary was sent to Bettiah. He arrived there on the 7th December 1745 and the Rājā assigned him a house with a garden near his palace, and allowed him to preach and make converts. This work Father Joseph Mary carried on, with the occasional assistance of a second Capuchin Father, until his death in 1761. When the English took Bettiah in 1766, Sir Robert Barker, who was in command of the forces, assigned the Mission about 60 *bīghas* in the fort and also a plot of land outside Bettiah, called Dasaiya Pādri, extending over 200 *bīghas*, for the support of themselves and their Christian converts. These grants were approved and renewed by the Governor-General in Council at Calcutta in 1786. The Mission is still in possession of these lands with the exception of about 10 *bīghas*, of which they were deprived in 1792 by the then Rājā. In 1892 Bettiah was made the headquarters of the Prefecture Apostolic of Bettiah and Nepāl, which was made over to the Capuchin Fathers of the Tyrolese Province. The Prefect Apostolic, the Superior Regular and three Capuchin Fathers have their residence in Bettiah, besides the Superioress and Members of the Sisters of the Holy Cross (Ingenbohl in Switzerland), who are in charge of the Fakīrānā orphanage and convent to the north-east of the railway station. In addition to Chuharī (q. v.), there are outstations at Chakhnī, two miles from Bagahā, at Rāmnagar, 24 miles north-west from Bettiah, at Rāmpur near the Bhiknā Thorī pass, and at Chainpatiā, 11 miles north of Bettiah.*

Bhainsalotan.—See Tribenī Ghāt.

Chakiā.—See Bārā.

Chakhnī.—See Bagahā.

Chānkīgarh.—The name of a remarkable mound in the Bettiah subdivision, situated 6 miles east of Rāmnagar, a short distance north of the road from Shikārpur to Rāmnagar. The mound, which stands about a quarter of a mile east of the village of Chānkī, is a mass of solid brick-work about 90 feet high, and is composed for the most part of large bricks, 14 inches square by 2½ inches thick. The whole mound from east to west is about 250 feet long, but of such a straggling shape that it is not easy to define its exact limits; its shape may, however, be roughly defined as resembling the letter L. The sides are perpendicular above a certain height, where they rise out of the debris which has accumulated from bricks, etc., constantly falling down. It was probably originally a fort, and the remains of some fortifications can still be seen, besides some insignificant shrines. Some sheets of water surround the mound, and to the south a broad winding path leads up to the summit. The mound is known locally as Jānkīgarh or Jānkikot, and local tradition asserts that it was a fort of king Janaka. Another tradition is that a Buddhist Rājā, whose palace was at Lauriyā Nandangarh, 11 miles to the south, had a favourite priest, named Tāntrik, for whom he built this fort; and while he kept a light always burning at Lauriyā, the priest kept a light on Chānkīgarh, in order that they might know that all was well with each other. Some excavations were made here more than 20 years ago by a Subdivisional Officer of Bettiah, but they only resulted in the finding of a cannon ball, an iron spike, and some copper coins; it is not known what became of these curiosities. The neighbouring village of Chānkī is remarkable for its length, for it extends for about 1½ mile from north to south. [Reports, Arch. Surv. Ind., Vols. XVI and XXII; Report, Arch. Surv., Bengal Circle, 1901-02.]

Chuharī.—A village in the Bettiah subdivision, situated on the road from Parsā to Laheriā, 6 miles north of Bettiah. The village contains the headquarters of a Catholic Mission, which is the lineal descendant of the great Capuchin Mission that succeeded in establishing itself at Lhāsa in the first half of the 18th century. In 1745, the heroic Father Horace

* I am indebted to the Very Rev. Fr. Hilarion, O. C., Prefect Apostolic, for information regarding the history of the Mission.

of Penna left Lhāsa, in despair at the order of the Tibetan authorities that he and his two companions might only preach on condition that they declared the Tibetan religion to be good and perfect, and returned to the Mission hospice at Pātan in Nepāl. Father Horace died broken-hearted some 6 weeks later; and the Mission continued there for 24 years longer, until the Gurkhas swept away the Newār dynasty and expelled the Capuchin Fathers. They then retired to Chuharī, where in 1769 the Rājā of Bettiah gave them and their Newār converts an asylum. There the Mission has remained ever since. It has an outpost at Chainpatiā and maintains at Chuharī an orphanage, a day school and industrial school for native boys, and an orphanage and day school for girls. The village also contains the Mission church and a Presbytery for the Curate and three other Capuchin Fathers.

Darwābāri.—See Bāwangarhi.

Dewar.—A village in *tappā* Rāmgīr in the extreme north-east of the Bettiah subdivision. The village contains a shrine at which two fairs are held yearly, one on the full moon of the month of Kārtik and the other on the Rāmnavamī in Chait. Local legend says that the place originally contained the fort of Arjuna Mahārājā, and that it was attacked by a predatory tribe. An Ahīrin, the sister of Krishna, was caught by them, while hiding her husband, and had her nose and ears cut off. She was then turned into stone. The idol now in existence has a broken nose, and this peculiarity has no doubt given rise to the legend. The offerings made at the shrine are the perquisites of a family of Thāru Gurus.

Jānkīgarh.—See Chānkīgarh.

Kasturiā.—A name given to a large mound of brick ruins on the west side of Saraiyā in the south-east of the headquarters subdivision, situated 16 miles east of Motīhāri. The mound, which is 160 feet long by 100 feet broad, is said to be the remains of a Chero Rājā's palace. It has been dug up in all directions for the large bricks of which it is composed, and the fields for half a mile round are also strewn with their fragments. To the west of the mound there is a large *pākar* tree (Ficus glomerata), about 15 feet in diameter, under which is a seated female figure, which the people call Durgāvatī Rānī, but which appears to be the goddess Durgā, as she holds the usual bow and arrow. The stone is much injured below, but the broken figure of a lion, on which the goddess is seated, is faintly traceable. She has eight arms, and the figure is clearly a representation of Durgā as Ashtabhujā Devī, or the "eight-armed goddess." The stone is partly enclosed by the tree, and is 3 feet 5 inches high and 2 feet 3 inches broad. The local legend is that Durgāvatī Rānī was the wife of one of the Chero Rājās. One day when she was seated under the *pākar* tree, a Banjārā came up to her, and tried to take off her bracelets and other ornaments. She prayed for assistance, and was at once turned into stone, with all her ornaments. [Reports, Arch. Surv. Ind., Vol. XVI.]

Kesariyā.—A village in the headquarters subdivision, situated in 26° 21′ N. and 84° 53′ E. in the extreme south of the district. The village contains a police station and has a population, according to the census of 1901, of 4,466 persons. Two miles to the south stands a lofty brick mound capped by a solid brick tower of considerable size, which clearly marks the remains of a Buddhist stūpa. The mound itself, which is now overgrown with jungle, is a ruined mass of solid brick-work, 62 feet in height, and 1,400 feet in circumference at its base; while the stūpa, which is in ruins, has a diameter of 68 feet at its base and a total height of 51½ feet; originally it was crowned by a pinnacle, which must have stood 80 or 90 feet high, or including the ruined basement, not less than 150 feet above the ground. General Cunningham was of opinion that it dates back to A.D. 200 to 700, and that it was built upon the ruins of a much older and larger stūpa. This ancient monument is known to the people as the *deora* of Rājā Ben, who is said to have been one of the five supreme Emperors of India and is therefore called Rājā Ben Chakravartti. It can hardly be doubted that the tradition of Rājā Ben preserves the story recorded by Hiuen Tsiang, according to whose account this stūpa was referred to a Chakravartti Rājā by the Buddhists of the seventh century. He states that somewhat less than 200 *li* (*i.e.*, about 30 miles) to the north-west of Vaisāli, which is the exact position of the Kesariyā stūpa, there was an ancient town which had been deserted for many ages. It possessed a stūpa built over the spot where Buddha had announced that in one of his former existences he had been a Bodhisatwa, and had reigned over that town as a Chakravartti Rājā. This stūpa is, in fact, one of the many memorial stūpas built by the Buddhists at places connected with some remarkable event in the life of Buddha.

Local tradition asserts that Rājā Ben had, by his austerities, become a Chakravartti or supreme ruler with superhuman powers, while his queen, Kamalāvatī, was able to stand on a lotus leaf when she bathed. The Rājā, it is said, was an ideal landlord, for he either took no rent for his lands, or only a *sūp*, *i.e.*, a winnowing basket of corn, from each cultivator. Unfortunately, one day he broke this excellent rule by ordering that every one should give him a piece of gold the size of a grain of barley; he immediately lost his supernatural powers, and the lotus leaf gave way under his queen as she was bathing, and she was drowned. The Rājā consulted his Pandits, who told him that she had been drowned because he had raised the old land rent; and he built the *deora* or stūpa, and going inside with all his family, closed the entrance by his magical powers and was seen no more. The site of the queen's palace is still pointed out in the shape of a mound called Rānīwās, about half a mile to the north-east of the stūpa; the tank in which she bathed is called the Gangeya Tāl, three-quarters of a mile to the east of the stūpa; and a large sheet of water, 3,000 feet in length, immediately to the south of the stūpa is called Rājā Ben's tank. The mound called Rānīwās, or the Rānī's palace, is however, really the site of an old Buddhist monastery. Excavations made there in 1862 disclosed the remains of small cells and of a shrine containing a colossal figure of Buddha; this statue was removed in 1878 by a Bengali employé of the Rāmgarh indigo concern. [Reports, Arch. Surv. Ind., Vols. I and XVI; Report, Arch. Surv., Bengal Circle, 1901-02.]

Lāl Saraiyā.—An indigo factory in the headquarters subdivision, situated 5 miles to the west of the Sugauli railway station. Lāl Saraiyā was at one time the most renowned indigo factory in Bihār, being the home of Mr. James Macleod, who was known as the king of planters, and was famous for his hospitality. The factory bungalow is situated on the bank of one ot the horseshoe lakes so common in this part of Bihār; and outside the door are the remains of the old race course, for Mr. Macleod's colours were at one time well known on the Turf in India and his stable contained 120 horses. The concern is also well known for its considerate treatment of the ryots. The name merely means the red *saraiyā* or *sareh*, *i.e.*, the belt of land furthest from a village.

Lauriyā Ararāj.—A village in the west of the headquarters subdivision, situated 4 miles north of Gobindganj thāna on the road from that place to Motīhāri. Population (1901) 1,107. It contains one of the lofty stone columns erected by Asoka in 249 B.C. The pillar, which bears in well-preserved and well-cut letters six of his edicts, is a single block of polished sandstone, 36½ feet in height above the ground, with a base diameter of 41·8 inches, and a diameter at the top of 37·6 inches. The weight of this portion only is very nearly 34 tons, but as there must be several feet of the shaft sunk in the earth, the actual weight of the whole block must be about 40 tons. This pillar has no capital, although there can be little, if any, doubt that it must once have been crowned with a statue of some animal. The edicts of Asoka are most clearly and neatly engraved, and are divided into two distinct portions, that to the north containing 18 lines, and that to the south 23 lines. They are in a good state of preservation, but the northern face of the pillar has suffered from the effects of the weather, and looks quite black, while the polish, which is beautifully preserved elsewhere, has disappeared. This ancient pillar has not escaped the vandals, one of the first of whom was Reuben Burrow, a distinguished mathematician and astronomer, and one of the earliest members of the Asiatic Society of Bengal, who had his name inscribed on it. This appears to be a favourite amusement of the scientist, for we also find his name chiselled on the Asoka pillars at Basārh and Lauriyā Nandangarh. In each case the date is the same, 1792, the year of his death. The villagers call the pillar *laur*, *i.e.*, the phallus, and the adjoining village is named after it Lauriyā ; here there is a temple of Mahādeo, one mile south-west of the pillar, which is the site of a large annual fair. [Reports, Arch. Surv. Ind., Vol. I.]

Lauriyā Nandangarh.—A village in the Bettiah subdivision, situated 14 miles north-west of Bettiah, with which it is connected by road. Population (1901) 2,062. This village contains some of the most interesting remains of the district, viz., a well-preserved pillar of Asoka, the ruins of a great stūpa, and some ancient sepulchral mounds. The following account of the pillar, which stands less than half a mile to the east of the village, is given by General Cunningham :—"Its shaft is formed of a single block of polished sandstone, 32 feet 9½ inches in height, with a diameter at base of 35·5 inches and of 26·2 inches at top. The capital, which is 6 feet 10 inches in height, is bell-shaped, with a circular abacus supporting the statue of a lion. The abacus is ornamented with a row of Brāhmanī geese pecking their food. The column has a light and elegant appearance, and is altogether a much more pleasing monument than the stouter and shorter pillar of Bakhrā. The lion has been injured in the mouth, and the column itself bears the round mark of a cannon shot just below the capital, which has itself been slightly dislodged by the shock. One has not far to seek for the name of the probable author of this mischief. By the people, the outrage is ascribed to the Musalmāns, and on the pillar itself, in beautifully-cut Persian characters, is inscribed the name of Mahi-ud-dīn Muhammad Aurangzib Pādshāh Alamgīr Ghāzī, San. 1071. This date

M

corresponds with A.D. 1660-61, which was the fourth year of the reign of the bigoted Aurangzib, and the record may probably have been inscribed by some zealous follower in Mīr Jumla's army, which was then on its return from Bengal, after the death of the Emperor's brother Shujā.

"The pillar is much thinner and much lighter than those of Bakhrā and Ararāj. The weight of the polished portion of its shaft is only 18 tons, or rather less than half that of the Bakhrā pillar, and somewhat more than half that of the Ararāj pillar. The pillar is inscribed with the edicts of Asoka in the same clear and beautifully-cut characters as those of the Ararāj pillar. The two inscriptions, with only a few trifling variations, correspond letter for letter. The Nandangarh pillar has been visited by numerous travellers, as it stands on the direct route from Bettiah to Nepāl. There are a few unimportant inscriptions in modern Nāgari, the oldest being dated in Sambat 1566 *Chait-badi* 10, equivalent to A.D. 1509. One of them, without date, refers to some petty royal family, Nripa Narayana Suta Nripa Amara Singh, *i.e*, king Amar Singh, the son of king Narayana. The only English inscription is the name of Rn. Burrow, 1792."

The pillar itself has now become an object of worship as a phallus or lingam, and offerings of sweetmeats and fruits are made before it by the villagers, who call it Bhīm Singh's staff (*lāthi*). There are no traces of any buildings near it, but there are two fine banyan trees close by, one to the north and the other to the south. The pillar, now over 2,000 years old, is in excellent preservation, and its massiveness and exquisite finish furnish striking proof of the skill and resource of the masons of Asoka's age.

About three-quarters of a mile west of the pillar and half a mile south-west of the village of Lauriyā is a huge detached mound, called Nandangarh, which commands an extensive view over the well-wooded country on every side. This mound, which stands about 80 feet high, is composed of bricks, some of which measure about 24 inches in length by 12 inches in breadth and 5½ inches thick. The space to the south was enclosed by a massive wall described as being 10 feet thick, and there are traces of the foundations of at least one small building on the top of the mound, which is about 250 to 300 feet square. It has been conjectured by Mr. V. A. Smith that this mound is the "Ashes stūpa," in which the ashes of Buddha's funeral pyre were enshrined. According to Buddhist tradition, after the cremation of Buddha's body at Kusinārā, the fragments that remained were divided into eight portions. The Mauryas of Piplivanna sent an embassy claiming a share of the relics, but the envoys only arrived after the division had been made and had to be content with the ashes of the funeral pyre. Over these they built a great stūpa, which is described by Hiuen Tsiang among others. It is impossible, however, to affirm this identification positively until an adequate survey of the entire group of ruins is made and systematic excavations are carried out. Dr. Bloch, on the other hand, is inclined to believe that this huge brick mound was some kind of fortification, or perhaps the citadel of an ancient city, and points out that round it the traces of an old ditch are still visible, and that the small brick buildings, of which there are traces on the terrace at the top, were perhaps watch-towers. It is open to question, however, whether the area on the top of the mound could accommodate a garrison or even a palace of any size. The mound is now thickly covered with jungle and trees, so that not even its shape can be made out; only a small path has been cut to the small plateau on the top. Local tradition says that Rājā Janaka lived at Chānkīgarh (Jānkīgarh), 11 miles to the north, while his sister was married in Lauriyā, and that the site of her dwelling is called Nandangarh, because she was the *nanad* or husband's sister of the Rāja's consort.

Even more curious are the earthen mounds, north of the village, on the western side of the Turkāhā stream. There are 15 mounds arranged in 3 rows, one running from east to west and the other two from north to south, parallel to each other, an arrangement which seems to show that they were erected according to some definite plan. They are known to be of great age, a small punch-marked silver coin having been found in one of them, which is anterior to the time of Alexander the Great and may be as old as 1000 B.C. General Cunningham was of opinion that they were the sepulchral mounds of the early kings of the country prior to the rise and spread of Buddhism, and that their date might be assumed as ranging from about 600 to 1000 B.C. They may, indeed, be the *chetiyani* or *chaityas* alluded to by Buddha in a question addressed to his disciple Ananda about the Vrijjians. "Ananda," he said, "hast thou heard that the Vrijjians, whatever the number may be of the Vrijjian *chetiyani*, belonging to the Vrijjian (rulers) whether situated within or without (the city), they maintain, respect, reverence and make offerings to them; and that they keep up without diminution the ancient offerings, the ancient observances, and the ancient sacrifices righteously made." * The

* A. Cunningham, Ancient Geography of India.

belief that they are tumuli or sepulchral barrows appears to have been confirmed by the discovery, about 40 years ago, of a leaden or iron coffin containing a human skeleton; while the more recent excavations of Dr. Bloch have shown without doubt that this belief is correct. The following account of these excavations is taken with some abbreviations from the Annual Report of the Archæological Survey, Bengal Circle, 1904-05.

The mounds are arranged in three rows of five each, varying in height from 50 to 20 feet. The first row runs from east to west; a little to the north between the first and second mounds in this row, stands the famous Asoka column with the lion capital. Then follow two parallel rows from north to south. The fourth mound from the north in the eastern one of these two rows is the place where the iron or leaden coffin with a human skeleton was discovered. The place of the fourth mound in the western one of the north to south rows is occupied by a cluster of five small mounds, only a few feet in height and hardly distinguishable from the fields round them. Their shape is now more or less conical, but it is probable that originally they were hemispherical, and that the action of the rain-water has washed off a good deal of earth from the top and thus changed their forms. There is generally round the base a large accumulation of yellow clay, the material used for building the mounds. This yellow clay, of which all the mounds have been made, is quite different from the white soil of the surrounding fields, and it is evident that it must have been imported from somewhere else. Time has made it almost as hard as stone, and to dig through the mounds is consequently slow work. There seems no doubt that the earth used in building the mounds has been taken from the bed of the Gandak, about 10 miles distant, numerous pebbles found imbedded in the clay leaving no doubt as to its real origin. A further peculiarity is that in three of the mounds opened the clay had been put up in thin layers with straw and leaves laid between them. In digging through the mounds, the earth broke off in flat cakes of a few inches thickness, showing on both sides clear marks of straw having been put between the layers of clay. The layers evidently consisted of broad strata raised one upon the other through the entire width of the mound, and no signs were found of their having been made by unburnt bricks.

Excavations were carried on by Dr. Bloch in four of the mounds. In the first mound opened a small deposit of human bones was found, mixed up with burnt wood, and a small gold leaf with a figure of a female stamped on it. This mound is the third from the north in the western line of the rows running from north to south. It is one of the highest of the mounds, its height exceeding 50 feet. In the centre was a hollow shaft, which had obviously been filled by a thick post of *sāl* wood, of which the stump was left, the remainder having been eaten up by white ants. The second mound opened was the first from the north in the eastern line of the rows, which yielded very little of interest. There was no deposit of bones, except some animal bones turned up here and there, but in the centre were found a great number of pieces of corroded iron. It is possible that they formed parts of a pillar running through the centre of the mound, like the wooden post in the first mound above. In the third mound opened, viz., the second in the western line of the rows, a deposit of human bones was found and a gold leaf with a female figure stamped upon it exactly like that found in the first mound. Here too was discovered the opening of a hollow shaft. The last mound opened was the third from the north in the eastern line of mounds aligned north and south, but in this no remains were found.

Dr. Bloch gives the following explanation of the use to which these mounds were put:—"The explanation of the facts revealed by my excavations will be found in the ancient Indian burial customs, described to us in the *Sutras* and *Prayogas* dealing with the ritual Their rules have been collected together and explained in Dr. Caland's well known work, *Die alteridischen Todten und Bestattungs-gebrauche* (Verhandelingen der koninklijke Akademie van Wetenschappen to Amsterdam, 1896). According to this excellent publication, the disposal of the dead in ancient India was divided into four separate acts, viz.,—(1) cremation; (2) collecting the bones of the cremated person and depositing them in an urn (*asthi sanchayana*); (3) expiation (*santikarma*); and (4) erection of the funeral monument (*smasana-chit, losta-chiti*). The fourth act is optional only, and is done some time after the bones have been deposited in the funeral urn and placed in the field under a tree. The urn is then taken out, and after the bones have been washed and several other ceremonies have been performed, they are placed upon the earth, the urn is broken and thrown away, and a funeral monument (*smasana*) is erected over the bones by piling up layers of bricks or clay. The height of such a grave generally does not appear to have exceeded that of a human body, and its shape was some form of a quadrangle. However, both *Apastamba* and *Hiranyakesin* also mention round *smasana* like the mounds at Lauriyā. In building up the *smasana* we find a Vedic verse employed where a post (*sthāna*) is mentioned. The meaning of this is not quite clear from the context or from the ritual, but I think the discovery of the two wooden posts, in two of the mounds above which the bones were deposited, shows that it refers to a similar custom, according to which a pillar was erected in the centre of the funeral monument and the bones placed above its top. The verse may be thus translated:—"I raise the earth around thee; that I lay down this lump of earth, should not do me any harm. May the manes hold this pillar for thee, and may *Jama* prepare a seat for thee in the other world." Again in another verse recited at the same occasion it is said:—"The piled up earth may stand firmly, may it be supported by thousand pillars."

"That there is a connection between the first and third mounds at Lauriyā and the *smasana* described to us in the Vedic ritual, cannot, I think, be doubted. The only difference is the height of the Lauriyā mounds. The straw placed between the layers of clay at Lauriyā even reminds us of the bushels of grass that are put upon the *smasana*, and as regards the gold leaf we must remember that pieces of gold are placed upon the openings of the dead body before it is cremated. Whether the second and the last mounds have served the same purpose as the first and the third is not quite clear. It is possible that they were erected as monuments of persons whose funeral urns could not be found. This case is provided for in the ritual, and it is prescribed that some earth then should be taken out from the spot, where the urn was supposed to have been deposited, and laid down instead of the bones. We may also think of the rules referring to persons who died on a journey and whose bodies could not be found. It is, however, likewise possible that the second and the third mounds merely served some purpose in connection with the cremation, which invariably was performed on the same place where the *smasana* was put up later.

"It is curious to find that Asoka erected one of his pillars close to a *smasana*, the haunt of ghosts and evil spirits in later times. The explanation of this is not difficult to find. Evidently these funeral monuments, probably containing the remains of royal persons, formed an object of worship, as we find adoration of the *chaityas* or funeral monuments of Chakravarttins or kings mentioned in ancient Buddhist literature. The worship of stūpas by Buddhists and Jains is nothing but an adoption of this popular form of grave worship. As a place which annually attracted large gatherings from far away, Asoka could not have selected a more suitable spot for the promulgation of his moral precepts. We thus have in the Lauriyā mounds an intermediate form between the *smasana* and the Buddhist stūpa or *chaitya*. That their date is anterior to Asoka's pillar seems highly probable, but I cannot say for how many centuries. It is a great pity that they yielded so little in the way of antiquarian finds. Only broken fragments of pottery and stone vessels turned up. The gold leaves may be looked upon as specimens of the ancient *nishka*, pieces of gold worn as ornaments and used as coins likewise. The ancient *smasana* was to the north of the town or village, and the mounds of Lauriyā likewise lie north of the Nandangarh, which may have been the citadel of an ancient city that once existed at that place."

At a distance of from 3½ to 6 miles to the west of Lauriyā Nandangarh, and both along and between two old river channels, hundreds of small grass-covered mounds or tumuli, varying from 2½ feet to 8 feet in height, are scattered here and there over the undulating grassy plain. These barrows are mostly of a subconical shape, but some few are shaped like a cup or a bowl turned upside down. The majority are situated near or along the banks of an old river bed, which divides into two branches to the west of Lauriyā, the eastern or larger branch being called the Harhā, and the western branch the Mausohimākhand. It is noticeable also that the great barrows of Lauriyā are situated near the northern bank of the Turkāhā and only about two-thirds of a mile to the south of another larger river. There was probably a purpose in this, as water had to be near at hand for the ablutions connected with the cremation of corpses, which was performed near the banks of such water channels, the ashes being afterwards deposited in the mounds close by. [Reports, Archæological Survey of India, Vols. I, XVI and XXII; Reports, Archæological Survey, Bengal Circle, 1901-02 and 1904-05; V. A. Smith, *Kusinārā and other Buddhist Holy Places*, Journal, Royal Asiatic Society, 1902.]

Madanpur.—A place in the Bettiah subdivision, situated on the bank of the Gandak, 10 miles north of Bagahā. Tradition says that Madanpur was formerly the palace of a king; it is now an almost impenetrable jungle, but there are many curious old brick remains similar to those found at Darwābāri and in the north-west corner of the district. A small footpath leads to a shrine in the midst of the jungle, where lives an old Sannyāsi, who never leaves his jungle retreat, but waits patiently for the villagers to bring him food. These jungles were the asylum of the Magahiyā Doms before the present settlements were founded.

Madhuban.—A village in the south-east corner of the headquarters subdivision, situated 20 miles south-east of Motihāri, and 5 miles north-east of the Chakiā railway station. Population (1901) 8,645. The village contains a police station and the residence of one of the most influential zamīndār families of the district. The founder of the family was Abdhūt Singh, the great-grandson of Rājā Ugra Sen Singh, the founder of the Bettiah Rāj, with whom *tappā* Duho-Suho and the villages of Madhuban and Shāmpur were settled as *nankar* in the time of Mīr Kāsim Alī Khān. At that time the family residence was in the village of Madhubanī, 8 miles east of Motīhāri, but his grandson Har Prasād Singh removed it to Madhuban, where his descendants have remained ever since. The estate is one of the largest in Champāran, having an area of 50,000 acres and an annual income of 2 lakhs. A large fair is held annually in the village in the month of Asin and lasts for 25 days. Large numbers attend it, and a brisk trade is carried on in the sale and purchase of cattle, horses and miscellaneous goods.

Mehsī.—A village in the south of the headquarters subdivision, situated 29 miles south-east of Motīhāri, on the main road from that place to Muzaffarpur. The village is said to have been the Sadar or chief civil station in Champāran, when the East India Company first acquired possession of it, and a Munsif's court was for a time located there: the remains of the court house and of one of the European bungalows are still visible. The place is noted for a strong flavoured tobacco, the seed of which is said to have been imported by one of the European officers stationed there, and also for strong and durable carpets (*darīs* and *satranjīs*) woven by the local weavers. Under the Muhammadans the village was long the seat of a Muhammadan Kāzi, and gave its name to the *pargana* of Mehsī, which was granted to one Mahrūm Khān by the Emperor Akbar.

The name Mehsī is accounted for by a quaint legend. It is believed that there was a Hindu *sādhu*, by name Mahesh Koiri, whose distinguishing characteristic was that he lived solely on milk. One Hālim Shāh, a Muhammadan ruler, having turned *fakīr*, came from the west to see the Hindu *sādhu* and was astounded to see him extract milk from a heifer for his refreshment. Needless to say, the Muhammadan magnate was much impressed by Mahesh Koiri's accomplishment, and caused the tract to be named after him. To this day the village contains a Hindu shrine and a Musalmān *dargāh*, which were built side by side under the express orders of Hālim Shāh, and all who would show honour to the one are asked to show equal honour to the other. Many miraculous feats are attributed to Hālim Shāh and his power to perform miracles is believed to have remained even after his death. It is said that when a Kalwār once attempted to tap a date-palm near the *dargāh*, in order to obtain the juice for the manufacture of intoxicating drink, which is forbidden to Muhammadans, blood flowed from the tree. There is also a tradition that there was formerly an inscribed stone at the gate of the tomb, with the magic aid of which thieves could be unerringly detected and stolen property recovered. Jang Bahādur, says the legend, removed this stone to Nepāl, and when the saint remonstrated, promised to erect a cenotaph in his memory. The original *dargāh* is a great place of pilgrimage, and an annual fair is held there, at which some thousands attend. It is visited by persons for all sorts of purposes, but mainly by those who desire to be blessed with children or who are suffering from some lingering disease.

Motīhāri.—Headquarters of the district, situated in 26° 40′ N. and 84° 55′ E. Population (1901) 13,730. Motīhāri is picturesquely situated on the bank of a lake (*mān*), which at one time formed a reach in the course of the Gandak. The river at this point has left two horse-shoe bends, which originally formed the neck of a loop in its channel, and the town is situated on the north side of the western bend. These two lakes never entirely dry up, and the depth in the rainy season is over 20 feet in places; but in the hot weather there is not more than two to three fathoms of water at any point. The head of the loop towards the south has silted up and is now under cultivation. In the rains, water is let in from the Gandak river on the north by a canal constructed by the Motīhāri Factory, and there is a small channel joining the two lakes, which keeps the water fresh. The western lake divides Motīhāri into two distinct portions. To the west are the European quarter and native town, and to the east are the various public offices and the railway station, beyond which again are the old race course and the present polo ground; adjoining the latter is the jail, erected about 20 years ago, on a standard plan, according to which the dormitories form the upper storey of the building, the basement of which contains the labour wards. A bund (*bāndh*) or embankment was built some 25 years ago in order to connect the town and European quarter with the Court buildings, which are situated near the station.

Leaving the station and approaching the town by the Bund road, one passes the dāk bungalow, and police lines, the latter being nearly opposite the station, while at a little distance to the right is a large two storied building which serves as a circuit house. Further along the road is the long line of the Court houses and offices, an imposing pile constructed in 1882, in front of which is a park surrounded by large trees; to the east of this and on the same side of the road are the Bar Library and

Munsif's Court. The road then runs along the top of the embankment across the lake, from which a picturesque view of the town can be obtained. On the left the still water reflects the houses of the bazar standing on a high bank with temples and palm trees, while to the north the view stretches away to green pastures and woods. On the right there is an uninterrupted view along the bank of the lake with the works of the Motīhāri Factory picturesquely situated on the water's edge in the foreground, and more pastures and groves of trees in the background. At the end of the embankment is a road leading on the right to the European quarter of the town and on the left to the bazar, and at the corner, where it meets the embankment, are the old hospital building, the Zilā school, the police station and the District Board offices.

The drive towards the European portion of the town past the Anglican church, which is half hidden among the trees, passes through a long and beautiful avenue of old trees. The road to Pīpra strikes off to the right, and at a short distance along this road is the entrance to the Motīhāri Factory; the road then passes between the two lakes through the neck of the loop. Continuing along the avenue of old trees which leads from the station, we come to the entrance to the Collector's house, originally built as a residence for one of the Mahārānīs of Bettiah, which is situated on the western lake. From the house a large *ghāt* leads down to the water and presents a pleasing view, for the lake stretches away in front and to the west, where the Civil Surgeon's house looks out from among the trees: to the east the Factory buildings on the other lake can be seen: and all round is what would resemble a great English park were it not for the palm trees seen here and there in the distance. On the side of the lake, a little way from the Collector's house, is the Gymkhāna Club with a swimming bath supplied with water from the lake. The tennis courts and golf links are in the park, which stretches from the Collector's house to the Club, and on the opposite side of this park is the planters' residential Club.

Opposite the house of the Collector is a road running through the village of Chitauni to Dhāka, and to the left, after passing through Mathia *Tolā*, we come to the Municipal Garden, with a large tank in the centre adorned with two fine bathing *ghāts* built by a wealthy *mahājan* of the town. A little further on is the cemetery, containing monuments recording the names of many well known planting families of Bihār and a stone obelisk, erected in 1864 by the residents of the district, to the memory of Major Holmes and his wife,

Dr. Gardiner (spelt Gardnier in the inscription), his wife and child, whose murder by the mutineers at Sugauli in 1857 has been mentioned in Chapter II. After leaving the cemetery the road leads on to Chauradāno and Nepāl. Turning to the left, we come to the Henry Bazar, a useful and profitable institution, which commemorates the name of Sir E. Henry, the present Commissioner of the London Police, who was for 5 years Collector of Champāran. Passing the bazar on the left, we come to the new hospital building, which is nearing completion: when finished, it will be one of the finest hospitals in the Province outside Calcutta. At this corner is the old civil station, containing the old jail, which is at present occupied by the opium godowns and offices, and the old club, which has been converted into a post office. From this point a road leads round the north of the western lake to the station, while the principal street of the town runs along the bank of the tank. The latter contains the houses of the principal merchants, many of them graceful buildings, with balconies along the front and the merchants' stores below.

A portion of the town is liable to inundation in a year of heavy rainfall when the Sikrāna rises in flood; at such times boats can ply up to the bazar. The name Motīhāri means a necklace of pearls, a picturesque name suggested by the pretty lake which nearly encompasses it.

Motīhāri Subdivision.—Headquarters subdivision, situated between 26° 16′ and 27° 1′ N., and 84° 30′ and 85° 18′ E., with an area of 1,518 square miles. The subdivision consists of an alluvial tract, in which the land is level, fertile and highly cultivated. The river Sikrāna, known in its lower reaches as the Burh Gandak, traverses this tract from north-west to south-east. The soil in the portion to the north of this river, comprising an area of approximately two-fifths of the subdivision, is a strong clay, known locally as *bāngar*, yielding very heavy rice crops in years of sufficient rainfall or in localities where irrigation can be carried on. South of the river, the soil is mainly a light sandy loam, not so suitable for rice, but yielding good crops of maize and various cold weather crops, such as wheat, barley, mustard, linseed, etc. Indigo is also still largely grown in this tract. Its population was 1,040,599 in 1901, as compared with 1,099,600 in 1891. The slight decrease was due to the famine of 1897, which stimulated emigration and diminished the fecundity of the people. There are 686 persons to the square mile, or nearly twice as many as in the Bettiah subdivision. There is one town, Motīhāri, the headquarters (population 13,730), and 1,304 villages.

Nonāchar.—An old fort in the headquarters subdivision, situated on the north bank of the Sikrāna, 5 miles north-east of Motihāri. The remains consist of an oblong mound, divided into four smaller sections by two roads running through it, one in each direction. At the place where they meet, an ancient tank exists, which is now silting up. All the four sides of each of the four smaller sections seem to have been protected by walls, which are covered with thick jungle. Local legend says that the fort is named after its former ruler, one Nonāchar Dosādh, who is the hero of a quaint legend regarding the Subhegarh fort in the Muzaffarpur district. Subhegarh, it is said, was the palace of Rājā Suhel De, who was the last of his race, having only one child, a beautiful daughter named Subahi Devī. After her father's death, she was sought in marriage by many princes, but she refused every one, and at last only consented to marry a man who should be able to count all the palm-trees in the fort. At that time, the whole place was covered with palm-trees, and the task of counting them seemed impossible. Many princes tried and failed, but Nonāchar succeeded by first tying a piece of string round every palm-tree, which is said to have occupied him for some months; and when no tree could be found without a string, he took off all the strings and counted them. He then claimed the hand of the princess, but she was so overcome with shame at the thought of being married to a man of such a low caste that she prayed that the earth would open and swallow her up. Her prayer was heard, and the earth at once opened under her.

Parsā.—Village in the Bettiah subdivision, situated 10 miles north of Bettiah. The village contains the headquarters of the Parsā indigo concern, which has outworks at Harpur and Serukahiā. This concern has recently started the manufacture of sugar with modern machinery, and a factory has been built at Pakhri, 5 miles from Parsā. The factory is an imposing, though far from picturesque, building, and its chimney, which is 107 feet high, can be seen for miles round.

Patjirwā.—A village in the Bettiah subdivision, situated 8 miles west of Bettiah. The village contains a shrine of extreme sanctity, which is said to have been erected by a chief called Durbijja Singh, whose wife and children committed *satī* after he and his sons had been killed in a fight. From that time onwards, in order to honour his memory, it has been laid down that within the *tappā* of Patjirwā none should sleep on a *chārpāi* or build a house of masonry. With such awe do the natives regard this shrine that it is said that they will not, within the whole of that *tappā*, build any house of masonry; and the death of a former

Subdivisional Officer of Bettiah, who committed suicide, is attributed to the fact that he had his tent pitched on the site of the shrine.

Pipariyā.—See Rāmpurwā.

Rāmnagar.—A village in the Bettiah subdivision, situated 13 miles to the north-west of Bettiah. The village contains the residence of an ancient family of zamīndārs, who trace back their descent to Ratan Singh of Chitor, who migrated to Nepāl, where he and his descendants carved out a small principality for themselves. Rājā Mukund Singh, the sixth in descent from Ratan Singh, divided the territory over which he ruled among his four sons. Prithwī Pāl Singh became Rājā of Butwal, Langi Singh Rājā of Makwānpur, and Rāj Singh was Rāāj of Rājpur, while another son, Burangi Singh, is described as being Rājā of "the mountains of Telhoni or Telahu." It is from this Rājā that the Rāmnagar family is descended. Owing, it is said, to the oppression of the king of Nepāl, the head of this branch took refuge in "the lowlands of the mountains of Tribenī" and established himself at Rāmnagar, where the family have remained ever since. They own one of the largest estates in the district, including the Sumeswar Hills and the once valuable forests on them. The title of Rājā was first conferred by the Emperor Alamgīr in 1676 and was confirmed by the British Government in 1860.

The only building calling for mention is a modern temple, a building with four heavy towers at the corners, which completely dwarf a central quadrangle. The building has been described as "something between a village church and a Hindu temple, and altogether about the plainest piece of masonry one would care to see." [Reports, Arch. Surv. Ind. Vol. XVI.]

Rāmpurwā.—A village situated near the village of Pipariyā, 32 miles north of Bettiah and 4 miles to the south of the Sumeswar Hills, in the extreme north-east of the Bettiah subdivision. Less than half a mile to the west of the village, and near the eastern bank of a stream called the Harborā, is one of the edict pillars erected by Asoka, which was discovered about 30 years ago by Mr. Carlleyle of the Archæological Survey of India. He learnt of its existence from some Thārus, who told him that, in the locality which they frequented in the Tarai, there was a stone in the ground like the pillar at Lauriyā, which they called Bhīm's *Lāth*. The Rāmpurwā pillar is similar to that of Lauriyā Nandangarh in the dimensions of the diameter of the shaft at top, viz., 26¼ inches; it is impossible to measure the diameter of the base, as it is buried in the ground much below the water level. As in the case of that pillar, both the shaft and capital are composed of highly polished sandstone, and the capital has a circular abacus ornamented with a row of geese pecking their food. It was originally surmounted with the figure of a lion, but this has disappeared, only the feet and part of the legs being left. The edicts on the pillar are, word for word, the same as those on the pillars at Lauriyā Ararāj and Lauriyā Nandangarh. Its base, a shattered stump 6 feet high, still stands *in situ*, midway between two low earthen mounds covered with brick fragments, evidently the remains of some Buddhistic monuments. The greater portion of the shaft now lies within a swamp, almost entirely under water, some 800 or 1,000 feet to the north of its base; evidently an attempt was made to remove it, but was given up on account of the difficulty and costliness of the task. Close to it stands the capital, which was disconnected from the shaft by Mr. Garrick in 1881, in order to take a photograph of it. These two masses of stone were connected by a solid bolt of pure copper, 24½ inches long, both ends of which were beautifully fitted into the stone without cement, a fact which shows that even in the age of Asoka the Hindus had discovered the destructive properties of iron when used as a fastening for stones. It is in contemplation to restore the fallen column to its original position. To the north, east and west of the pillar, there are the remains of some brick ruins buried in the ground.

The Thārus of the neighbourhood tell a curious story to account for the origin of the broken base of the pillar standing between the two mounds. They say that Bhīm was carrying two loads of earth in two baskets suspended from a pole across his shoulder; when he reached this spot, the pole broke, and the two loads of earth consequently fell down on the ground on either side, and thus formed the two mounds; while the broken pole stuck in the ground in the midst, and became petrified, and thus formed the broken pillar. It has been suggested that the destruction of this pillar, like the injury done to that at Lauriyā Nandangarh, is due to some zealous followers of the army of Mīr Jumla, which was then on its way back from Bengal after the defeat of Sultān Shujā, the brother of Aurangzib. [Reports, Arch. Surv. Ind., Vols. XVI and XXII; Report, Arch. Surv., Bengal Circle, 1901-02.]

Raxaul.—A village in the extreme north of the headquarters subdivision, situated 17½ miles north of Sugauli. The village contains a police outpost and a station on a branch line from Sugauli; the line under construction from Bairaguiā to Bagahā will also run through the village. It is situated close to the boundary between Champāran and Nepāl, and opposite to it is the town of Bīrganj, which is the headquarters of the Nepalese *zilā* of Bārā. A bungalow belonging to the Nepalese Resident is close to the railway station, and a large volume of traffic from Kātmāndu passes through the village, as it is situated on the direct route from Nepāl to British territory.

Sāgardih.—A mound situated close to the village of Sāgar in the headquarters subdivision, 13 miles to the south of Motīhāri and at a distance of 4 miles from Pīpra on the road to Kesariyā. The mound, which undoubtedly marks the remains of a Buddhistic stūpa, is 37 feet high with a circular base nearly 200 feet in diameter; but it is now thickly overgrown with jungle, so that it is difficult to form an accurate idea of its original shape. The excavations made by General Cunningham have shown, however, that the stūpa stands on a paved terrace raised 20 feet above the ground. He was of opinion that it was built over the remains of an older stūpa which had become ruinous. Between the foundations, and in the very midst of the remains of the earlier stūpa, he found the roots of a palm tree still preserving their original upright position, from which he concluded that the ruins of the old stūpa must have been overgrown with jungle before the mediæval stūpa was built, and that the trees were cleared away and the ruins levelled to receive its foundations, leaving the roots of this single palm embedded in the bricks of the older stūpa. From the general appearance, as well as from the relative proportions of height and diameter, General Cunningham concluded that it must be a mediæval building, probably of the 9th or 10th century A.D. The former stūpa must have been several centuries older, as a long time must have elapsed before it became so ruinous that only its foundation was left, to be overgrown with palm trees. The great paved platform, 20 feet high and 175 feet in diameter, on which the present stūpa was erected. must date back to the same time. It was faced with a wall of brick all round, and as the bricks of this wall were all of the smaller size found in the later stūpa, the wall itself is most probably of the same age.

The mound which is called Bhisa, *i.e.*, simply the mound, is attributed to Rājā Sagara, the solar hero, and is therefore also known locally as Sagargarh or Sagara's castle. It stands on an elevated piece of ground, 500 feet long by 300 feet broad, on the eastern bank of an oblong sheet of water called Gayā Pokhar. A short distance to the south-east there is a fine large tank 1,000 feet square, which is called simply Pokhar or the tank, and sometimes Bauddha Pokhar, a name which seems to point to the Buddhistic stūpa close by. Its position in the midst of a vast plain of low-lying rice fields is not an inviting one, as the country all round it must be a wide swamp in the rainy season.

On the eastern embankment of the Bauddha Pokhar, there is a small shrine of the Grām Devatā, or village godling, before which the villagers make offerings of flowers and sacrifice a young goat or sheep. At the foot of the mound stands a small brick tomb of a Muhammadan saint, Ghulām Husain Shāh, who is more commonly known by the name of Mallang or the madman. It is a small brick building, only 13½ feet square, but it has 15 *bīghas* of land attached to it, and is about 100 years old. A few hundred feet to the east there are two bridges on the high road, one of them with six piers and two abutments, built of materials taken from the old stūpa on the mound 50 years ago, when the road was being made. There is no tradition connected with the Sāgardih, except the common story told at many other places that travellers used to find cooking pots lying ready for their use, but an avaricious Baniyā having carried off some on his pony, the cooking vessels have never been seen since. This probably dates back to the old Buddhist times when travellers received hospitality in the monasteries. [Reports, Arch. Surv. Ind., Vol. XVI; Report, Arch. Surv., Bengal Circle, 1901-02.]

Sārangarh.—A village about 2 miles distant from Nonāchar. The name has been applied in some reports to the latter, but the village does not contain any ancient remains.

Simrāon.—A village situated on the north-eastern boundary of Champāran, 6 miles north of the Purnahiā factory in the Motihāri subdivision. The village, which contains remains of the ancient capital of the Simrāon dynasty, is now in Nepalese territory, the boundary running along the southern wall. The form of the city was a parallelogram, surrounded by an outer and inner wall, the former being 14 and the latter 10 miles in circumference; traces of the walls are still visible. On the eastern and western sides several moats may also be traced, and inside are the ruins of massive buildings. The remains of the palace, of the citadel, and of the temple of the tutelary goddess have basements of finely carved stones of great size, some being 5 feet long by 1½ feet wide, and a superstructure of polished bricks. The citadel is now a mound in the north of the city called Kotwālī Chautārā, and the palace is represented by another mound called Rānīwās in its centre. In the neighbourhood of the latter is a ruined causeway made of large burnt bricks, and vestiges of the same causeway elsewhere seem to show that the streets of the city were made of the same costly material. A large tank called the Isrā tank, about three-quarters of a mile from the north-east corner of the city wall, is still in good preservation, and close to it is a *math* with a temple of Kankali bearing an inscription, the date of which corresponds to 1747 A.D. Another *math* at the place called Rānīwās contains a large temple built in the Nepalese style. These buildings are modern, but contain some pieces of ancient statuary. [Reports, Arch. Surv. Ind., Vol. XVI; Report, Arch. Surv., Bengal Circle, 1901-02.]

Singhāsani.—A village in the headquarters subdivision, situated 7 miles to the north of Sugauli, a short distance to the east of the Gadh river. Half a mile to the west of the village is a large mound, 130 feet long by 100 feet broad covered with broken bricks, to which the villagers give the name of Unchadih. This mound is believed to be the remains of an old fort, and has 4 larger mounds at the 4 corners, which may have been bastions but are more likely the foundations of towers. A road about 14 feet broad leads up to the north face of the mound, which contained the entrance to the fort. This road passes right through it and can be traced for nearly half a mile in a south-westerly direction; it is occasionally used by bullock-cart drivers travelling from one village to another with their wares. The villagers have no traditions concerning these remains, except that they mark a ruined fort. Mr. Garrick was of opinion, however, that "the name of this village would almost show it to have been at some remote period directly connected with royalty or the seat of Government; perhaps a capital city once stood on this site, albeit, in the early history of India, there were such a plurality of petty chiefs governing small tracts of country that the existence of a throne (*singhāsan*) did not always tell of a large city." [Reports, Arch. Surv. Ind., Vol. XVI.]

Sītākund.—A village in the headquarters subdivision, situated near the Pīpra railway station, 10 miles to the south-east of Motīhāri and half a mile to the north of Madhuban on the Sikrāna river. The village contains the remains of an ancient fort, the shape of which is an irregular square, 450 feet long on each side, with large round bastions at the corners and in the middle of each face. The ramparts of the fort are formed of two separate brick walls, with 8½ feet of earth filled in between them; the outer brick wall is 10 feet thick, and the inner one 3 feet, so that the total thickness of the rampart is 21½ feet. On the east, west and south there was a single entrance, and on the north there were apparently two gates; but the rampart on this face is nearly obliterated, so that one can only make a guess at the position of the gates by the depressions on the edge of the mound. The brick walls are still from 10 to 12 feet in height, but they must have been much higher originally; as the earthen rampart is generally about 20 feet in height, the whole height of the rampart with its parapet could not have been less than 30 or even 35 feet. In some places, on the west and north, there are traces of a moat. Altogether, the Sītākund fort must have been a place of some strength when guns were unknown, and thick lofty walls could only be attacked by escalade.

Inside the fort is a holy tank, to which the name Sītākund peculiarly applies, as Sītā, the wife of Rāma, bathed there. It is a deep circular pond surrounded by brick walls with 4 *ghāts* leading down to it. A great *melā* is held here on the Rāmnavamī, when several thousands of pious Hindus assemble to do honour to Rāma and Sītā. There are several temples and shrines round it; the principal temple, which stands near the western side of the tank, is a white-washed building, with octagonal turrets at the four corners and a domed roof. It enshrines 8 well-preserved images, viz., images of Sūrjya, Hanumān and Vishnu; an image of Rāvana, with 20 arms and 10 heads, five of which only are shown on the carving; another of Mahishamardinī or Durgā in the act of killing a buffalo demon; and two images of Ganesh, one seated with 4 arms, and one dancing with 8 arms. On the southern rampart of the fort, close to the middle bastion, there are two small places of worship under trees, one dedicated to Garh Devī and the other to Baran Bīr; the former is a tutelary goddess of the fort, and the latter a deified ghost or the spirit of a man who met a violent death. On the top of the western rampart, immediately opposite the principal temple, and under the shade of a magnificent tree, there is a small terrace called *Jogi-kā-baithak* or the hermit's seat; and in the northern part of the fort there are a few tombs (*samādhs*) of Hindu ascetics (*jogis*). [Reports, Arch. Surv. Ind., Vol. XVI.]

Sugauli.—A village in the headquarters subdivision, situated in 26° 47′ N. and 84° 45′ E. on the road to Nepāl, nearly midway between Motīhāri and Bettiah, being 15 miles from the former and 18 miles from the latter place. The place, which contains a railway station and District Board bungalow, is of some historical interest, as it was here that the Nepalese treaty of 1815 was signed. It was the headquarters of General Ochterlony during the last campaign against the Nepalese and, after that date, was the site of a cantonment. In the mutiny of 1857 the 12th Regiment of Irregular Horse commanded by Major Holmes was stationed at Sugauli. As soon as the first symptoms of unrest appeared in Bihār, this officer declared for prompt and vigorous repression;

but up to the last he retained full confidence in the fidelity of his own men and freely scattered them, in little parties of thirty or fifty, throughout the neighbouring districts. But one day in July, when he was taking his afternoon drive, accompanied by his wife, they were met by a party of sowārs or troopers, and butchered on the spot. The remaining Europeans at Sugauli, except one little child, were then murdered, and the great body of the regiment broke out into open mutiny of the worst kind.

The only building of any interest is a large Hindu temple, called the Mahārājā's Mandil, standing in spacious grounds, which is of modern date, being only about 100 years old. The old cemetery is interesting, and there is a fine encamping ground in which there are some large trees. The village stands on a low piece of ground close to the Sikrāna which often floods the adjacent country; there is an embankment built many years ago to protect the cantonment from inundation, but it is no longer maintained. On the banks of the Sikrāna close by are the ruins of the officers' mess house and a summer residence built by one of the Mahārājās of Bettiah.

Sumeswar.—A fort in the Bettiah subdivision, situated on the summit of the Sumeswar Hills, at a height of 2,884 feet above sea-level. The fort, which stands on the edge of a sharp precipice, is now in ruins, but its remains are well defined, and reservoirs cut out of the solid rock, in which water was stored for the use of the inhabitants, can still be seen; a temple bell of remarkably sweet tone, which is an object of considerable veneration, also hangs in the ruins on the east of the fort. From the ridge upon which Fort Sumeswar is situated, a magnificent view of the snows and of the intervening valleys and low hills situated in Nepāl can be had; the ridge here forms the boundary between Champāran and Nepāl. An inspection bungalow has been erected about 200 feet below the crest of the ridge, and residents of the district occasionally reside there when they require change of air, as the temperature ranges about 10° lower than in the plains.

Tribenī Ghāt.—A *ghāt* or passage over the Great Gandak at the extreme north-western corner of the district at the point where the Great Gandak first touches upon British territory; one side is in Tribenī in Nepāl, and the other in the village of Bhainsalotan in British India. It is situated at the end of a road, which runs from Bettiah through Bagahā crossing the Tribenī Canal at Sidāo, past the old police outpost of Harnātānr, and across numerous hill-streams flowing from the Sumeswar range. The approach to Tribenī Ghāt along this road is exceedingly picturesque. At Darwābāri it enters a dense forest, the beauty of which in the rains it is difficult to describe; the undergrowth is thick, and the branches of trees, overhanging the road and festooned with long creepers, form a natural arcade. Nor are there want of signs of animal life; at times a lazy python may be seen curled round some tree stump, a *sāmbar* may occasionally be spied in the jungle, barking deer often come into sight in the more open parts, and at night the roar of a tiger may be heard. In the midst of the jungle is a lonely temple, which wandering Sannyāsis often make their home. Half a mile further on, the traveller comes suddenly to an opening in the forest, from which he looks down upon the grey waters of the snow-fed Gandak flowing swiftly between long stretches of white shingle. On the other side of the river is a picturesque village of white houses, with larger buildings in the centre, which in the distance look like Swiss chalets. These are the buildings attached to the court house and office of a Nepalese official stationed at Tribenī, or as it is also called Shāopur; and a little further down the stream is a large wood yard with a steam saw mill worked by the Nepalese Government.

The name Tribenī means the three rivers, and is derived from the fact that three streams unite here soon after they quit the hills, viz., the Great Gandak, the Pānchnad and the Sonāha. The place is considered sacred on this account, and also because it is believed to be the site at which the fight commenced between the lords of the forest and the water, Gaj and Garah, the elephant and the crocodile. According to the Srimat Bhāgabat, there was in olden times a vast lake round the Trikut hill, which had, as the name implies, three towering peaks, crowned with dense forest and infested by wild animals. In this lake lived a crocodile of enormous size; and one day when a huge elephant came with a herd to bathe there, the crocodile caught him by the leg and tried to drag him into deeper water. The struggle continued for thousands of years, all the crocodiles and elephants joining in the contest. At last, the elephant, beginning to weaken, prayed to the supreme god, Hari, to help him. His prayer was heard, and Hari saved him from the grip of the crocodile in the presence of Hara and other gods. According to Hindu mythology, the crocodile had in a previous life been a Gandharva chief, named Huhu, and the elephant, a king of Pāndya, Indradyumna by name. A short way up the picturesque valley of the Gandak is the traditional site of the battle, where the people still point with awe and wonder to some deep holes in the limestone, some of which are the exact shape of the foot of an elephant, while others resemble the imprints of an alligator's foot. These curious holes are probably due to the action of water churning round some hard stone embedded in the limestone; but the people believe that they were made by Gaj and Garah in the soft mud when the fight began, and then were turned into hard stone and will remain for ever. A large fair is held at the point where the Pānchnad and Gandak met at the time of Māgh Sankrānti in February, when a temporary village of grass huts springs up on a broad expanse of shingle in the river bed, and thousands of villagers flock in to bathe and trade. The site of the fair is half in Nepāl and and half in British territory, and an iron post marks the boundary. On the opposite side of the river in Tribenī itself a brisk trade is also carried on during the fair, one of the most conspicuous features of the bazar at this time being piles of Nepalese oranges brought down for sale.

At the point where the District Board road ends there is a temple built by the Bettiah Rāj looking down upon the stream, and also the remains of an old traffic registration station now removed to Bagahā. On the other side of the Pānchnad are a Nepalese shrine and a police outpost in charge of a Havildār. The Gandak forms the boundary between the two Nepalese Commissionerships of the Eastern and the Western Tarai, and the outpost on the other side of the Pānchnad is under Bīrganj, while the outpost at Tribenī is under Butwal. A little way up the Pānchnad, opposite the point where the Sonāha comes down, is a small shrine dedicated to Sītā, as there is a tradition that it was here that Sītā watched the fight between Rāma and his sons, Lava and Kusha. The beds of these two streams present some scenes of great natural beauty. A narrow limpid stream wanders from side to side between the shingle; on both sides the banks rise to a height of 50 to 100 feet, covered with vegetation and crowned with leafy trees; and all round are hillocks with a thick growth of *sābe* grass.

Passing along the narrow bed of the Kālāpāni, an ominous name given to a stream which flows into the Pānchnad a short distance below its confluence with the Sonāha, we come to a hill, on the top of which are the remains of the plinth of an old bungalow, now almost inaccessible through the growth of weeds and creepers. All round are dwarf trees, the leaves of which seem strangely familiar, for this is all that remains of a tea garden which Mr. Gibbon, Manager of the Bettiah Rāj, tried to start many years ago; the place is now the home of *sāmbar* and occasionally of tigers and leopards. Both the Pānchnad and the Sonāha wash down small fragments of gold, and it is a common sight to see gold washers working at curious little dams of sand in the beds of both streams.

Near the village of Bhainsalotan, at a distance of about a mile and a half down-stream from Tribenī Ghāt, are the head-works of the Tribenī Canal and the bungalows and offices of the engineering staff. The name Bhainsalotan means the buffaloes' wallow, and is apparently derived from the fact that the place used to be the haunt of the wild buffaloes of the Tarai. With its combination of hill and river scenery, it is one of the most picturesque spots in the district.

Unchadih.—See Singhāsani.

INDEX.

A.

B.

D.

E.

F.

G.

H.

I.

J.

N.

O.

U.

V.

W.

Z.

B. S. Press—15-6-1907—10802—524—Wm. D'C.

U.

V.

W.

Z.

B. S. Press—15-6-1907—10802—524—Wm. D'C.